Democracy and Education in the 21$^{st}$ century

T0199919

# Social Strategies

Monographien zur Soziologie und Gesellschaftspolitik
Monographs on Sociology and Social Policy

Vol. 54

Edited by: Ueli Mäder & Hector Schmassmann

Jordi Feu & Òscar Prieto-Flores (Eds.)

# Democracy and Education in the 21st century

## The articulation of new democratic discourses and practices

**PETER LANG**

Bern · Berlin · Bruxelles · New York · Oxford

**Bibliographic Information published by the Deutsche Nationalbibliothek**
The Deutsche Nationalbibliothek lists this publication in the Deutsche
Nationalbibliografie; detailed bibliographic data is available in the internet
at http://dnb.d-nb.de.


Library of Congress Cataloging-in-Publication Data
A CIP catalog record for this book has been applied for
at the Library of Congress.

Several chapters of this book have been translated by Michael Weiss.

ISSN 1424-0467 • ISBN 978-3-0343-3085-5 (Print)
E-ISBN 978-3-0343-3086-2 (E-PDF) • E-ISBN 978-3-0343-3087-9 (EPUB)
E-ISBN 978-3-0343-3088-6 (MOBI) • DOI 10.3726/b11577

This publication has been peer reviewed.

© Peter Lang AG
International Academic Publishers
Bern 2018
All rights reserved.

Printed in Germany

**www.peterlang.com**

# Table of Contents

# Preface

*In the past few decades, our society* has witnessed unprecedented changes that give us the sense that we are witnessing a metamorphosis that is either interesting or disturbing, depending on which point of view you look at it from. The traditional conception of representative democracy is now facing a crisis of social legitimacy evidenced in many contexts around the planet by social protests demanding that human agency have greater control over matters that affect our lives. Some of these protests range from the Arab Springs (various, depending on each context) to the demands of 15-M in Spain, Occupy Wall Street in the United States, the *Umbrella Revolution* in Hong Kong or Iceland's Saucepan Revolution among others. Many of these citizen protests denounce the concentration of economic power in large corporations, the increase in economic and social inequalities and the complicity of the political class with the hegemony of economic power. These demands are not only reactive, of denunciation, but also contain multiple specific proposals concerning which political and economic reforms can promote greater social justice and a strengthening of democracy.

At the same time, however, other emerging social movements also openly criticize globalization and the need to become entrenched again in nation-states. Most of these movements generate a nativist anti-immigration or anti-Islam discourse, achieving some significant changes such as the departure of the United Kingdom from the European Union or the reinforcement of economic protectionism. These conquests are based on discourses that tend to connect emotionally with their followers by relativizing notions of truth and falsehood, reinforcing the differences between "ones" and "the others" and spreading an image of loss of national identity and sovereignty.

While the clamour for a deepening of democracy or xenophobic retrenchment are not new chapters in our history, what is new is the informational context in which these outcries are spread, as well as the use that these social movements make of internet and social networks. The fact that more information than ever before is available to everyone, and that the reliability of this information is questionable in many cases, inspires us to seek educational responses that provide citizens with a critical spirit and that enable schools to address existing social conflicts through a research process based on dialogue and cooperation. In this respect, the "classics" of education such as John Dewey or Paulo Freire, who have demanded the need for all citizens (workers, peasants, immigrants or refugees included) to experience democracy and empowerment, are more alive than ever. Having said that, however, many questions and debates arise between education professionals, academics and politicians on how to deepen democracy in educational centres, going beyond theory and discourse. When reference is made to the democratic school, this adjective connotes multiple interpretations according to the context and the interlocutor being referred to. From the DEMOSKOLE group, we understand that democracy in schools goes beyond participation in representative bodies and that we must advance in enhancing and strengthening this in educational centres, especially, in how it is lived and experienced in first person by all the agents that participate in the reality of education. To this effect, from the University of Girona and the University of Vic joint work began in early 2010 with the objective of identifying and analyzing specific cases in which schools and institutes are working on democracy and whether, in some cases, as Erik O. Wright would say, real utopias can be identified in the world of education. More explicitly, this can be understood as the institutionalization of practices that challenge neoliberal hegemony and promote emancipatory spaces. Despite being imperfect realities and practices, what unites these practices is the deepening and sustainability over time, beyond specific charismatic people who can lead these projects or educational centres.

The main objective of this book is, then, to describe how educational initiatives are emerging that are hopeful in terms of strengthening democracy in a real way in a convulsive world like the current one. Recently, some of the neoliberal educational reforms that have been implemented in many countries have fostered, in a macro-systemic way, the weakening of democratic practice in various ways. On one hand, they tend to devalue the structures of representative democracy in schools (school boards for example) to give more powers to the directors of educational centres while promoting training programs to manage schools as private businesses. On the other hand, some reforms have encouraged schools to be governed by an external council of selected or assigned citizens who have the authority to ensure that the school is accountable to the logic of the market and competition. While it is true that bureaucratization of public school in modern states has tended to defeat the purpose of community and family participation in schools; there is evidence of schools and educational contexts that have been able to institutionalize participation mechanisms in which students, families and the community have a voice and participate actively in the majority of the decisions of the centres. Sometimes, these experiences of direct democracy have had to be developed outside the public education system as a response movement and to not adapt to the rules of the system. At other times, teachers, families and students have been able to find gaps in the education system to create ad hoc structures that enable democratic participation in a sustainable and prolonged way. This is a challenge in a context where priority is given to the bureaucratisation of the system and decision-making according to accountability standards (based on standardized tests). For this reason, education professionals are needed with a critical capacity to know how to interpret the world they are in and with the ability to relinquish or share the power granted to them by the system with other agents, especially those who tend to have less of a voice.

In the first chapter, Feu, Serra, Canimas, Lázaro and Simó-Gil present a proposal for a theoretical framework for the analysis of democratic processes in educational centres that goes beyond describing who governs and how this power is shared and exercised. According to the authors, we must go beyond democratic governance to understand how democracy takes place in a specific space. Analysis of democracy in schools must be sufficiently thorough to identify other significant and related elements, including, for instance, how "the other" is recognized (people belonging to a cultural minority or counter-hegemonic group), how conditions of social inequality and equity are treated and, finally, how to promote a series of values and virtues that favour democratic participation. Schostak then analyzes the recent growth of cooperative schools in the United Kingdom that are governed by respect for the values of mutual aid, democracy, equality and solidarity in a capitalist and competitive context. It is interesting to observe, the author says, how schools can favour counter-democracy, understood as the research practice that students can undertake to identify the false truths promised by governments and delve deeper into one's own truth. In the third chapter, we travel to Iceland where Jónsson describes in detail how just before the economic collapse of 2008 an educational reform was approved in which the neoliberal values of privatization and the emphasis on individualism were central. He also points out, though, how the economic crisis and the democratic context of the Saucepan Revolution stimulated a new curriculum in 2011, where greater emphasis is placed on the moral and community objectives of education. These community and moral values are fundamental in the next chapter where Fielding presents his concept of radical democracy. Educational centres should not only try to promote democracy but must also create spaces, and generate roles and relationships to make it possible. In this direction, he provides us with a typology of ways of interacting between adults and young people in educational contexts that either fosters more instrumental or market relationships, or civic relations and democratic comradeship, which favour egalitarian relationships between adults and young people. Taking the voice of the students into account is the axis of the chapter by Messiou where she describes, through illustrative examples, a series of innovative strategies that have been put into practice in school contexts in different countries that favour schools that are more inclusive. For his part, Collet analyzes the importance of including families and the community in school as well as students. The participation of all stakeholders must be intrinsic in schools and should be carried out through the three areas detailed in this chapter: inclusion, equity and empowerment. In turn, Prieto-Flores, Feu, Serra and Lázaro present case studies of schools that deepen democracy through institutionalizing new forms of governance. The authors examine in depth how some educational centres analyze or expand the existing representative bodies stipulated by law to give a voice to more people, especially individuals from traditionally excluded groups, or generate new ones. This chapter explains the strategies followed by these centres. Next, Simó-Gil and Tort analyze how democratic participation occurs in secondary schools. Specifically, they emphasize challenges facing secondary education in promoting democracy in four areas: tutoring and assemblies, a more community-based approach to the curriculum by fostering service learning, agreement on the spaces and times for learning and teacher participation in leadership and democratic management of the centre. To conclude, the last chapter shows how countries with a high degree of democratization of their societies address the training of their teachers.

We hope, therefore, that in this book you find relevant information that will help to reflect and debate on the deepening of democracy in schools; on the context of economic crisis and prosperity, the intrinsic values of the capitalist society in which we live and how they can be translated to education, but also on the contrary, how education can become a niche of resistance and change. This resistance and change involves giving visibility to strategies implemented by some primary and secondary schools that promote greater presence of the voices of both students and families in the decision-making and the practical and everyday life of the centres. These realities would not be possible without the excellent and anonymous work of the teachers, students and families that have the capacity to de-bureaucratize the educational space and to endow it with meaning. This book is a small tribute to the effort of these people to move towards a more humane and just education and society.

Jordi Feu and Òscar Prieto-Flores, University of Girona

Jordi Feu, Carles Serra, Joan Canimas & Laura Lázaro
*University of Girona*

Núria Simó-Gil
*University of Vic-Central University of Catalonia*

# Democracy and Education: A Theoretical Proposal for the Analysis of Democratic Practices in Schools[1]

Many authors reflect on the role of schools in promoting democracy, but they almost never address the controversy implicit in the concept, and proposals elaborated from the educational sphere are generally unrelated to current philosophical, politological and sociological debate on democracy. Hence, the hegemonic meaning of the term, which is shared in our schools (with exceptions that we cannot overlook), tends to be simple, ambiguous, diffuse, and often situated halfway between the banal and the defense of values where virtually everything fits. *Democracy*, in education, is associated indiscriminately with governability, altruism, equality, the common good, collaboration and participation, without any precise criteria to establish the relationship of each of these concepts with democracy.

This situation is not new nor is it exclusive to the field of education. In 1852 Auguste Blanqui had already called for a clarification of "what is a democrat" and declared that we found ourselves "before a vague and trivial term, with no precise meaning, an elastic term" (Blanqui 2006, p. 172). One hundred sixty years later, Wendy Brown (2011), among others, argues that this vagueness has even increased. Jean-Luc Nancy

---

1   This article is part of the research project "Democracy, participation and inclusive education in primary schools" (EDU2012-39556-C02-01/02) carried out by the research team Democracy and Education: Demoskole, and funded by the Ministry of Economy and Competitiveness.
    This chapter is derived from an article published in Studies in Philosophy and Education, doi:10.1007/s11217-017-9570-7.

(2011, p. 58) also considers that "the signifier 'democracy' has become an exemplary case of absence of meaning" and, still more radically, Jacques Rancière (2011, p. 78) claims that for as long as the word *democracy* has existed "the only consensus that exists consists of the idea that 'democracy' means different and opposing things"[2].

Given this situation, it is undeniable that democracy as a concept remains highly attractive today; broad sectors of society identify with it, and groups and movements appear in the political sphere that rally to the cause of democratic regeneration, democratic radicalism or a more authentic and "true" democracy[3]. It is therefore important to clarify what we mean when we refer to democracy in education and it is imperative for the concept we are going to employ to be consistent with the conceptualization of the term in other fields. As we argued in the article *Dimensions, characteristics and indicators for a democratic school* (2017), the concept of democracy which we support integrates the postulates of the three generations of human and social rights, and aligns with the principles of republican, deliberative and participatory democracy. We start, then from the contributions of authors including Taylor (1979), Fishkin (1995 and 2009), Habermas (1999), Sandel (1998), De Francisco (1998), Pettit (1998), Elster (2001), Viroli (2002), Barber (2004), Skinner (2004), Martí (2006) and Subirats (2011), who in one way or another exercise a critique of the model of representative liberal democracy, considering it elitist, competitive and rigid in the distinction it establishes between governors and governed, and considering the citizenry to be insufficiently represented.

Thus, in the following section we expose how the research team understood democracy (and democracy in the field of education),

---

2    According to other authors, the issue is not the lack of definition of the concept, but the degradation of democratic practices. Thus, Daniel Bensaïd (2011, p. 16) states that popular sovereignty today lies hidden behind democratic formalism, and Sheldon S. Wolin (2008) speaks of a fugitive democracy, a mere episodic expression of the legitimate rights of the people.

3    "Democracy now" and "they call it democracy, but it is not" are some of the most popular slogans chanted in the 15M demonstrations in Spain, just as they were in other countries like the United States, with the OWS (Occupy Wall Street) movement that began in New York, or the United Kingdom, with the OL (Occupy London) movement in London.

interweaving classical aspects (such as governance) with less common ones (such as inhabitance and otherness), and others that are very present in the area of education (values).

## Democracy: four dimensions to take into account

The first thing we must recognize is that we use the word democracy to describe a form of government in which the sovereignty of political power resides in the citizens and in which, consequently, structures of participation and free and informed decision making are established and organized. We call this dimension of democracy *governance*[4]. However, a description of the forms of government is not sufficient to characterize democracy. It is necessary to delve into the conditions that enable the exercise of popular sovereignty and free and informed participation and decision making.

To identify these conditions, it is helpful to look at the three generations of human rights systematized by Karel Vasak in 1977. According to this Czech-French jurist,

> "while first-generation rights (civil and political) were based on the right to oppose the State and those of the second generation (economic, social and cultural) on the right to place demands on the State, those of the third generation currently being proposed to the international community are rights of solidarity" (Vasak 1977, 1984).

As we know, first-generation human rights were formulated at the end of the 18th century, in the Declaration of the Rights of Man and of the Citizen of 1789 and in the Bill of Rights of the United States of America in 1791.

---

4    We use the concept *governance* in its most generic sense, of "forms of government", and more specifically to refer to processes, devices or mechanisms designed for decision making. We are not referring to the concept of *governance* as it has been defined since the 1990s as a "new form of government characterized by the interaction of institutions at different levels and by public administrations interacting and working in network with civil society or private organizations" (Rhodes 1997; Subirats 2010).

They focus mainly on governance, that is, on liberty and participation in political life and on the forms and limits of the exercise of power. However, it soon became evident that democratic governance alone was not sufficient for living together, that this required certain living conditions, and economic, social and cultural rights. We will call this second dimension of democracy *inhabitance*, since it deals with the conditions in which people inhabit. This second generation of human rights, together with the first, was embodied in the Universal Declaration of Human Rights of 1948.

As of the 1980s, and despite the fact that first and second generation human rights had by no means been fully achieved, it in turn became evident that governance and inhabitance were insufficient for living together; that mutual recognition and fraternity with others, as well as respect for the planet were also necessary, whereupon rights began to be formulated including the rights to self-determination, difference and peace, and the right to a preserved, healthy and sustainable environment not only for contemporaries, but also for future generations, etc. For our purposes, we will call this dimension of democracy *otherness*, as it deals with recognition of the other and of the different, with all the complexity associated with this term.

In each of these three dimensions of democracy the *ethos* (character, way of being and of living in the world) of individuals and collectives surfaces. Without specific values, virtues and characters it is impossible to articulate governance, inhabitance and otherness. Without humanist values, virtues and characters governance turns into particracy or bureaucracy, inhabitance becomes complacency, and otherness is impossible. These dimensions are brought into play in approaching democracy as a form of associated life. As Bernstein (2010, p. 251) states when analyzing Dewey's work: "Democracy is the personal way in which an individual lives life and only becomes a reality when practiced in our day-to-day existence".

Consequently, in this article, when speaking about democracy, we will take into consideration the four dimensions of any democratic project: governance, inhabitance, otherness and *ethos*.

## Democracy as governance

Democracy as governance refers to the structures and processes through which political decisions are made and the public sphere is managed, as well as to a method and rules of coexistence. In modernity, this sense of democracy is embodied in the liberal tradition, in the first generation of human rights and the rule of law.

This dimension is what generates greater consensus among theorists of democracy[5]. Thus, for Bobbio (1986, p. 9) the minimum definition of democracy consists of "a set of procedural rules for collective decision making in which the broadest possible participation of stakeholders is envisaged and fostered". From this perspective, democracy is a form of social organization that attributes ownership of political power to individuals recognized as citizens who form a society. Generically, it is a form of social coexistence in which its members are free and equal and social relations are established according to contractual mechanisms. More particularly, it is a form of State organization in which collective decisions are adopted by the people (by those who are recognized as citizens) through different mechanisms of participation.

However, beyond the consensus generated around democracy as a particular form of government, discrepancies and questions arise when establishing the specific characteristics that democratic governance should have[6]. For example, how should popular sovereignty be translated

---

5    Never a complete consensus: from Marxism it has always been considered that liberal democracy, which left economics outside the scope of popular sovereignty, focused on formal aspects (*possibility* to choose and to be elected) and renounced substantive aspects (under this form of democracy it is possible that the whole of the *demos* may not be able to decide on fundamental aspects that affect their existence and that frequently remain unresolved); hence, it was considered to be a somewhat less than democratic form of government that must be overcome in favor of the process of emancipation they pursued for the whole of humanity (Marx, 1975 [1843]; MacPherson, 1973).

6    Apart from the usual distinction between direct, indirect or representative democracy and participatory democracy, the proposal of "deliberative democracy" (Bessette, 1980; Habermas, 1998; Blattberg, 2003; Talisse, 2004), which places emphasis on the examination of public debate and the reasons of justice and general interest, seems especially appropriate for the field of education (for the educational dimension it entails). This model can be contrasted with the model of

to making concrete decisions? Or, to what degree should the principles of democratic governance be extended?

### Democracy as inhabitance

The humanist and socialist tradition, and more recently new social movements, have considered that political freedoms alone were not sufficient, that democracy is not only *governance* but *inhabitance* as well, that political participation in conditions of freedom and equality is not only a procedural question, but also material. Hence, debate surrounding democracy showed concern for the conditions in which people live and propounded that governance requires basic conditions of quality of life and well-being for all people in order for it to be truly democratic. Without the attenuation or elimination of certain inequalities, any pretense of participation in political life on an equal basis is mere fantasy; for political life to be egalitarian, it must be based on economic, material and health conditions, and access to information, training and security. This is what we mean when we talk about *inhabitance*.

The opening of the concept of *democracy* towards issues that go beyond governance became evident in the second generation of human rights, which vindicated as fundamental the right to education, health, work, housing, culture and creativity, and began to materialize, albeit in a timid and limited way, in the so-called welfare state.

Recently proposals have been made that attempt to specify human rights and identify what is required for a life worthy of human dignity. The "Capabilities Approach to Human Development" of Amartya Sen (1999, 2009) and Martha Nussbaum (2011), for example, moves in this direction. This approach is based on the consideration that personal and political governance (to choose and act) require capabilities that

---

democracy based on negotiation, which starts from the capacity to reach agreements or establish counterparts based on the power and negotiating capacity of each actor and in which the common good may prove to be secondary. To understand the distinction between the deliberative and the aggregative models (not necessarily liberal), Young (2000), Ovejero (2003) and Hanson and Howe (2011) are particularly enlightening.

Nussbaum (2011, p. 21) defined as follows: "I call these states of the person (not fixed, but fluid and dynamic) internal capabilities. They are to be distinguished from innate equipment: they are trained or developed traits and abilities, developed, in most cases, in interaction with the social, economic, familial, and political environment". One of the most interesting contributions of Amartya Sen in the development of economic and social indicators is the concept of the capabilities approach: people must have the capability to convert their rights into real events, such that a government should be judged on the specific capabilities it provides to its citizens, for example to be able to vote[7]. These capabilities range from access to education, to citizens having a means of transportation that allows them to arrive at polling places. Only when these barriers are overcome can it be said that citizens can exercise their personal choice. Martha Nussbaum's[8] work develops, explores in depth, and in some cases modifies this line began by Sen.

Different theorists of democracy also refer to the conditions of inhabitance as an essential prerequisite for us to be able to speak of democracy. One of them is Paolo Flores d'Arcais who states:

> A citizen, first and foremost, is a body, a *bios*. To exercise power, they have to be able to live. Even the most intolerant of metaphysicians would grant this 'materialism'. If there are no guarantees for the *bios*, there is no possibility of will or decision. The *bios* is the first '*chez soi*', original and inalienable, of the individual citizen in relation to society: the beginning of political equality and, to start speaking meaningfully, physiological equality of the vital minimum. (Flores d'Arcais 2005, p. 29).

Flores d'Arcais considers that this vital minimum includes food, housing and health care and believes that these factors are the "inalienable

---

7    His approach based on "capabilities" ties in with the idea of positive freedom (the actual ability of a person to be or do something), instead of negative freedom (the absence of prohibitions).

8    Nussbaum identifies ten core capabilities, which have to do with (1) longevity, (2) physical health, (3) physical integrity, (4) the senses, imagination and thought, (5) emotions, (6) practical reason, (7) membership, (8) the relationship with other species, (9) play, and lastly, (10) control over one's environment. (Nussbaum, 2012). Of these ten core capabilities identified by Nussbaum, governance covers only certain aspects, while the remainder refer to *inhabitance* and otherness. (Nussbaum, 2011).

material foundation of abstract equality (for instance, of political equality) between citizens" (2005, p. 30). To not guarantee this basic inhabitance causes some to live below the minimum while others live in the privilege of disproportionate wealth, and democracy suffers from this, because "the sick, and perhaps even more than the hungry, are absolutely dependent: they cannot dissent, nor even decide" (2005, p. 30).

As Flores d'Arcais points out, it is not about taking advantage of discussing democracy to interpolate social objectives; it is a question of recognizing that equality goes beyond the formal equality of "one person, one vote". Furthermore, he asserts that equality must reach aspects in which education plays a fundamental role, because in order to deliberate and decide we need to know.

For Flores d'Arcais, access to training and information are fundamental aspects of democracy. Savater (1999) also arrives at similar approaches. He considers that, beyond democratic isonomy (equality before the law and equal ability to participate in the enactment and abolition of laws), the democratic project contains, more or less explicitly, the ideal of achieving other forms of equality (1999). He justifies this in two ways: *(i)* because it is necessary that all members of society have equal opportunities to realize their abilities, and *(ii)* because for democratic isonomy to be effective and efficient it is necessary that all people have a sufficient degree of personal independence regarding their most imperious needs.

Therefore, he asserts that democratic decisions have to be oriented towards a more complete and thorough equalization of social conditions. Savater warns of the tension that in any democratic system is generated between the principle of equality and the principle of freedom, which refers to two democratic traditions. On the one hand, the republican, which emphasizes participation in the political life of the community, advocates a virtuous and responsible citizenry[9] able to take control of their destinies, and seeks to encourage participation, deliberation and the public good and to abolish any form of domination. On the other hand, there is the liberal tradition, which gives priority to individual freedom and the inviolability of private life. Undoubtedly, our proposal

---

9    Talking about citizenry is not easy, because this concept depends, in part, on the
      political project and the ideology that supports it.

is closer to the republican conception than the liberal,[10] or what Barber (1984) has defined as "strong democracy": a system where citizens actively participate and the government is not in the hands of the few, where there is the will to correct some of the undesirable consequences of inequality, discrimination and domination, and where mechanisms of social inclusion and deliberative processes appear as fundamental.

To the minimum conditions that enable participation, and which we can relate to certain ideas of social justice, another may be added: the quality of reception, coexistence and welfare of the contexts where participation develops (in the educational setting they have been called "climate of the school" or "climate of coexistence"). If, as we have stated, our option is based on a republican, participatory and deliberative conception of democracy, we must consider that everything that favors or is predisposed to participation contributes to the quality of democratic processes.

However, in order to practice democracy, it is not enough to merely promote and ensure participation (first dimension), nor basic conditions of material and environmental well-being for all (second dimension). It is also necessary to recognize the other in their diversity and provide them with adequate answers, for which the policies of the first modernity are no longer sufficient, because in their universalist configuration they ignored singularity, which brings us to the third dimension of democracy, otherness.

*Democracy as otherness*

Recently, the humanist tradition has insisted and advanced in the study of responsibility towards the other. This third opening of the word *democracy* is reflected in the third generation of human rights: protection of minority groups or those discriminated against, respect for cultural diversity and, in general, for the choices people make in the most diverse areas of their lives (sexuality, religion, diet, etc.) in an increasingly

---

10    The texts of Pettit (1997a, 1997b), Ovejero *et al.* (2004), Sandel (1998, 2004) and
      Agulló (2014) adequately describe the two traditions, while helping to position
      our proposal in relation to them.

heterogeneous society. This dimension nullifies the democratic paradigm of numerical power through which the majority imposes their will on minorities, replacing it with the paradigm of reasonableness and respect for singularities. As authors of reference of these approaches we can cite Charles Taylor (1994), Bill Kymlicka (1995a, 1995b), especially concerned about respect for minorities, practices and policies of recognition and protection of community rights; and Henry Giroux (2005) who applied some reflections on these issues to the field of education.

Within this perspective we can include all those actions, policies, programs and attitudes that enable the normalized, dignified and positive recognition of persons and non-hegemonic groups that because of this condition are easily rendered invisible or negatively represented (stigmatized). Otherness refers to the recognition of the "other". There are those who, like Axel Honneth, refer to three-dimensional recognition: emotional (through relationships of love and friendship, which make self-confidence possible), legal (through equality and legal protection or rule of law, which allow an elemental self-respect) and social (through social consideration and assessment, which make self-esteem possible) Non-recognition, disparagement, humiliation, failure to respect dignity or exercising violence against the identity of a person or group, can cause, states Honneth, their "psychic death" or "social death", but also the reaction and struggle in their different forms of expression (Honneth, 1997).

The principle of equality is the recognition that all people, regardless of their singularities, have the same rights. It is not, as some pretend, the nullification of singularities in order to make us all homogeneous. Linguistic, sexual, cultural or any other kind of diversity must be recognized and respected, provided they do not violate fundamental rights of others, and at the same time, it must be ensured that certain discourses based on diversity do not serve as a basis for establishing principles of inequality (Taguieff, 1990). All of this leads us to the need to clarify the values to promote in a society that seeks to be democratic.

## Democracy as ethos: values and virtues

In the introduction we noted that to define our model of democracy we understand that along with governance, inhabitance and otherness we contemplate *ethos*, since that without values, virtues and certain characters it is impossible for governance, inhabitance and otherness to function in accordance with democratic standards. Thus, *ethos* (largely, that which education has been addressing for centuries) is an integral and fundamental part of the other three dimensions.

This proposal is consistent with the republican tradition, with which we have already expressed our affinity. From this tradition, it is considered necessary to cultivate the virtue of citizens if we want the community to take control of its own destinies (Sandel, 1996), and it is assumed that citizenship not only entails rights for the individual, but also duties.

Public virtues are intimately related to the sustaining of liberty, virtues understood as "capabilities that each of us must possess as a citizen: capabilities that allow us to willingly serve the common good" (Skinner 2004, p. 106). Philip Pettit also considers that laws require the support of "forms of virtue, good citizenship, or civility" (1997b, p. 326), in so far as they ensure greater respect for the law, improve their application and favor their submission to collective interests.

Concerning the defense and promotion of civic virtues, there are notable differences in the discourse of current republicans (Ovejero *et al.* 2004). Some continue considering them as the only way to elevate the character of citizens and tend to a certain perfectionism, while others defend them for purely instrumental reasons, as a means to promote deliberation in the service of social justice (for example Sunstein 2004). Agulló (2014) states that all advocates of republicanism agree that civic virtue is the "backbone" (Giner, 1998, p. 2) of republican democracy, and that there cannot be genuine deliberation (nor valuable or desirable participation) without citizens who are aware of their duties and responsibilities, competent, active, well informed and willing to make a commitment to act in the service of the public good (Peña 2000). Agulló, in turn, cites Rubio Carracedo (2005), who states that only an elevated sense of democracy enables politics based on popular sovereignty to function properly.

On the other hand, Ovejero, Martí and Gargarella (2004) caution that, while liberal discourse has traditionally been more reticent to speak of virtues (in that they would be linked to specific conceptions of "the good", which the State should refrain from supporting), several authors of liberal inspiration have begun to reflect on the role of civic virtues based on liberal principles and cite Macedo (1990), Galston (1991) and Rawls (1993).

The values to be promoted diverge from one author to another, but there is a degree of consensus around qualities such as responsibility, commitment, prudence, continence, tolerance, courage, respect for others and their freedom and opinions; and also with regard to capacities such as knowing how to listen and express oneself, searching for and selecting information and knowing how to interpret and contrast it, developing critical and independent thinking and resolving conflicts peacefully. The concretion of these values and capacities in real life is not unequivocal, since, without invoking cultural relativism, they are embodied in particular and diverse cultural contexts.

## Democracy in the classroom: the four dimensions of democracy in the field of education

Thus far we have established a way of understanding democracy that is consistent with some of the current approaches being dealt with in disciplines such as political science, sociology, legal theory or philosophy; and this theoretical framework now allows us to analyze the dilemmas and uncertainties faced by schools in view of the challenge of promoting democratic educational practices.

### Governance in educational contexts

To analyze school governance mainly involves analysis of all of the bodies and processes related to decision making, which in turn involves studying the relationships between the different agents of the educational community in terms of both the interpersonal dimension and the search for common or collective interest. Thus, the analysis of governance in schools requires analysis of the functioning of bodies established by the administration (institutional bodies), those established by each school (their own bodies), and the more or less informal and spontaneous practices that in one way or another influence the decision-making processes. These governance bodies and processes can be differentiated by the type of participation of each of the agents, their representativeness or the competences that are attributed to them. Thus, it is of great interest to analyze in each school how crucial questions are resolved such as: What forms of participation and/or representation are encouraged? Which aspects can be decided upon and which decisions are considered to be the province of only one particular body? How do participation and decision making affect the hierarchy between teachers and students?

Analysis and proposals of this type are posed, for example, in the Proyecto Atlántida [Atlantis Project], which formulates proposals for a school in which all educational and social partners (local social agents, participatory structures of families and governing bodies of the centers) share responsibility for its operation (Luengo 2006). In an interesting article, Alvarez (2004) offers a critical review of the functioning of the governance mechanisms of public and *concertada* [private establishment financed with public funds] schools, analyzes the official political bodies of the center and what he calls "micro politics", and offers some suggestions for improvement aimed at training for participation and change in the dynamics of governance. Jordi Garreta, in a study on associations of parents (2008), provides abundant data and recommendations on the role that these associations have in the governance of schools and in educational activity in general, and calls for internal democracy and open structures to facilitate their participation. Edelstein (2011) is another author interested in governance, which he conceives of as a prototype of democratic government (an idea that is related in some ways, with Freinet), and proposes learning *through democracy* as a form of "learning democracy". *Learning through democracy* involves, among other things, student participation in the processes of government articulated through *self-government practices* as a tool that offers the possibility of collecting the expression and discussion of the wishes of students in the classroom and in the center.

As Flutter (2007) affirms, assessing the voice of the student body is a complex task. To ensure that the voice of students will be heard involves the broad participation of all students in all areas of decision making of the school (both in organization and curriculum, and in determining the educational mission and philosophy). In the words of Sutherland (2006, p. 8): "[s]tudent voice and student participation in schools need to be part of a collaborative ethos that embraces all members of the school community".


## Inhabitance in educational contexts

In speaking of *inhabitance* in the school context we are referring to the set of actions that make the educational community, and especially students, feel good and be able to fulfill their main task: to be autonomous citizens, with good judgment, able to relate well with others, to be happy and be able to successfully complete the various stages of the education system. This is a broad and diverse principle that we have centered around three issues: actions designed to provide a good reception for the community (especially students, teachers and families); strategies that favor educational success for all; and lastly, those relating to educational infrastructures and human, economic and pedagogical resources.

Actions related to reception refer to actions that are carried out to facilitate participation in the center of students and families with difficult living conditions (with deficits of *inhabitance*), in order to mitigate as much as possible the interference that these situations cause for them. This includes ease of access to the center (one can hardly speak of political equality if access to certain centers is conditioned by the payment of fees or if families have difficulty accessing school material), aid for access to certain services (one wonders whether it makes sense to talk about school success or participation of families when some students do not have their daily meals guaranteed), scheduling meetings on days and at times so that working families may attend, taking specific actions so that parents from disadvantaged groups can serve on the school board, and the existence of channels or protocols to detect and address problems that may occur in the family and have repercussions on children.

Second, the strategies set in motion by the school to achieve the educational success of all students encompass actions aimed at capacitating all members of the educational community, especially students, but also their families. For example, educational actions and support in the classroom so that all students may acquire the skills and knowledge necessary to develop their capabilities and live in society. This aims to ensure that all students, regardless of their social, economic or geographical origin, may achieve school success in the terms set out by Ainscow *et al.* (2004).

And last, the actions and strategies referring to educational infrastructures and human, economic and pedagogical resources. This includes taking care of all those aspects that promote a positive atmosphere, making the stay in the educational center easy and enjoyable and facilitating the relationships that are established within it, which contribute to the quality of life and well-being. For example: conditions of habitability of schools, ease of access to the center, ease of contact and relationship with its professionals, establishment of a climate of coexistence and cordiality, existence of a positive link between all educational agents and the school, amenity and comfort of the architecture and attention to the decoration of the center, etc. Only in these conditions is reciprocity in the interpersonal relations between students, teachers and other educational agents possible. As Thornberg and Elvstrand (2012) point out, "Only when understood in this way can the trust be built that allows relationships in which all the participants, in this case pupils and teachers, feel that they are full partners". And as expressed by Simó, Parareda and Domingo (2016, p. 2), "In the realm of education, the quality of the shared life is described as the school atmosphere, which involves two fundamental aspects: the minimum conditions that make possible the participation of each and every one of the members of the school community, and the level of receptiveness, the quality of the shared life and the sense of well-being of the contexts in which participation occurs."

Many authors have stressed these aspects linked to the discourse of democracy and democratic quality in education. Gutmann and Thomson (1996), for example, focus on the first aspect that we mentioned when they argue that to participate in a deliberative democracy there is a general need for certain minimal resources, such as housing and access to healthcare. In the same vein, Apple and Beane (1995) mention the need for structural and institutional inclusion accompanying equal access to education in democratic schools. Serramona and Rodriguez (2010) suggest the need for cultural inclusion of families to empower them to participate, and in a similar way Alvarez (2004) alerts us to the necessity to train students for participation. Meira Levinson (2012) be-lieves that civic involvement of students and, therefore, the possibility of learning about democratic citizenship, presupposes levels of social and ethnic integration in the schools and areas where they are located, and the study by Brady *et al.* (1995) shows that socioeconomic status is included among the predictors of political participation of citizens (in their analysis they go beyond the school environment), evidenced in the possession of resources such as time and civic skills.

Other authors link democracy, equality and academic success. For example, Guarro (2005) asserts that a democratic school is a just school, committed to the democratic reconstruction of its culture to create citizens, properly integrate all students, without discrimination of any type, and provide an education that allows them to live in harmony and actively participate in society. Feito (2009, 2010) argues that a democratic school has to be committed to comprehensiveness and inclusion (it must work towards the academic success of students in the compulsory education stage and should adopt educational strategies that contribute to achieving this goal). Also, Meira Levinson (2012) and Diane Reay (2011) advocate inclusive education and take a position against *tracking*, to the extent that this does not contribute to position students in a situation of maximum equality, and actually does just the opposite. In fact, Reay builds on the work of R. H. Tawney (1964) and extends this argument to advocate for a common school in order to promote the same capabilities in all students, which she considers essential for navigating the world in which we live, understanding it and positioning ourselves before it judiciously.

## Otherness in schools

As we have seen in some examples from the previous section, it is sometimes difficult to draw a clear distinction between what corresponds to *inhabitance* and what corresponds to otherness, among other things because frequently the groups considered as "different" turn out to be, moreover, those suffering from the worst conditions of *inhabitance*, and both axes are mutually interfering or reinforcing. In any case, we understand that otherness in the area of education is embodied in the practices, discourses, initiatives, policies or projects that are established in order to recognize (respect, welcome, include) and positively assess the "other" (the other who is minority, unconventional, counterhegemonic, etc.). In this meaning, democratic practice not only consists of "tolerating" the other, but in giving them visibility and "normalized" treatment, resituating the relations of power and domination between the hegemonic and the peripheral. This exercise involves understanding the other in all their complexity and taking into account their own frame of reference, as well as their cultural and symbolic universe.

The majority of initiatives aligned in what has been called *intercultural education* (or *critical multiculturalism*, in the British tradition), and the practices of reception and attention to diversity from an inclusive perspective, can be described as initiatives that seek to work on one of the aspects we consider fundamental in any democratic project: otherness. A separate issue is the effectiveness of such practices and the undesirable effects that can be generated and that have been intensively studied and denounced by a large proportion of the researchers who we can situate in this tradition[11]. In this direction, works including those of Palaudàrias (2002), Bertran (2005) and Garreta (2009), among many others, go into depth on this dimension of democratic practices, focusing on analysis of the participation of immigrant families in schools, while studies by Palaudàrias and Feu (1997) analyze reception and recognition at school (it is somewhat more difficult to find works on inclusion and recognition of other forms of diversity).

---

11   Primarily based on the work of Taguieff (1990). In Spain, San Roman (1996) includes many of the contributions of the French philosopher, and Carbonell (2000), has effectively transferred them to the field of education. Serra (2002) exposes the criticism to the first multiculturalism and presents the basic axes of critical multiculturalism and interculturalism. Authors like Delgado (2003) move away from the optimism or possibilism of others, and continue to raise profound criticism of both multicultural and intercultural approaches.

*Ethos and education: the treatment of values, virtues and
capabilities in the classroom*

The fourth and final dimension is that of values, attitudes and competences that enable us to participate fully and responsibly in democratic processes. We have already mentioned that values are an area that
seems particularly educational, scholastic even; there are many authors
who insist that democratic education consists of an education in values and think of it as an element of ethics. What varies substantially
from one author to another is how these moral values, these attitudes
and the ability to implement them are transferred to students. Manuel
Barbosa (2000), for example, establishes three basic models: the model of transmission of knowledge and values, according to which content is transmitted through the explicit curriculum integrated in one or
more subjects; the model of training democratic habits, which seeks
to develop democratic routines and attitudes through experience and
implementation of democratic practices in schools, and the model of
direct confrontation with socio-political reality, which aims to develop
democratic values and attitudes through the exposure and involvement
of students in real social problems. Guarro (2002, 2005) as well as Barbosa (2000) and Edelstein (2011) contribute abundant bibliography on
authors who have elaborated proposals along these lines, and on projects and programs that have been developed and on researchers who
have analyzed the limitations and problems of some of these proposals.
One aspect that seems particularly relevant to highlight is the notion of
citizenship that we relate to this way of understanding democracy. In
this connection, Lawy and Biesta (2006) and Biesta, Lawy and Kelly
(2009) contrast the concepts *Citizenship-as-achievement* and *Citizenship-as-practice*. In the first, the skills and capabilities learned in school
are those that students need when they leave school and become future
citizens, while the second concept understands students as citizens involved in the existing socio-political, economic and cultural order. Thus
the conditions in which students experience the school institution, and
the interpersonal relations that develop there, shape their way of understanding and living life. Accordingly, we share with Biesta and Lawy
(2006, p. 43):

Citizenship is no longer a solely adult experience but is experienced and articulated as a wider shift in social relations common to all age groups. It is reflexive because it feeds back on itself, and is relational because it is affected by different factors, including social and structural conditions that play upon it. As such it cannot be simply learned in school or in any other institution but is common to all situations.

# Conclusion

The proposals for analysis of democracy in the sphere of education and proposals for implementation of what is intended to be a democratic education encompass very diverse fields: from forms of governance to the commitment to comprehensiveness and inclusion; from a curriculum centered on democratic values to the defense of recognition or the commitment to interculturalism; from academic success for all to the development of the critical capacity of students. But this was the starting point of our article; the aim was to show the extent to which such heterogeneous proposals could be framed as proposals for promoting democracy in education.

At the beginning of the article, we observed that very few of the works on democracy and education made an effort to link their proposals intended for the educational sphere with an idea of democracy sufficiently comprehensive so as to be acceptable for those disciplines that have traditionally worked on, and continue to work on, this concept. We believe that throughout these pages we have shown how, from the republican and deliberative concept of democracy (two currents of democratic thought still fully relevant and recognizable in current political and academic debate), we can establish and delimit this notion of democracy that is at once coherent, acceptable and comprehensive. This is a notion that unfolds in four dimensions: governance, inhabitance, otherness and *ethos*, which any democratic project should consider and which has the virtue of collecting the process of progressive recognition and expansion of human rights, as has been analyzed and systematized by Karel Vasak (1977, 1984). And lastly, it is a conception of democracy that allows us to position ourselves clearly before the current crisis of the concept of democracy and democratic practices. Put another way, we believe that the multifaceted concept of democracy identified here is current, relevant, well-established, defensible from different disciplines, comprehensive and at the same time committed and ambitious, the precise opposite of the simplicity, ambiguity, laxness – and in some cases, the banality – that we denounced in the introduction. In short, it is far from the vacuity referred to by Wendy Brown (2011) and from what, according to Nancy (2011), was a signifier without meaning.

Undoubtedly, the multifaceted conception of educational democracy that has been presented here can be controversial. We would even dare to say that it should be, especially if we want to take it as a starting point to analyze what a democratic education or school should be. The possibility to translate the different dimensions of the concept of democracy to the educational sphere allows us to establish broad (but at the same time coherent) and ambitious criteria to work on the analysis and proposals of what has come to be called the "democratic quality" of our schools. We understand that with the delimitation of the concept we have proposed it is possible to analyze the coherence of heterogeneous and seemingly disparate practices and proposals, such that it is easier to establish what we mean when we talk about democracy in education or which aspects we should pay attention to and which aspects we can influence to contribute to improving the democratic quality of schools.

JOHN SCHOSTAK
*Manchester Metropolitan University*

# Truth, Lies and Propaganda: The Challenge for Democratic and Co-ooperative Education

Democratic education, children's rights and child centred teaching compete with national demands to top the global league tables particularly in numeracy, literacy, science and information technologies. Within this context, it has always concerned me that education too often is reduced to the social function of reproducing society rather than critiquing and transforming it. What I want to argue here is that education is critical in creating the conditions for a free and equal society, what Rosanvallon (2013) refers to as the society of equals. What sort of society we want depends crucially upon the relation between the prevailing political institutions, discourses, and practices in conjunction with the forms of education that take place not only in childhood but also throughout adult life as a member of 'the public' (Schostak 2018). The socialist utopian Robert Owen, a key pioneering figure in the history of the co-operative movement, saw education as essential to changing society from one based on greed and competition to that of equality and co-operation. Moreover, education was seen as vital by the Rochdale Pioneers whose shop set up in 1844 has led to a worldwide movement. A report for the United Nation's Secretariat (Dave Grace and Associates, 2014) estimated there were now 2.6 million co-operatives in 145 countries impacting upon the lives of a billion people. Its combined assets were worth around US$20 trillion with about US$3 trillion in revenues. If this were treated as an economic unit, it would be the world's 5th largest.

It is the movement's global economic structure sustaining a view of community and social reformation that potentially provides the dimension lacking in the experiments in democratic schools whether Susan Isacks (c.f. Willan 2011), Dewey (1916, 1938) or Summerhill (Neill 1973). Dewey's experiment has had a profound influence but according to Mayhew and Edwards who taught at his laboratory school, he became increasingly pessimistic about the prospect of democratic schooling. Similarly, Fielding and Moss (2011) in their introduction to the Italian edition of their review of the legacies of democratic schools expressed pessimism. It is this pessimism that has to be overcome. It can be done so I argue by combining the economic and community building power of the co-operative with the insights of the legacies of democratic schooling in conjunction with the contemporary political debates around radical democracy.

Democratic education has failed to enter the mainstream, I suggest, due to the larger political environment which in Bouton's (2007) and Rosanvallon's (2013) view, since the eighteenth century democratic revolutions in America, France and Saint-Domingue (now Haiti), are designed to tame democracy, that is, to make it work for the rich elites not the many. The debates concerning the development of democracy – essentially how to manage the relation between the rich and the rest – in the early years of the twentieth century were dominated by factors leading to the world wars, their consequences, and the threat of communism to market capitalism. The key question concerned how to protect the freedoms of the property owning individual from the totalitarian impulses of state communism and fascism. This debate was central to the Paris colloquium called in 1938 following the publication of Walter Lippman's book *The Good Society* (1937). Attending the conference were Friedrich Hayek and Ludwig von Mises, both central to the development of neoliberalism. Indeed Hayek's, influential book *The Road to Serfdom* (1944) was, he claimed, influenced by Lippmann. Lippmann essentially argued that the world is so complex that the work of governance is best left to experts. Along with Edward Bernays, a nephew of Sigmund Freud, both were major figures in the emergent public relations industry that campaigned equally for business interests and political interests. Both saw the public as the objects of manipulation and both saw education as central to democracy. Bernays (1928) drew little distinction between education and propaganda. For him the teacher had a "twofold job: education as a teacher and education as a propagandist" whereby the teaching profession had "the right to carry on a very definite propaganda with a view to enlightening the public asserting its intimate relation to the society which it serves" (*ibid*, p. 137).

And more generally the propaganda-educational relation further blurs at the level of state leadership:

> The important thing for the statesman of our age is not so much to know how to please the public, but to know how to sway the public. In theory, this education might be done by means of learned pamphlets explaining the intricacies of public questions. In actual fact, it can be done only by meeting the conditions of the public mind, by creating circumstances which set up trains of thought, by dramatising personalities, by establishing contact with the group leaders who control the opinions of their publics (Bernays, 1928).

Thus:

> Is this government by propaganda? Call it, if you prefer, government by education. But education, in the academic sense of the word, is not sufficient. It must be enlightened expert propaganda through the creation of circumstances, through the high-spotting of significant events, and the dramatisation of important issues (Bernays, 1928).

For Bernays, propaganda whether good or bad could not be escaped, because "in some form [it] will always be used where leaders need to appeal to their constituencies" (*ibid*, p. 123). In short, the blurring between propaganda-education raises the crucial question of truth.

The question is exemplified by two related but different political campaigns, one in the UK to leave the European Union and one in America to elect the president. In educational and propaganda terms the critical element in each case was the blurring of lines between fact, fantasy and lies. As, in a slip of the tongue, senior White House advisor Kellyanne Conway put it, there are 'alternative facts' (Pengelly, 2017). The implication was one could choose the facts that suited and supported the narrative being promoted. This is at once an educational and a democratic issue that undermines any notion for the existence of objective evidence that can be robustly contested through rational public debate. Rather than search for the truth concerning a reality that resists our desires and fantasies about its nature, one only has to identify alternative facts that support the desired perception of reality. For this, the American talk show host Stephen Colbert had in 2005 invented the term 'truthiness' which he defined as "something that seems like the truth – the truth we want to exist" (The Washington Times, 2016) or on another

occasion as "believing something that *feels* true, even if it isn't supported by fact" (Latour, 2016). Colbert then extended his understanding of
the concept in the light of Trump's presidential campaign by inventing
the term 'trumpiness'. Distinguishing the two terms, Latour writes:

"Truthiness has to feel true, but Trumpiness doesn't even have to
do that". Colbert referenced a *Washington Post* article from June, many
Trump supporters don't believe his wildest promises – and they don't
care. That now serves as the definition of the term (Latour, 2016).

This definition of Trumpiness is similar to the more general and
earthy term discussed by Frankfurt (2005) where he distinguishes between truth, lying and bullshit. Both the liar and the honest person share
a notion of the true and the false but the bullshitter he is neither on the
side of the true nor on the side of the false. His eye is not on the facts at
all, as the eyes of the honest man and of the liar are, except insofar as
they may be pertinent to his interest in getting away with what he says.
He does not care whether the things he says describe reality correctly.
He just picks them out, or makes them up, to suit his purpose.

The issue at stake for democratic education and its contribution to
public life is how to create the conditions under which individuals can
engage with each other in the critical examination of the values, beliefs
and what counts as 'knowledge', 'expertise', 'evidence' and 'understanding' through which their behaviours and the organisation of their
everyday lives are shaped and managed? Nothing better exemplifies
elite driven judgement on the 'masses', the 'public' than Robert Lowe's
critical campaign that led to the 1870 Education Act in the UK following the extension of voting rights to some members of the lower classes.
The purpose of this education was so "that they may appreciate and de-
fer to a higher cultivation when they meet it," and thus "I believe it will
be absolutely necessary that you should prevail on our future masters
to learn their letters" (cited by Sylvester, 1974). This deference to the
'cultivated' elites, or later, to experts, as advocated by Lippmann and
Bernays, has been variously implemented in the political campaigns,
mass media and mass education systems of westernised democracies
resulting in maintaining inequality even while professing democracy
and equality of opportunities (Marsh, 2011). This subterfuge conforms
to another characteristic of the Trump and Brexit campaigns: gaslighting. As Duca (2016) explains:

"Gas lighting" is a buzzy name for a terrifying strategy currently being used to weaken and blind the American electorate. We are collectively being treated like Bella Manningham in the 1938 Victorian thriller from which the term "gas light" takes its name. In the play, Jack terrorizes his wife Bella into questioning her reality by blaming her for mischievously misplacing household items which he systematically hides. Doubting whether her perspective can be trusted, Bella clings to a single shred of evidence: the dimming of the gas lights that accompanies the late night execution of Jack's trickery. The wavering flame is the one thing that holds her conviction in place as she wriggles free of her captor's control.

To gas light is to psychologically manipulate a person to the point where they question their own sanity, and that's precisely what Trump is doing to this country.

How might education counter the forms of liberal democracy that sustain the gaslighting of populations?

## Schooling and Education as Counter-Democracy

Dewey's book *The public and its problems* (1927) was in response to the issues raised by Lippmann in his 1927 book *The Phantom Public* (see Dewey, 1927). For Lippmann the public was basically a phantom since the real decisions were to be made by experts. No one, he argued had the time or sufficient expertise to deal with the full complexity of society. Hence, there should be experts for each issue and the consent of the 'public' to the decisions of the experts was to be manufactured through media campaigns. Dewey agreed with the diagnosis, but thought a more productive and substantive democracy could be produced through engagement with educators. Unfortunately, Dewey might have won the philosophical debate among educators, particularly as modelled by his laboratory school (Mayhew and Edwards, 1936), but he did not win the more general propaganda war (Labaree, 2010) that resulted in a more technical 'scientific' approach to schooling where children were to be measured, sorted, and engineered through performance driven forms of teaching and learning. In short, the realities of children were to be sub-jected to and manipulated by the powers of educational engineers – all, of course, in their best interests. And periodically, the success of that manipulation can be evidenced through testing, creating a sense of the real by highlighting only what can be tested rather than the experience that is felt, or the imagination that enriches the world. In short, it sys-tematically reinforces a reality that is counter to the values underpinning democracy – principally freedom and equality – that are fundamental to ensuring that individuals are not dominated by the powerful, manipulat-ed to meet ends that are not of their choosing, and exploited.

Counter-democracy is a term employed by Rosanvallon (2012) to refer to practices such as protest, investigative journalism, investigative tribunals that hold the powerful to account and resist the manufactured realities of governments that promise freedoms and equalities yet in countless ways do not deliver. It counters the hollowed out democracy that enables elites to impose authoritarian structures throughout the or-ganisations that impact upon the everyday lives of the majority (Schos-tak and Goodson, 2012). And that, of course, includes the majority of mainstream schooling that institutionalises hierarchical forms of dis-cipline and control whether of behaviour or of knowledge, whether of learning or teaching as a model for a social order underpinned by elite driven understandings of what counts socially, politically, economically, culturally as 'expertise'. In these hierarchies everyone who is anyone finds their place, significance and meaning and sense of subjectivity as a member of the social order. This is what Rancière (2004) calls the 'police' state, an order that is not simply reducible to the agencies of the police. It refers to the totality, like a social envelope, or an egg, where each part is a part of the whole and thus contained by the shell of the whole. Against this, as individuals, as members of a crowd, a mass, a mob, a multitude, however, we are not part of the structure of the whole. Apart from their social functions, their levels of wealth, their class power or powerlessness, individuals are just one individual among others, equal in being no more and no less than others in their individual existences. This for the social 'policed' order is dangerous. In this sense, individuals are 'a part of no part' as Rancière calls it. The mass is not functionally a part of the machineries of the social order, unless it is reconstituted say as 'consumers'. But to step outside of that social functionality is potentially revolutionary. It is the moment when all can change. It is *the political*, as Rancière calls it. It is the moment when people see that as in aggregating their powers as equals they can either continue to constitute the given or change it. Thus, it is equally a moment of learning, a moment of education that breaks the bounds of the forms of schooling that prepare them to enter a given social order.

Counter-democracy operates from this moment of awareness where an individual either counters the movement towards greater democracy in order to reinforce the given, or counters the given political forms of democracy in order to open them up to greater accountability to the people in their aspect of being a part of no part, that is, of being free and equal individuals. In this moment of ambiguity between maintaining the bounds or breaking the bounds, schools play a pivotal role.

At the extreme, as Willard Waller (1932) remarked, there is a 'natural' enmity between teachers and students as the one stops the other from doing what they want to do. The teacher, in this role, teaches the appropriate bounds and schools are constitutive of disciplinary hierarchies, whether those are organised through legitimate means or illegitimately and abusively. At their worst, schools align with and constitute the psychological and social forms, behaviours and values that Harber (2004) shows underpins the most hateful and violent regimes in the world. At their best, they are institutions of child rearing instilling values that underpin the boundaries required for a civilised and peaceful society. Education, in the sense I am using here, escapes the child rearing function that is founded upon elite adult driven curricula, in order to activate its root meanings of *educare*, to 'draw out', 'lead out, 'bring forth' the expressions of the free and equal powers of individuals. Its related latin root, educere, also gives us 'educe' which according to etymonline <https://www.etymonline.com/word/educe> around 1600 meant to "bring into view or operation" and from 1837 "to draw a conclusion from data". Combining these meanings of drawing out, bringing into view and into operation define how I want to use the term education. To 'educate', in the sense being created here, brings into view and into operation the powers of individuals that enable them to draw conclusions from the data of their senses and their intellectual imaginations to act in the world. A philosophical grounding begins with Spinoza (2004) who provides a political ethics of organising powers that lead directly to democracy, a democracy, that is, of powers. If one power, like reason, is privileged over another, like imagination, then the benefit to be provided by the full development of imagination will be diminished. In his reasoning, the freedom of all powers to come to full fruition, thus the freedom of all individuals depends on their being treated equally. Here equality is not to be confused with homogeneity but rather is the equality that comes with difference, that is, heterogeneity. It is from heterogeneity that forms of social organisation are constituted that are faithful, as Rancière (1999) would put it, to the disagreements the stem from differences in ways of seeing the world, differences in desire, and differences in demands. In terms of our uniqueness of view, our existential alone-ness, our finitude we are all equal. As to our social position at birth, our physical and mental capacities we are all unequal. For some that inequality results in privilege, wealth and power and a life of ease inherited from social class differences. For others, there is poverty, misery and a life of struggle. From this point of view, education to create the society of equals is radical, insurrectionary, revolutionary. From the perspective of those whose wealth, privilege and political power is underpinned by the status quo, the perception that reality can be otherwise must be countered at all costs. This, in turn, makes schools – the 'part of the whole' where the young are prepared for their future in society – a battleground for constituting what is, or is not real, realistic, right and socially 'good'.

## Constitutive practices

There is an emotional dimension to the experience of reflection upon one's experiences that can be expressed as joy, pleasure or pain. The laws, traditions and norms of a society act to reward the expressions of powers that sustain the social order as it is and punish those expressions of powers that are a threat. How then are the social and organisational practices, procedures, and mechanisms to be constituted that engage with boundaries in ways that increase the freedom of all individuals?

It is a question that fundamentally engages with the truth about one's experiences in the world. This is the most difficult question to explore and answer. It is variously the goal of investigative journalists attempting to uncover what the powerful are hiding, social and political theorists who seek what prevents the accomplishment of the 'good society' and indeed, psychologies of all kinds that seek to heal the wounds of living. Exploring such truths necessitates courage, a courage that teachers would have to find in order to explore and engage with the truths of their selves and the young people who are both their equals as living beings among all other living beings as well as their students, bearing socially defined, prescribed and proscribed 'roles' who are in the process of being fitted for present and future roles and service in society. The dilemma was illustrated perfectly for me when a school student of 13, 14 years old Nicky Wragg had brought a student teacher to the headteacher of the school to complain that the teacher had acted unjustly (Schostak, 1983/2012). The recording of the interactions provided a narrative structure formed from the typical relations, discourses, behaviours and courses of action available to the 'dramatis personae' (Schostak 1983/2012, Schostak and Schostak, 2012). In brief, the resulting story took place at lunchtime in a school that served a community of extremely high unemployment a level of unemployment that remains excessive today after nearly 40 years when I first visited for my doctoral fieldwork. It was the custom of the school that teachers sat informally with students for their meals. On this occasion, a student teacher told a student – Nicky Wragg – to take the teacher's dirty dishes to the other end of the dinner hall to where they would be washed up by kitchen staff. Nicky refused and the two argued. Nicky's case was that it was his free time thus the teacher could not command him. Hearing the case the headteacher saw it as an outrage that a school boy thought he was able to pass judgement on a teacher. The arguments continued until the deputyhead took Nicky into his office in order to try and calm him down. Nicky wanted to bring in his mum, his social worker and anyone else who he though might support him. The deputyhead said he would be pleased to meet them. However, it would be of no use, said the deputyhead, because:

> 'I think it's one of the reasons why you're upset isn't it? That you've made such an awful fool of yourself.'

> 'I've not.'

> 'Oh yes you have.'

'I'm right, everyone is…'

'But Nicky, you're not right. This is the thing. You're not right. Your *quite* wrong. And you're going to have to learn that you're quite wrong. One way or another son you're going to have to learn. I'm confident… I know you pretty well by now Nick Wragg don't I?'

'Sir, yeah.'

'Yeah. And I'm confident that I know that one reason why you are so upset at this moment is because you realise you made such an *awful* fool of yourself, haven't you?'

'Sir no.'

'Yes you have Nick.'

'I'm in the right.'

'Well that's just you dreaming and I'm not going to argue with you at all… Sit there until you've calmed down.' (Schostak 1983/2012, p. 14)

What is the truth? This little narrative is driven by all the elements of the gaslighting strategy. Each attempt by Nicky to call upon elements that he experiences as 'real', 'true', 'right' are shifted by each of the teachers involved to present the reality constituted by the prevailing powers. Indeed, in a telling exchange the headteacher remarked 'You're trying to fight a war old boy. And rather a silly war to fight. It's a bit like the Isle of Man declaring war on the United States'.

What is remarkable is that Nicky, confronted by the might of this intimidatory structure, does not shift. He was punished, of course, but reluctantly by the deputyhead because as he told me later, he had spent months constructing a good relation only to have it blown apart by the attitude of the headteacher. Unfortunately the deputy headteacher was also negating the reality he felt, as he negated the reality Nicky felt.

None of this could have happened without already historically constituted forms of practice, organisation, social roles, law and authority of which the school was a product. Nicky's clinging to his experiences and the alternative relatively fixed points in his life acted like the dimming of the gaslight to point to another explanation, however dimly understood, that could unravel the opposing 'reality' maintained by the teachers. He clung to his truth. Indeed, the reality that the school was too often covering over was acutely seen and expressed by another teacher:

> [...]sometimes y'see John, what [the pupils] are telling you is so flaming true and
> real that you don't want to hear it, because, it's, it's absolutely loaded, loaded with
> problems. What, what some kids are telling me in not so many words is that they
> loathe and detest this system that we're forcing them through [...] They throw into
> doubt the whole purpose of what these schools are for and what we're sending
> pupils here for in our present society anyway. (Schostak 1983/2012, p. 215).

Many staff in the school, commendable for its sustained attempts to address the wider community issues faced by the students, felt they were at such an impasse where doubt was clouding the purpose of schooling.

It is at this point where the courage – and it does take courage – is needed to transition from schooling to education. There are examples of such courage to be found in the legacies of democratic experiments (Fielding and Moss, 2011). Whether it is a Herbert Kohl (1967) learning from his 36 children to trust them, or a Jonathan Richmond (1982) learning how children and adults can 'become their own experts' the courage to engage differently have taken place and will take place. Indeed, if as equals mutually engaged we can become our own experts, is the teacher role necessary or an impediment? This was a question clearly raised by the School of Barbiana (1969) where there were no teachers as such, only young people who taught each other. In fact, it was these examples and the questions they raised concerning schools and their roles in young people's lives that led me to develop what we termed the listening and talking project and that the children themselves called: sorting it out. Perhaps what I was experiencing, like others confronting the impasses of contemporary schooling, was what Lissovoy (2018) calls a 'pedagogy of longing'. However, more than this I wanted a pedagogy of action, perhaps that insurrectionary moment seen by Lissovoy as fundamental to a process of real change. Action research seemed to offer an approach, especially given that I was a member of the Centre of Applied Research in Education at the University of East Anglia where the proponents of teacher as researcher (Lawrence Stenhouse) and later action research (notably John Elliott and Bridget Somekh) were pioneers in the UK. However, the action research I wanted was one that was not just focused on the research and reflective capabilities of teachers who set the agenda but levelled the relations between adults and young people thus opening agendas and reframing organisational relationships so that, as Clark (2018) writes, an 'education in spite of it all' can be undertaken.

The listening and talking project (Schostak 1989, 1990) focused on problems and how they were to be resolved. The problems were often unanticipated and as much to do with social and emotional problems as academic problems. That is to say, they did not easily form neat subjects, or required skills as set out in the levels of attainment expected in national testing. In short, the agenda of concerns arose from the everyday experiences of the school as a community within a wider community. That is to say, the educative process began by systematically reflecting upon the everyday curriculum of a given individual or group. Here is an early videoed example:

*scene*: it is a first school classroom, there are just under 60 children in a large room which has been used as two classrooms. There are two teachers and one welfare assistant. It is nearly dinner time and the children have just cleared up their work. One of the teachers has just praised them and the excellence of their work and clearing up their work quickly and neatly. She goes on to say:

> *T:* Before we have our lunch, could I just speak to for a moment..
>
> *p:* yes
>
> *T:* Um... Quite a few people have come and said that other -people are bothering them. I think people came and said me that Alan was bothering them and people came and said to me that Mary was bothering them. What do you think you should do in that situation? What do you think is the best thing to do, Jill?
>
> *Jill:* Go on the carpet.
>
> *T:* Go on the carpet and sort it out. You can just say to the person "You are bothering me, please come with me on the carpet and we can sort it out. Now, what are you going to do it you can't sort it out, it's too hard? What do you think you could do then? Jane?"
>
> *Jane*: Come and fetch you.
>
> *T:* Yes, come and fetch some help and then we'll, we'll help. There's no point in coming and saying to me "Alan did this and Mary did that", because I'm not going to sort it out for you. OK? So, let's try that and see how it goes. Alright?

The project idea began simply enough. A teacher had made the observation that quarrelling children were very often seen shortly after hand in hand as friends, as if nothing had happened. How did they sort out their problems? This was a school that took children from the nursery age of

3 through to the primary or 'first school' period from 5 to 8 years old. As the project evolved it became clear even very young children could engage in 'sorting it out' across a wide range of activities, whether these were behavioural issues, resource issues arising when scarce resources were wanted by several people at once, or whether it was about what to do when class work had been finished and the child did not know what to do next. Each time, the teacher would say something like, 'now that's an interesting problem, how can we sort it out? Have a think about it and come back and tell me when you have a solution.' What was remarkable was that children, regardless of age, became increasingly creative, self responsible and self-organised in every area of school life. In order to research the ideas more fully, a new school was found where the staff agreed to experiment with the new way of working. Again, it was transformative. Indeed it resulted in an evidenced based policy development for the school. The school had box files of transcripts from audio and video recordings of classroom activities and discussions. From this they developed policies for the school grounded in the evidence as shown from an extract from their school policy on social development:

1. At every stage create opportunities for children and teachers to be explicit about problems and possible solutions.
2. At every stage encourage the children to contribute to the solution of problems. <*At a whole school level the tape of the football assembly is a good example of both of these. The children were given the opportunity both to lay out the problem, and to discuss possible solutions.*>
3. Encourage the children to say what they are thinking. The teachers and other staff too need to say what they are thinking. <*There are plenty of examples on the tapes of the children having the opportunity to say what they are thinking. The whole talking out procedure is designed to do precisely this too. As far as staff are concerned the democratic mode of discussion and decision making is designed to that end, but the principle also applies between staff and children.*>
4. Make time in the school day, in and out of the classroom for discussion with the children. <*Look for opportunities for ordinary friendly social interrelationships and chat between staff and children. It is*

> *important that our focus is positive not negative, and problems will then be reduced to their proper perspective.>*

5.  Make sure that the solution of problems is one of our priorities. The rationale is that personal and social development is of crucial importance to the development of any learner, child or adult. *<This very much needs to be read in conjunction with 4. The evidence of the fourth year children on the interview tape reinforces the importance of this. Learning in groups is clearly tied in with their social learning.>*

Point 2 referred to the constant problem that during playtime the children who were playing football would sometimes kick the ball over the wall used as a goal that separated the playground from the houses behind. The neighbours regularly complained. The children involved discussed the problem and came up with several possible solutions. However, each solution would involve stoping other children from using that part of the playground when they were playing football. To address this issue the children called a general assembly of the school and put the possible solutions to them. From the assembly children then posed questions before voting possible solutions. A solution was agreed and put into practice. It worked. The whole event had been videoed and became a key piece of evidence concerning how to build the practices and forms of organisation necessary to solve both personal and larger social problems within and outside of the school.

Point 3 and 4 refers to the general procedure that had become common throughout the school and had been made explicit when the fourth year children decided that it was important to create a film of how they operated the 'sorting it out' procedure because new children and their parents would need to know about this. The film was subsequently shown to the new intakes of parents and children as an induction into the cultural and organisational practices of school, practices that included children, teachers and support staff in their relationships to each other. In undertaking the sorting out procedures, the teachers were facilitative and neutral by not making the decisions for the children, nor forming judgements about the decisions made. This, in itself, was a major contrast with the earlier Nicky Wragg episode where the realities of the youngster were challenged and manipulated by the adults involved. What the experiment

revealed was that education is indeed possible when democratic relations are constituted by the collective discussion, decision making, action and monitoring of consequences by all. Whether the problems to be
addressed were behavioural, social or academic the broad procedures
involved in working through problems were the same. Lessons whether
focusing primarily upon subjects to with maths, science, language, humanities or sports were all constructed on the same principles of sorting
it out whether done as an individual, group or collective activity; sorting out what project to be developed, how to develop it, what resources
would be necessary. The sorting out procedures were constitutive of new
forms of practice for the members of the school, creating procedures,
mechanisms and legitimising restructured relationships between adults
and children that were more equal, creative and free. However, it did not
last. Increasingly from the late 1980s the UK educational context became inspection and performance driven that created a harsh climate for
democratic freedoms in schools. And of course, staff leave, whether to
new jobs or simply retire. More than the courageous creative innovations
of a few teachers and their schools is required. What is it?

## Steps Towards the Freedom to Act Differently

Freedom is not given. It is socially constructed according to the purposes, interests and needs of many conflicting parties. In unequal societies,
the freedoms of the few are privileged over those of the many, and in
particular, those of the poor, the 'others' who are discriminated against
according to gender, ethnicity, faith, and physical and mental ability. If
freedom and equality for all are to survive then the forms of organisation that materially, socially and legally support this are vital. This returns us to the co-operative movement. Its significance resides precisely
in its independence yet capacity to co-exist with competitive, capitalist
markets and societies.

Although there are schools that operate upon co-operative principles around the world, the first co-operative school in the UK was established in 2008. It was set up under the 2006 Education and Inspections

Act that enabled the development of 'trust schools' as a way of gaining some degree of independence. Following this, other schools followed leading Mervyn Wilson the then Principle of the Co-operative College to remark in 2012, "We're now the third largest association of schools in England after church run schools, a ranking which has largely gone unnoticed" (Birch, 2012). Currently, there are about 600 co-operatively organised schools whose constitutions employ the agreed values and principles of the co-operative movement (see the Schools Co-operative Society: <http://co-operativeschools.coop/about/values-and-principles/>. These values include: self-help, self-responsibility, democracy, equality, equity and solidarity. There is much optimism that spaces will be created within schools for democratic debate and decision making that includes both students and teachers and encourage co-operative forms of learning in order to experience democracy through relations of mutuality, equity and solidarity (Davidge, Facer, Schostak, 2015).

However, the articulation of these values depends on whether material, organisational structures are radically changed from hierarchical authoritarian forms of control to horizontal relations of equality. As an example, Davidge (2017) in her ethnographic based study of a co-operative school discussed the excitements, hopes and resistances to change raised by the development of a school mobile phone use policy. The young people undertook research in order to develop the policy, interviewing both teachers and students. At the point of presenting an agreed policy the headteacher simply used her authority to quash the initiative. It left the students feeling bruised and angry. Another more subtle use of authority was employed in a co-operative school that used the latest digital technologies to aid the monitoring of learning as well as behaviour (Schostak, 2014). The students could make choices about how well they were working, which groups they were to work with, and how fast they progressed from topic to topic. They recorded their choices on a smart board at the front of the class. Although they felt engaged, they were essentially complicit in a top-down monitoring system that could be checked by any teacher at any moment and presented during parents' evenings for discussion. Effectively, this was micro-control of behaviours. The monitoring was, of course, asymmetrical; it did not work from the ground up where students and parents could monitor the practices of the teachers. As Bentham (2001) the originator of the panopticon model of the prison put it in 1797 "The more strictly we are watched, the better we behave." However, the democratic revolutionaries of his time were more concerned not with elite control over the rest, but the suspicion that the elites would abuse their powers. Thus they were concerned to create the forms of organisation that would keep them in check. The key to this many thought was the development of an effective public opinion. Hence "Bergasse, who served as a member of the Constitutional Assembly in the early days of the French Revolution" wrote that public opinion: "is truly a product of everyone's intelligence and everyone's will. It can be seen, in a way, as the manifest consciousness of the entire nation" (Rosanvallon 2012, p. 68). This intelligence, will and manifest consciousness was of course precisely what the wealth elites like Robert Lowe did not want and that Lippmann and Bernays saw as the focus for the manufacture, engineering and manipulation of consent – all features that have characterised contemporary 'democracies'. However, the opposite – that is an active and engaged public – was what was activated during the listening and talking project, particularly well illustrated in the whole school assembly called to solve the football problem. The conditions for such an approach are formed whenever individuals are called to reflect upon their collective action and decision making experiences. For example, in the listening and talking project a class theme had been set to create interesting games that could be played by a small group of players. It was up to the children to invent these. They separated into groups and at the end of the session, when the games had been created, each group described their ideas to the whole class. One game was considered by them to be the most interesting. The inventors were asked how they came up with the idea. One child said, we all discussed it, came up with ideas and then chose the best. I asked the rest of the group if that was their experience too. After a moment one boy said, 'no it wasn't like that. I gave an idea but wasn't listened to.' It turned out that one child was more extrovert than the others and led the session, choosing his own ideas. I asked the whole class, 'that's interesting has anyone an idea about how to deal with this issue?' The answer from the whole class included the suggestion that each individual in a group could take turns giving their ideas and then the group could vote on the suggestions. It was simple and perhaps commonsensical. But until the class as a whole made the suggestion it had never been operated. From then on, without any instruction from the adults, the children adopted the democratic solution in their groups.

Rather than a pedagogy driven by adult authority, the school as a whole adopted what may be called a pedagogy of inclusion. The inclusion of different views enabled truths to be established, drawn from the realities of their powers of reflection on lived experience and from their imaginations, thus prefiguring in concrete terms Bergasse's sense of public opinion as the will, intelligence and manifest consciousness of all. However, before such an experiment can become the ground for wider social renewal, it needs to be embedded in and sustained by a comprehensive politically, socially, culturally and economically grounded movement like the co-operative schools movement with its relations to the wider cooperative movement. Together, the dream of education contributing to a democratically formed society of equals can, perhaps with sufficient courage, become reality.

Ólafur Páll Jónsson
*University of Iceland*

# In Search of a Democratic Society: The Icelandic Kitchenware Revolution and an Educational Response to a Socio-Economic Collapse

In the fall of 2008 and into 2009 Iceland became the focus of rare international attention, first when the entire financial system collapsed like a house of cards and again when the government stepped down after public protests where people banged on pots and pans in front of the parliament for several days. Later, when the sea of troubles began to calm, attention was again on Iceland due to various responses to the collapse many of which were not only focused on the economic disaster that had just unfolded but rather on the moral and political decline that had taken place prior to these unruly events. Thus, the collapse of the financial system was not seen as the core problem but rather a symptom of a much deeper social and moral issues. The two responses that caught most international attention were the trials and convictions of several high powered bankers and financial executives (see Birrell, 2015; Milne, 2016), and the crowdsourcing of a new constitution (Kinna, Prichard & Swann, 2016; Landemore, 2014; Ólafsson, 2014; Siddique, 2011). The focus of this chapter, however, is the educational response to the collapse which has not received much international attention.

The constitutional procedure illuminated some of the themes and concerns which were central, even if not always stated explicitly, in various moral and political responses to the collapse. Although most people, academics, politicians and the public alike, agreed that the Icelandic constitution was in many ways outdated and unclear on certain basic rights, legislative structures and political procedures, revising it had turned out to be very difficult. After the collapse, the call for a new constitution became louder and widespread, and with the record low trust towards the government and the parliament, the idea of involving the general public in drafting a new constitution seemed to many not only natural, but also a vital step in the direction of rebuilding social trust and a communal feeling of belonging.

The first large public meeting related to the constitutional revision was held in November 2009, organized by 300 volunteers and involved around 1,500 people (0,5% of the entire population). This forum identified certain basic values which should guide the reconstruction of a democratic society in Icelandic (integrity, equal rights, respect and justice) and laid out nine themes of special significance (education, family, welfare, economy, environment, sustainability, opportunities, equality, public administration) (see <http://thjodfundur2009.is/english/>). Writer and journalist Alda Sigmundsdóttir captured the spirit of the event in a blog post immediately after the event:

> I have to say that I'm proud of my fellow citizens for the civil action that has been undertaken since the meltdown last year. First we had the Saturday afternoon demonstrations [which initially were met with precisely the same disdain in some circles that you see towards yesterday's National Assembly – but in the end, of course, almost everyone wanted to own a part of them], we had the civic action meetings on Monday nights, we had the Kitchenware Revolution, and now we have the National Assembly [often referred to as "national forum"]. Which incidentally differs from the rest in that people are attempting to lift themselves above the endless bickering, anger and negativity and to approach the reconstruction of this society in a proactive, unified manner. I will go so far as to say that, even if nothing else comes out of this, it has given this society a sense of momentum and hope, and a chance to think about what we DO want, as opposed to always focusing on what we DON'T want (Sigmundsdóttir, 2009).

The national forum was not part of the constitutional process itself though crucial in lending credibility to the idea of involving the general public in a work on a new constitution. In June 2010, the parliament passed a law delineating a public procedure for the constitutional revision. The procedure began with a national forum (*ice. þjóðfundur*) of around 950 people <http://www.thjodfundur2010.is/english/>. The work was continued by a constitutional committee consisting of seven members (ice. *stjórnlaganefnd*) who compiled the results of the national forum for a constitutional assembly (ice. *stjórnlagaþing*) which would be formed by 25 people selected in public elections in November 2010 <http://stjornlagarad.is/english/>. The whole procedure generated a great deal of interest in

Iceland and for the election to the assembly 522 candidates showed interest in participating. After some bumps on the way, a constitutional council (*ice. stjórnlagaráð*) of 25 people began work on April 6th, 2011. Four months later the council presented a draft of a new constitution to the Icelandic Parliament.

This public process – what foreign activists and scholars would later refer to as crowdsourcing of a new constitution – was, in part at least, symptomatic of the low trust towards the government and the parliament after the collapse. In February 2009, a poll indicated that around 13% of the population trusted the parliament compared to, for instance, 80% trust towards the University of Iceland and the police (see <https://www.gallup.is/frettir/92-landsmanna-treysta-landhelgisgaeslunni/>). The procedure encountered many obstacles along the way and was, in the end, terminated after the 2013 elections without any revisions to the constitution (Gylfason, 2013; Landemore 2014, 2016; Ólafsson, 2016).

The educational response to the collapse differed from the constitutional process in the sense that it was initiated and carried out from within the Ministry of Education although relying on input and work by a wide variety of people from the educational system. After the parliamentary elections in February 2009 a left-wing coalition government was formed with the Minister of Education, Katrín Jakobsdóttir, coming from the Left-Green Coalition. Among the first things Katrín Jakobsdóttir did in the Ministry was to initiate a thorough revision of the national curricula for preschools (2 to 5 years), compulsory schools (6 to 16 years) and upper secondary schools (16 to 20 years) with a strong emphasis on democracy, human rights, equality, sustainability and other moral and political values. These changes garnered little public attention to begin with. It was only with the publication of the new national curricula in 2011, followed by publication of supporting documents and various other initiatives, that the new curricula entered public discourse. The changes, which were in some respects profound, were generally well received although teachers, principals and other people working in the educational sector were somewhat perplexed as to how to implement the new curricula.

The positive attitude with which the new curricula was met derived no doubt from people perceiving the strong democratic emphasis as a moral and political response to the collapse directed at the very roots of the problem, namely the withering away of communal values such as

respect, fairness and honesty, and lack of democracy, integrity, responsibility and criticality. Thus, although very different in nature from both
the prosecution of the bankers and the crowdsourcing of the constitution, the writing of the new curricula resonated well with those other re-
constructive initiatives as a moral and political response to the collapse.

Various other initiatives took place which did not catch the eye
of international media; most of them revolved around certain basic
values, either political or moral, such as fairness, participation and respect (Ólafsson, 2014, 2016). Such initiatives, for instance the project
on allowing residents of Reykjavík a direct say on how to spend part
of the budgeted funds in their own neighbourhoods (see <http://www.
betrireykjavik.is>), were often conceived of as attempts to improve or
revitalize democracy with a focus on direct or participatory democracy.


## The collapse


In October 2008, the Icelandic economy collapsed so dramatically that
Paul Krugman, the Nobel prize winner in economics, described it as "one
of the great economic disaster stories of all time" (Krugman, 2010). The
disaster had been a long time brewing but the general public only discov-
ered how serious the situation was on October 6 when the Prime Minister
of Iceland, Geir H. Haarde, gave a special address on Icelandic National
Radio and Television saying that the entire financial system was collaps-
ing. Haarde first discussed the international financial turmoil, the fall of
large investment banks in the USA, and then turned to the situation in
Iceland saying:

> In the threatening situation that now prevails on the world's financial markets a
> great risk would be involved for the Icelandic nation in any attempt to keep the
> banks afloat with a lifeline. [...] If the worst came to worst, there would be a real
> risk, dear countrymen, that Iceland's economy would be sucked into the turmoil
> and the result would be a national bankruptcy[1].

---

1    Haarde, Geir H. (2008). Prime Minister's address due to special circumstances in
     the financial market. Special broadcast on Iceland's National Radio and Television.

The Prime Minister asked people to remain calm in the coming difficult days which turned out not to be easy when a sea of bad news washed away any possibility of optimism. The three main banks in Iceland were bankrupt and the country's stock exchange was wiped out. Iceland is one of the smallest independent states in the world, with only around 300.000 inhabitants, and yet the collapse of the three banks was the world's third largest collapse after Lehman Brothers and Washington Mutual (Sigurjónsson & Mixa, 2011). The banks had been privatized in 2003, when they were small, local, commercial banks, but grew to become international commercial and investments banks with the combined balance sheets amounting to ten times that of Iceland's GDP's (Sigurjónsson & Mixa, 2011).

During the first weeks of the collapse (*ice. hrunið*), as these events were referred to, the events were experienced primarily as a financial crisis: The banks were closed, the currency plunged, there was no fixed exchange rate, foreign banks simply refused to recognize the Icelandic króna as a viable currency, people travelling abroad were unable to use their credit cards, and so on. However, as the days went by and people came to know more about the extent of the collapse – the warning signs that had been ignored during the previous years, and the corrupt practices of the bankers and politicians – the collapse was not only perceived as an economic disaster but as a symptom of a sick society where the moral and political foundations of the community itself had withered away (Árnason, Nordal, Ástgeirsdóttir, 2010b; Jónsson, 2009). Sociologist Jón Gunnar Bernburg described the situation in the following way:

> During this time the media bombarded the public with news about scandalous practices and alleged criminal behaviour in the financial sphere. Through intricate patterns of cross-ownership, the banks had seemingly invested in themselves to conceal their problems and maintain high stock values. Major shareholders in the banks had apparently borrowed enormous amounts from their own banks. News came out about high-up bank employees being granted relief on huge loans that they had been encouraged to take to buy bank shares during the good times. The emerging image was that of a thorough corrupt financial system (Bernburg, 2016, p. 6).

---

Reykjavík, October 6th, 2008. Translation into English by Jón Gunnar Bernburg (Bernburg, 2016).

In the following weeks, regular Saturday protests were organized by a musician and long standing gay rights campaigner Hörður Torfason. The protests took place in Austurvöllur, a small green square in down-town Reykjavík right in front of the Icelandic parliament. Initially there were few protesters but the number grew steadily and soon several thousand protesters would gather to listen to speeches where the government's framing of the crisis as an international event was challenged. Instead, it was argued that this was a local catastrophe caused by widespread corruption, criminal activities and gross negligence on the part of the bankers as well as various politicians and public officials. Each protest ended with the same demand: The resignation of the government, the dismissal of the Director of the Financial Supervisory Authority and the dismissal of the Chairman of the Board of Governors of the Central Bank. The Chairmain, Davíð Oddsson, had been prime minister of Iceland for the right wing Independence Party from 1991 to 2004, a time during which the main banks in Iceland had been privatized. But, despite the continuation of the protests and increasing participation, many people were pessimistic that anything would happen. The government showed no sign of resigning and with it in place, these two public officials would remain in their posts.

But the patience and persistence of Hörður Torfason eventually paid off. In early January he had mounted a small protest right in front of the Parliament building. And right there a police officer asking him to move away gave him an idea:

> [A police officer] came to me and asked me to move away from the building to the other side of the street. I asked him why? He told me my speech had disturbed parliament members who were having a meeting inside the house. I was very surprised [...] the house was so badly sound-insulated! [...] I thanked him for giving me a very [good idea]. The idea was to ask people to meet up in front of the parliament building on January 20 when the parliament members returned from their holidays and bring their pots and pans so the parliament members would hear us clearly. Now was the time to make ourselves as visible as possible to them; for too many months and weeks we had simply been ignored (Bernburg, 2016, p. 55).

Then, when Parliament resumed after Christmas recess on January 20, a mass protest broke out in front of the Parliament building where people banged on pots and pans, shouted slogans and made so much noise that the proceedings inside the building could not continue. The protests went on day and night for the next few days and on January 26, Prime Minister Geir H. Haarde announced that the government was stepping down. A temporary, minority government of the two left-wing parties was formed and soon politics became as normal as it could be in a country that was essentially bankrupt and had resorted to the aid of the International Monetary Fund to maintain a basic functioning status. In the spring elections were held where the two left-wing parties gained a narrow majority and formed a new government. Among their first tasks was to fire the Director of the Financial Supervisory Authority and the Chairman of the Board of Governors of the Central Bank.

For many people in Iceland the collapse was not just a financial or economic event but a symptom of much deeper problems related to morality, community and the political fabric of society. Hörður Torfason described the situation thus:

> Prior to the collapse people lived on some cloud [...] if you tried to talk to them about the structure of society they had no interest, but rather asked "Where did you buy the sweater?" or "Did you get a new car?" They talked in money and about having things (Bernburg, 2016, p. 41).

The collapse changed this overnight as if people suddenly realized that it was not enough to have things if one has lost the community itself. The writer and social critic Einar Már Guðmundsson described the sea-changes in the following way:

> There we were in October 2008 and *it just became so clear how absurd it all had been,* like the insider trading and how the banks had been run and how the neo-liberal religion had become widespread in the society and then [... *the collapse]* just happened and people start giving speeches, and there are people everywhere talking about these things and meeting; *there emerges this longing among people to meet and to express themselves and listen to others and mirror oneself in the experiences of others.* (Bernburg, 2016, p. 48, original italics).

After the collapse many people experienced a deep loss; they had taken for granted that they lived in a democratic society, which respected the rule of law and was rooted in strong communal ties, but all that vanished in a spur of a moment (Jónsson, 2009). The energy that surfaced during the kitchenware revolution and the wide-spread participation was doubtless due to a feeling, common to Icelanders from all walks of life, that the very foundations of Icelandic society was threatened.

In December 2008, the parliament organized a special research commission for investigating the failing of the banks along with a working group on the ethical aspects of the collapse. In April 2010, the commission published its findings in 9 volumes (around 3000 pages) detailing bad management, excessive risk taking, lack of regulation and government supervision, insider trading, extensive cross-ownership and market manipulation (Special Investigation Commission, 2010). An English summary of the report of the working group on the ethical aspects of the collapse concludes with the following paragraph:

> The main conclusion of the Working group are that although several individuals, in the financial, administrative, political and the public sphere, showed negligence and sometimes reprehensible action, the most important lessons to draw from these events are about weak social structures, political culture and public institutions. It is the common responsibility of the Icelandic nation to work towards strengthening them and constructing a well functioning democratic society (Árnason, Nordal & Ástgeirsdóttir, 2010b).

In the Icelandic report of the working group on the ethical aspects (volume 8 of the report on the processes leading to the fall of the banks) the authors reported on what would be essential to remedy the situation and avoid new collapses in the future:

> From a moral point of view it is, in the long run, most important to strengthen the democratic structure of society and public institutions; improve business morality, governing practices and working habits, improve professionalism and moral character. Conditions for moral dialogue among the citizenry about common goods must be improved. Real social responsibility must be emphasized and pervasive self-interest and narrow individualism must be resisted. The moral upheaval of society should primarily be focused on strengthening these factors and it is a long term project which requires input from people from all parts of society (Árnason, Nordal & Ástgeirsdóttir, 2010a, p. 243, English translation Ólafur Páll Jónsson).

Some of the tasks that are listed here, such as improving moral character and conditions for moral dialogue among the citizenry about common goods, were understood to have direct implications for public education. The new curricula for preschools, compulsory schools and upper secondary schools, published in 2011, can be seen as both an acceptance of the causes of the collapse and a direct response to it by highlighting the values which should guide the reconstruction of society.

## The Icelandic educational context before the collapse

New law on public education had been passed in 2008 shortly before the collapse and a revised version of the national curricula was in the making. The law had been written during the years when the financial system was flying high and individualism and neo-liberalism was the call of the time. This is evident in the law itself, for instance in the sections on school management, possibility of privatization, focus on individualized learning outcomes and the absence of communal and moral objectives for education. However, after the new left-wing government was formed in 2009 the existing drafts for the new national curricula were scrapped and a completely different approach was taken where the neo-liberal perspective of previous decades was challenged and democracy, equality, human rights and sustainability were presented among six fundamental pillars of all education from preschool up through upper secondary education (Sigurðardóttir, Guðjónsdóttir & Karlsdóttir, 2014).

Although the new curricula published 2011 struck a new tone with the six pillars emphasizing a strong democratic and critical role of the education system, it presented in many ways a return to ideas that had shaped important educational changes in 1970s and into the 1980s. In 1974 the parliament had passed a progressive law on compulsory education with strong emphasis on democracy and inclusion (Compulsory School Act, 63/1974). The law declared that the main purpose of schooling was to prepare students for participation in a continually changing democracy, also that all children, including those with disabilities, should have access to suitable education in their local school district. The law also required schools to abandon tracking and streaming students according to reading ability, which had been standard practice in many of the bigger schools in Reykjavík. Education scholar Ingólfur

Á. Jóhannesson describes the development in the 1970s as a systemic modernization based on democratic principles:

> If we look at late twentieth-century educational history in Iceland from this perspective, we see that the reform efforts of the 1970s and 1980s were aimed at modernizing the Icelandic education system, with an emphasis on primary education (6 to 16 years). The reform was based on child-centred, humanistic, and egalitarian views which I will call the democratic principle. These views are apparent in cooperative learning methods, integration of subject matter, evaluation as process rather than product, and many other 'progressive' views in education (Jóhannesson, 2006, p. 105).

Even if the Compulsory School Act of 1974 was radical in its democratic and inclusive vision for schools, it had received wide support in the parliament and did not generate any strong divides along political lines (Jónsson, 2014). However, when implementation work had been under way for almost ten years, fierce debates rose concerning the rationale of the educational reform. On the surface the debate concerned the teaching of Icelandic history in compulsory schools but when reading the over 70 newspaper articles and letters and the extensive debates in the parliament (Guttormsson, 2013), it is clear that the substance of disagreement was not merely a single subject in the curriculum for compulsory education but the nature of Icelandic identity and the grounds for social cohesion. The reformers were criticized for abandoning traditional conceptions of Icelandic history and identity in favour of constructive conceptions with little grounding in traditional Icelandic values. They, conversely, argued that history as a school subject had been a glorification of heroic masculine identity which could not stand up to scrutiny and was disconnected from the everyday reality of children and adolescents (Edelstein 1988/2013; Halldórsdóttir et al., 2016). Both parties to the debate agreed that education was important for constructing personal and political identity and maintaining social cohesion, but disagreed about the role of "Icelandic" values and traditions toward this end (Edelstein 1988/2013; Guttormsson 2013; Halldórsdóttir *et al.*, 2016).

Some of the critics charged the reform of being a leftist conspiracy against liberal and traditional Icelandic values but such criticism had little foundation in the actual reforms. Wolfgang Edelstein, researcher at the Max Planck Institute in Berlin, who had lead the educational reform and the ongoing implementation, responded to this charge:

> It is a complete nonsense that the social studies [which in the new curriculum replaced history and some other traditional subjects] is an attempt at some leftist indoctrination. Anyone can see this in a trice just by looking at the textbooks. The social studies are a deliberate attempt to fulfil the intention of the Compulsory School Act [from 1974], and in so far as this subject is political, it is "civic," democratic and is grounded in individual well-being (Edelstein, 1984, p. 18, English translation Ólafur Páll Jónsson).

In these debates about history teaching in compulsory schools two conflicting conceptions of political identity emerged. On the one hand, was a deliberative and constructivist conception promoted by the reformers, inspired in part by John Dewey (works such as *The School and Society* and *Education and Democracy*) and Jerome Bruner (in particular *The Process of Education* and the MACOS teaching program). On the other hand, was a republican conception emphasising traditional national values and cultural heritage (Jónsson, 2017). The latter view was best formulated by Arnór Hannibalsson, a professor of philosophy at the University of Iceland:

> There are few things that are more important to a nation than its history. It is the history along with the literature and other arts which is the primary moulder of national identity, gives people an answer to the question: Who am I? The history is particularly important when the life of a nation is undergoing great changes so that the new generation can relate to the life of the ancestors and the national tradition is maintained (Hannibalsson, 1983, p. 25, English translation Ólafur Páll Jónsson).

The views of Hannibalsson and others who argued in favour of traditional history and history teaching in compulsory schools fit well with what Jürgen Habermas refers to as republicanism or republican conception of democracy. According to this conception a central feature of politics – and, consequently an important task for comprehensive education – is the generation of collective self-understanding grounded in traditional values. Thus, Habermas says:

> [...] ethical discourse aimed at achieving a collective self-understanding – discourse in which participants attempt to clarify how they understand themselves as member of a particular nation, as member of a community of state, as inhabitants of a region, etc., which traditions they wish to cultivate, how they should treat each other, minorities, and marginal groups, in what sort of society they want to live – constitute an important part of politics (Habermas, 1998, p. 244).

Within the republican paradigm questions about what it is to belong to a nation become central. Habermas returns to this a little later when he says:

> According to the republican view, democratic will-formation is supposed to take the form of an ethical discourse of self-understanding: here deliberation can rely for its content on a culturally established background consensus of the citizens, which is rejuvenated through the ritualistic reenactment of a republican founding act (Habermas, 1998, p. 246).

In contrast to the republican conception of political identity as grounded in – or even determined by – the history of the nation and national traditions, the educational reform in the 1970s was based on the idea that political identity should be formed through discourse among students and in the interactions between school and the wider society. In line with this the new law and the national curriculum emphasized democratic practices, where communication and interaction within the schools – and between school and society – was of special concern. The reform also extended to the definition of school subjects, teaching practices, methods of evaluation, school administration and more. The philosophical and educational ideas behind the reform are well described by Wolfgang Edelstein in a paper written in the wake of the reform.

> Although social studies (*ice. samfélagsfræði*) should be unified in structure and content it draws resources from various subjects. It should mediate understanding of social phenomena, knowledge of the social structure and its changes, but also help students to explore their own position in society and find their own niche. The social sciences are products of relativism and, yet, social studies should contribute to a firmer cultural identity among students who are facing social and cultural uncertainty. It should help students to get a sense of direction in the liquid world of social changes and strengthen their cognitive abilities to deal with the challenges of growing up in a society of changes. It should help students to select a responsible value base without eliminating their own responsibility by the indoctrination of specific values. It should mediate political understanding and critical media literacy without prescribing specific interpretations (Edelstein, 2013, p. 59).

The reformers saw a subject such as Icelandic history as offering opportunities to reflect critically on contemporary society rather than simply providing the students with facts – and myths – about the past. Rather than grounding individual and national identity in a predetermined national heritage, the reformers saw identity as developing through the interactions of different individuals. Moreover, the various school subjects should not be looked upon as a well from which knowledge and ideas could be poured, but an instrument for the cultivation of attitudes and skills for exploring and developing individual identity for personal fulfilment and participation in a continually changing democratic society.

This epic saga of the educational reform in Iceland ended with the defeat of the reformers as the implementation work lead by Wolfgang Edelstein was simply terminated by the Ministry of Education. However, the broad curriculum changes that had already taken place remained intact and many of the people who had worked with Wolfgang Edelstein on the reform became faculty member at the University of Iceland and Iceland Education University (since 2008 School of Education at the University of Iceland) and continued to influence teachers and the educational field through teaching and research. Although Edelstein did not have any formal role within the educational sector in Iceland, his influence continued to be strong through frequent visits and personal ties with faculty at the University of Iceland and Iceland University of Education.

Over the next ten years or so the clash between the deliberative and the republican conceptions seemed to be forgotten while the society as a whole became increasingly influenced by consumerism and neo-liberal ideology with a liberal conception of democracy silently replacing the republican and the deliberative conceptions, which had clashed so dramatically in the winter of 1983 to 1984. Those social changes influenced school policy in the 1990s and into the 21st century when many of the democratic principles from the 1970s were abandoned or silenced in favour of more technical, managerial and market oriented ideology. Jóhannesson describes the situation in the following fashion:

> The technological views of the late 1990s and the beginning of the twenty-first century have become discursively connected to market themes, for instance, competition, individualism, budget reform to use money more efficiently, the student as consumer (of, for instance, special educational needs), private enterprise in education, etc. This new discursive tendency is also characterized by talking about education as consensus-building and emphasizing that matters are technological

(including the belief that it is easy to change schools or to medically diagnose
special educational needs). There is more emphasis on management, for instance,
in the increased role of the principal. In addition to the 1970s belief in defining
goals and objectives, the technological view now is also characterized by beliefs in
self-evaluation and efficiency in education (Jóhannesson, 2006, p. 105).

But history is rarely without complications and in 1994 Iceland signed
the Salamanca Statement on inclusive education and, as such, committed to some strong democratic principles. Thus, educational policy in
Iceland during the 1990s became a mixture of principles pertaining to
inclusive education, on the one hand, and principles that were highly
individualistic, market-oriented, managerial and technological, emphasising competition, outcome-based evaluation and diagnosis as a basis
for educational support, on the other (Dýrfjörð & Magnúsdóttir, 2016;
Jóhannesson, 2006; Jónsson, 2011; Marinósson & Bjarnason 2014;
Sigurðardóttir, Guðjónsdóttir & Karlsdóttir, 2014). The net result was
a silencing of the democratic principles that influenced the educational
reform in the 1970s and into the 1980s. This is, partly at least, in line
with a general trend as Marinósson and Bjarnason note in a chapter on
special education in Iceland:

> In the last few decades, the major change in Icelandic education policy has been
> away from state control of education towards local responsibility; away from
> curriculum guided by content towards one assuming that teaching is guided by
> objectives; from bureaucratic control of schools towards their self-evaluation
> and accountability; from a social pedagogy towards an individual, competitive
> one; from annual budgets to contractual management of schools; from a so-
> cial to a technical conception of change and development; and from a central
> administration towards the devolution of responsibility for administration and
> finances monitored through performance indicators (Marinósson & Bjarnason,
> 2014, p. 299).

Marinósson and Bjarnason further observe that this development
conceals certain complexities and contradictions such as between the
policy on inclusion, on the one hand, and a policy of competition and
accountability, on the other.

# The rise of neo-liberalism and liberal conception of democracy

In the 1990s and into the 21st century educational discourse had turned increasingly technical and individualistic, focusing more than before on tests, comprehensive objectives and quality control while the underlying conception of democracy changed from either deliberative or republican to what Habermas refers to as liberal:

> The crucial difference between liberalism and republicanism consists in how the role of the democratic process is understood. According to the "liberal" view, this process accomplishes the task of programming the state in the interest of society, where the state is conceived as an apparatus of public administration, and society is conceived as a system of market-structured interaction of private persons and the labour. Here politics (in the sense of the citizens' political will-formation) has the foundation of bundling together and bringing to bear private social interests against a state apparatus that specializes in the administrative employment of political power for collective goals (Habermas, 1998, p. 239).

Following the Salamanca Statement on inclusive education in 1994, inclusion became a central issue in both educational discourse and policy in Iceland. However, inclusion was often understood in individualist and technical terms in line with the growing individualism within Icelandic society and the emphasis on quality control and accountability, education as a preparation for the job market, and more emphasis on choice for parents (Dodds, 2013, p. 139; Jóhannesson, 2006). Thus, the emphasis on social values such as democracy and equality that characterized the educational reform of the 1970 gave way to individualistic policy based on efficiency and accountability. Jóhannesson describes the educational policy in the following way:

> Accountability, not only in terms of money but student performativity, is another important part of school policies in modern Iceland as well as elsewhere. The goal of the new national curriculum is to "produce" strong individuals and independent learners, who are able to learn more in a shorter time; this is important so that they can compete in a market society that is a part of a global system. Standards are created and compared in international comparison studies. The subject matter is centred in the new Icelandic primary school curriculum, the precision of goals is

supposed to make it easier to standardize assessment, and schools are judged on how they score in the league tables (Jóhannesson, 2006, p. 114).

A little later he adds:

> The conjuncture of the vision of inclusion, the technological approach to defining differences, and the market-oriented approach in financing education (e.g., management by results) creates a silence about equality in other terms, such as gender, residence, class, and culture (Jóhannesson, 2006, p. 114).

The ideological changes that occurred within the educational system reflected widespread and powerful changes in Icelandic society in general – not only in the economic and political fields. The whole society had taken a liberal, individualistic turn where more and more aspects of society were taken over by market oriented language (Dýrfjörð & Magnúsdóttir, 2016; Nussbaum, 2010; Skúlason, 2008). The role of the state was widely seen as that of an instrument to aid private enterprise, regulations were lifted and public agencies were judged by the efficiency and flexibility of the market they were supposed to regulate. This vision of the state fits with Habermas' description of the liberal state as an "apparatus that specializes in the administrative employment of political power for collective goals," with the "collective goals" often defined by the economic elite, not least the newly rich and powerful bankers and big business owners. "Important values" were those values which promoted economic wealth and consumption. For instance, risk taking was considered a virtue among the businessmen and among the general public greed was not considered a vice, but a virtue since it promoted economic growth. The anthropologist Kristín Loftsdóttir describes the pre-crash time in the following way:

> The Icelandic "economic miracle," as it was called at the time, began in the mid-1990s when Iceland adopted strong neoliberal economic policies that promoted the gradual liberalization of banks and capital flows and emphasized global integration as demonstrated by the adoption of the [European Economic Area] treaty in 1994 (Loftsdóttir, 2015, p. 4).

Although the ideology at the time was increasingly neo-liberal, it was also interpreted in nationalistic terms glorifying the "golden age" view of the early Icelandic settlement that had dominated history textbooks up to the educational reform in the 1970s. These nationalistic terms were not something one had to dig for, they were the very terms in which the Icelandic "economic miracle" was talked about as Loftsdóttir notes:

> Of particular interest is how the economic expansion was interpreted in highly nationalistic terms by the media and leading politicians and became incorporated into Icelandic social discourses. Across diverse social contexts, the economic boom was attributed to the special characteristics of Icelanders. For example, the success of the Icelandic entrepreneur overseas is expressed in terms such as *útrás* (outward expansion [or outvasion]) and *útrásarvíkingur* (Business Viking[or "out-vasion Viking"]). When economic success was attributed to individual qualities in the entrepreneurs, the populace nevertheless claimed them as Icelandic entrepreneurs, and as such their success reflected on the character of Icelanders as a whole (Loftsdóttir, 2015, p. 9).

The president of Iceland at the time, Ólafur Ragnar Grímsson, even traced the economic success of the Icelandic bankers to the age of settlement. In a talk in January 2006, which was part of a lecture series by the History Society of Iceland, President Grímsson said:

> It is interesting to consider the question of how elements in our culture and history have played a part in our overseas ventures, how qualities we have inherited from our ancestors give us, perhaps, an advantage in the international arena and how perceptions and habits that for centuries set their stamp on our society have proved valuable assets for today's achievers on the international stage (Grímsson, 2006, p. 1).

In this lecture, as well as in many other talks which he had given on both sides of the Atlantic, he stressed this "Icelandic heritage" as an explanatory factor for the "economic miracle".

These nationalistic ideas of Viking spirit and economic heroism that beset the political and economic sector were not without criticism. From within the academia, historians, philosophers and economists criticized these ideas for neither having any foundation in the historical past (Jóhannesson, 2015), nor being suitable for the present day society (Árnason, Nordal & Ástgeirsdóttir, 2010a; Skúlason, 2008). But this criticism fell on deaf ears until the collapse. After the collapse, it echoed in every corner of society.

## An educational response to the collapse

The new curricula for preschools, elementary schools and upper secondary schools from 2011 were directly influenced by the kitchenware revolution and aimed at moving the education system away from the neo-liberal and managerial path it had been on for the last two decades, towards a course guided by democratic and critical principles. This is particularly clear in the six pillars of education defined in the curricula all of which reflect a strong communal and democratic vision of schools and education: (1) democracy and human rights, (2) equality, (3) sustainability, (4) creativity, (5) health and well-being and (6) literacy (Ministry of Education, Science and Culture, 2012a, 2012b, 2012c). Katrín Jakobsdóttir, the Minister of Education in the left-wing government from 2009 to 2013, described the work on the new curricula in an interview:

> When our government came to power in May 2009, the work on the curriculum was in its initial stages and the approach was traditional, i.e., to focus on the subjects taught and list the fields that should be covered on different levels of education. But, from the very beginning, my main question was how do we put into practice the ideas of democracy that are the focus of our legislation? The legislation contained lots of nice words, but I wanted to take these words further in order to give guidelines of how they could be realized in the classroom (Hannesdóttir, 2013, p. 8).

She then adds how she saw the schools as being fundamental institution in a democratic society:

> My vision was that the school had to be a basic democratic institution, that we needed to describe in more detail what this involved, and that I had to develop methods to make this happen (Hannesdóttir, 2013, pp. 8–9).

The idea behind the six pillars was to identify the core values on which the educational system should rest. In light of the neo-liberal and nationalistic ideological upheaval in the years prior to the collapse, it was natural that an educational response to the situation would not merely focus on technical aspects of education – such as teaching methods, learning outcomes and school organization, quality control and competitive measures – but seek to revitalize core values for the entire educational system as a fundamental structure in a democratic society. Katrín Jakobsdóttir describes this in the following words:

> I set up a small focus group that included academics, philosophers, and curriculum specialists, as well as teachers and headmasters. Their job was to identify the basic values upon which our educational system should rest—not only the subjects such as languages, mathematics, literature, and so forth, but the pillars on which our democratic educational system should rest. These values needed to have such a wide application that they could be relevant to children in preschools, elementary schools, and high schools as well as to secondary school students studying in technical colleges—to learners in the whole educational system (Hannesdóttir, 2013, p. 9).

The issuing of the new curricula was followed by the publication of short books (64 pages each) on each of the six pillars, authored by experts in the field, where the ideas behind the pillars were further explicated and given practical interpretation to help teachers adopt them (see <http://vefir.mms.is/flettibaekur/namsefni/lydraedi.html/>). Each booklet began with an address from the Minister of Education in which she emphasized the importance of schools for developing critical citizens:

> It is of fundamental importance to cultivate the knowledge, skill and attitude which strengthens the ability of individuals to become critical, active and competent participants in a society characterized by equity and democracy. The fundamental pillars are, among other things, meant to improve this. All people should have access to education which helps them to put reasonable restraints on authorities, whether within finance, politics, media or in other sectors. Schools are in fact the only institutions of society which can guarantee coming generations an opportunity to prepare for participation in an active democracy, practice critical and creative thinking, and meet varying social and cultural circumstances (Jakobsdóttir, 2011, p. 3, English translation Ólafur Páll Jónsson).

Icelandic teachers faced increased workload and stress after the collapse, experiencing the social unrest that shook the whole society both directly and through the children and their parents while, at the same time, having to face direct cuts to school funding and restriction of various support services. This resulted in student-teacher ratios in preschools, compulsory schools and upper-secondary schools increasing in a school environment, which had already seen increased workload related to more paperwork for teachers and principals (Dýrfjörð & Magnúsdóttir, 2016; Halldórsdóttir et al., 2016; Lárusdóttir, 2014). Still, teachers generally received the new curricula with an open mind although somewhat perplexed as to how to respond to these new emphases in their daily work. This positive attitude was, in part, due to the curricula amendments being seen as part of an attempt to revive the values and visions for a democratic society that had been lost in the pre-collapse years.

In light of the development before the collapse – not only within the educational system, but in society as a whole – one can appreciate Katrín Jakobsdóttir's, as the Minister of Education, emphasis on fundamental values where democracy and criticality take a central stage. Various other educational initiatives took place, such as a program initiated by Páll Skúlason, the eminent philosopher and former rector of the University of Iceland, on strengthening teaching in ethics and critical thinking in elementary schools (Haraldsdóttir, 2011). The project sought to map the field, made the case for more philosophical teaching and learning in elementary schools, and introduced a website which served as a resource for teachers in preschools, elementary schools and upper secondary schools <https://gagnryninhugsun.hi.is/>. More concrete initiatives were taken in individual school districts (for instance in Garðabær, see Haraldsdóttir, 2015) or in individual schools. However, such initiatives were often dependent on enthusiastic individuals as the budget of both the state and the municipalities was extremely limited in the years following the collapse, as Katrín Jakobsdóttir noted towards the end of her tenure as Minister of Education in 2013.

> We wanted the teachers to have continuing education courses, seminars, and conferences where the new ideology is introduced. We wanted to have lots of training for the teachers where the schools could send their staff to familiarize themselves with these ideas, but we did not have the money to do it. In fact, the ideal would have been to have a training session in each school – also not possible because of financial constraints.
>
> One of the most serious problems with the implementation is the limited budget with which we must work. We have published guidelines and idea booklets for each of the basic values, and more guidance is being prepared. But the process is too slow. We, therefore, had to extend the implementation and give it more time. We are now working on a 3-year implementation period (Hannesdóttir, 2013, p. 10).

Although the national curricula were written within the Ministry and thus distanced from the individual teachers working with the children

and adolescents in schools, Katrín Jakobsdóttir recognised the importance of involving the teachers themselves.

> By the time we had the pillars or foundations for our school system, the work on im-
> plementation had started. I should add here that the Icelandic teaching professionals
> are very well educated, creative, and hard working – but inevitably they called for
> guidance. How did we want this to be carried out? How could the individual teacher
> or school implement these democratic ideas? Teachers are positive, but only a very
> few have jumped into the deep end of the pool (Hannesdóttir, 2013, p. 11).

And a little later she stressed the cooperative nature of the reform process where the teachers were not only participants, but played a central
role:

> We considered the curriculum to be a cooperative agreement between the gov-
> ernment and schools, but personnel in each school must develop the methods that
> they consider will best suit them (Hannesdóttir, 2013, p. 11).

After parliamentary elections in 2013, the right wing Independence
Party and the centrist Progressive Party, which had been widely blamed
for the collapse 5 year earlier (Indriðason, Önnudóttir, Þórisdóttir &
Harðarson, 2017), formed a new government with the Minister of Education coming from the former party. The changes that followed were
pronounced. The previous curricula was not abandoned but the six pillars were silenced. Emphasis was again placed on individualistic elements, such as reading, student retention and PISA scores, as well as on
economic and technical features such as efficiency and accountability.

## Closing remarks

The educational history of Iceland since the beginning of the 20th century
has been, by and large, a history of a democracy coming of age. When the
first law on public schooling was passed in 1907 one could not claim the
existence of any formal educational system in Iceland, even if the majority of people were literate and had been so since the eighteenth century
(Guttormsson, 1990). This first comprehensive educational legislation

was ahead of the system at the time, and subsequent legislation continued to be so towards the end of the century. Iceland gained independence from Denmark in 1944 and with new comprehensive legislation on primary and secondary education in 1946, one can see how people conceived solid education of the general public to be a precondition for both cultural and economic independence that extended beyond a mere political status (Halldórsdóttir, *et al.*, 2016). This development culminated with the next comprehensive legislation in 1974 when democracy and inclusion in education became both an explicit and a central concern for legislators. After a decade of implementation this radical reform came to a halt and the democratic principles were gradually silenced. They were never explicitly challenged, quite the contrary, every law and every new curriculum repeated the clause from the 1974 Education Act declaring that preparation for a life in a continually changing democratic society was the central purpose of compulsory education. But since the 1990s and into the 21st century those words lost their power and became little more than a dead letter (Halldórsdóttir *et al.*, 2016; Jónsson, 2017). The idea of learning for democracy in a democracy was not connected to the rest of the curricula; evaluation was not related to this idea as it had been in the 1970s but was increasingly summative and standardized, objectives were predefined and the educational process was increasingly steered by detailed objectives and sub-objectives, educational support was based on diagnoses and individualized treatment rather than on inclusive pedagogy, etc. This development followed trends that were visible in large parts of Europe and North-America, and not only in schools, but in the wider societies as well.

With the collapse in October 2008, there suddenly was no "normal" any more, and people realized that the norms by which they had been living in the previous years were anything but "normal". And so, a communal search for a new grounding began with people talking to each other, whether at home or public meetings, about fundamental things such as the basic values of the society, the meaning of democracy, and the importance of a shared community. The post-collapse years were, thus, characterized by a widespread search for a meaningful life in democratic society. It was as if the Socratic principle, that only the examined life is worth living, had become the norm by which people now lived. The radical educational response to the collapse – with the definition of the six pillars of education for all schools from preschools up through upper secondary schools – resonated well with the spirit of the time. But not only did it resonate with other initiatives and the mood of the time, it also aimed at taking things further. By defining democracy, human rights, sustainability, equality, literacy, creativity and wellbeing as fundamental pillars of all education, the Ministry of Education strove to give criticality, self-reflection and the continued search for a democratic society lasting momentum so that it would not simply be a short-lived reaction to a shocking event but a principle for change. This initiative resonates well with Wolfgang Edelstein's perception of the post-collapse challenges. In a paper from 2011 titled "Education for Democracy" he says:

> The importance of learning democracy in school is linked to the present crisis, a crisis that presents the system in which we live with perilous challenges and risks, for which both governments and citizens in general are ill prepared. Beyond the recent crisis of the financial system that determines the present social and economic experience and the political disillusionment of millions worldwide, political scientists, have identified serious threats to the very foundations and basic components of democratic systems: the corrosion, as Münkler calls it, of the *sociomoral resources of democracy* (Edelstein, 2011).

Although nine years have passed since the collapse and six since the publication of the new curricula it is still too early to judge what impact this educational response has had, let alone whether the impact is a lasting one. With a right wing government back in power in 2013 – and again in 2016 after continued scandals on the political scene – the radical work has not been continued and many feel that the spirit of the pre-collapse years is returning, where people seem to be more interested in having things than cultivating communal ties and moral and political values. It is challenging to live by the Socratic principle; it is strenouos to live an examined life, whether as an individual or as a whole society.

MICHAEL FIELDING
*University College London Institute of Education*

# Radical Democracy and Student Voice in Secondary Schools

If we are to develop, as best we can, approaches to secondary schooling that are inspired by ideals of radical democracy I think we need to begin by addressing a number of preliminary issues.

Firstly, we need to say a little about what we mean by radical democracy and distinguish it boldly from its contemporary neo-liberal distortions that have colonised so many countries around the world.

Secondly, we need to underscore the importance of education as an essential element in democracy's creation and renewal. Too often schooling marginalises or corrupts both education and democracy and through that double betrayal we create disillusionment and despair.

Thirdly, we need to interrogate the notion of student voice, granting it only transitional legitimacy. Inspired by education in and for radical democracy we need to develop a more profound mutuality between teacher and student that positions voice within a context of resolve, hope and profound transformation.

Having offered these three starting points for reflection I then offer two frameworks that I hope will be a helpful basis for dialogue and future action. The first framework is my *Patterns of Partnership*, developed over the last 20 years as an intellectual and practical intervention intended to name real-world actions and practices that illustrate the lived reality and generative vitality of different ways in which adults and young people in schools can and do instantiate and prefigure a democratic way of living and learning together.

My second framework, *Schools for Democracy*, offers a wider institutional and social schema to which Patterns of Partnership contributes and by which it is sustained.

In *Tripwires of Integrity* I reflect briefly on ways in which we might sustain our commitments to education in and for participatory democracy in times which have little understanding and even less commitment to its future reality. I conclude by insisting that 'Democracy is not only something to fight for, it is something to fight with' and that '[S]ome change have to start now else there is no beginning for us.'

## Democracy, education and student voice

### Democracy

We live in difficult times: as I have argued recently, (Fielding, 2016) democracy has been swallowed by the gluttony of neo-liberal consumerism and regurgitated as an emetic scramble for easy and endless acquisition at the cost of a narrowing of vision, a corrosion of generosity and human sympathy, and an impoverishment of much that distinguishes democracy as an ennobling as well as an enabling way of life. Unsurprisingly, the consequences for education are as disastrous as they are for democracy. As the great US philosopher, Martha Nussbaum, reminds us, "Education based mainly on profitability in the global market magnifies (democracy's) deficiencies, producing greedy obtuseness that threatens the very life of democracy itself." (Nussbaum, 2007, 40).

There are, of course, quite different traditions of democratic thought and action. My own position draws on participatory traditions and is mindful of contributions from those like Benjamin Barber who insists that "Voting is the least significant act in a democracy" (Barber, 1987, 187) and Michael Sandel who bravely and uncompromisingly insists that

> Democratic governance is radically devalued if reduced to the role of handmaiden to the market economy. Democracy is about more than fixing and tweaking and nudging incentives to make markets work better (it) is about much more than maximising GDP, or satisfying consumer preferences. It's also about seeking distributive justice; promoting the health of democratic institutions; and cultivating the solidarity, and sense of community that democracy requires. Market-mimicking

governance – at its best – can satisfy us as consumers. But it can do nothing to make us democratic citizens (Sandel 2009).

For me democracy is a way of living and learning together, not merely a mechanism for taking joint decisions and holding each other to account. It is, as Sandel insists above, a means of 'cultivating the solidarity, and sense of community' that presumes and enhances the principles of freedom and equality. Participatory traditions require not just the recognition of rights which ground and secure the formal entitlements of democratic citizenship. They also insist on a deeper, more profound set of dispositions which give rights their point and nurture the lived realities of generous, caring human encounter. Issues of power, of rights, of justice are, of course, foundationally important. However, they are not enough. Justice is never enough: it is a necessary, but not a sufficient condition of human flourishing. Justice, and indeed any form of politics, is for the sake of something else, for the sake of creative and joyful relations between persons.

Procedural traditions of democracy rightly insist on the importance of structures and processes. What they tend to ignore or disregard are prior questions which return us to purposes, to the nature and needs of democracy as a way of living good lives together. Structures are not ends in themselves: their justification lies in the purposes they are intended to realise. For me structures and procedures should be expressions of democratic fellowship, means by which we encourage, deepen and extend certain kinds of human encounter that incorporate rights and entitlement, but come before them, underpin them and go beyond them. It is these kinds of encounter that delight in an open reciprocity of difference, that celebrate a restless commonality, as open to surprise as it is to re-assurance which lie at the heart both of democracy's presuppositions and its deeper aspirations.

## Education

Just as participatory traditions emphasise democracy as a way of leading good lives together its companion education traditions retain that holistic, other regarding orientation and, as a means of remaining true to those aspirations, insist on the distinction between education and schooling. Here schools and schooling have a derivative justification. Their legitimacy must be interrogated and established by reference to deeper educational purposes. Schooling, as the present depressingly testifies, too often betrays or distorts or damages the possibility of its educational aspirations. High-performance schooling, to which many of our countries subscribe, marginalises education, narrowing its aspirations, diminishing its daily realities, often through the incorporation of student voice as a disciplinary device.

For us to retain our integrity, deepen our understanding, and widen the scope of our democratic aspiration we must return again and again, in the pressured realities of our daily work, to educational purposes that express and enact democracy's aspirations and grant schooling its always provisional legitimacy.

If, as John Dewey argues in his *Democracy and Education*, "democracy is more than a form of government: it is primarily a mode of associated living, a conjoint communicated experience" (Dewey, 1916 / 1944, 87), then we need to develop ways of working and learning together in schools that honour, instantiate and further those aspirations.

In similar vein, Alex Bloom, one of the most important pioneers of radical democratic education in my own country, insists that because education is "fundamentally a matter of relationships", our primary concern must be "with the practice of right human relations … He is educated who is able to recognise relationships between things and to experience just relationships with persons." (Bloom, 1952, 136). For Bloom, as for Dewey, education was a way of being and living in the world, and "since this ars vivendi cannot be taught, it must be learnt. And it can be learnt only through and by actual living. Through living one learns to live. School therefore should be a place where such learning is not merely possible but is made possible" (*Ibid*).

Unless democracy shapes the way we live and learn together, we will fail to achieve our wider democratic aspirations and the enabling educational encounters that nurture their growth and development.

## Student Voice

Given the kinds of commitment to participatory traditions of democracy and to their educational manifestations as a way of living and learning together advocacy of student voice also takes on a distinctive form and rationale. Certainly, the kind of consumerist, neo-liberal approach that in large measure explains and expresses its popularity in many countries across the world is, for a number of reasons, at odds with the approach for which I am arguing here.

Firstly, such approaches are primarily a means of pressurising those involved into a higher productivity, measured in ways that narrow their focus, indiscriminately intensify working practices, and reduce the likelihood of exploratory approaches to learning. In short, they are anti-educational. Secondly, they have nothing whatever to do with democracy as a form of intergenerational learning, shared responsibility and future possibility. Thirdly, they are too easily prone to the dangers of condescension, tokenism and the perpetuation of exclusion, privilege and injustice.

If student voice is to have a legitimate place in education in and for democracy it must be firmly located within frameworks, roles and dispositions that require and enable a mutuality of endeavour.

The frameworks, the structures of discussion, dialogue and democratic engagement, must be there. Likewise, we must develop roles that express and generate confidence and commitment in all participants, sometimes leading to what the great Brazilian social theorist, Robert Unger, calls 'role jumbling'. (Unger, 2004, 563) Here students are also teachers and teachers also students; a 'radical collegiality' (Fielding, 1999) of democratic endeavour.

But so too – preceding, informing and generating future transformation of structures and roles – must be the kinds of relationships, dispositions and attitudes that expresses our care for and delight in each other as persons, not just as citizens. Structures, procedures and roles are for the sake of something else: their legitimacy is always provisional, always dependent on the values and vision that author their emergence.

For participatory democracy to become an educational reality and a societal possibility we must move more deliberately, more courageously and more insistently to an intergenerational unity of purpose which not only requires a multiplicity of student voices (rather than the singularity of student voice), but also sees an active interdependence and reciprocity, a more profound mutuality between teacher and student.

## Patterns of Partnership

Too often publicly funded school systems demonstrate a complacent, even lazy, espousal of democracy as an orienting dynamic. There is little or no recognition of schools' overt responsibility to educate young people and the adults with whom they work to embrace, understand and joyfully develop together their capacities as democratic citizens, still less in their deeper obligations to create and sustain living communities which initiate, develop and sustain the dispositions and contexts of daily encounter that exemplify and prefigure democracy's ultimate aspirations. In the last quarter century even the rise of the 'student voice' movement owes significantly more to the now hegemonic neo-liberal myopia of market-led customer orientation than it does to traditions of civic education, let alone its more radical counterparts in the democratic schools movement.

In an effort to reaffirm the possibilities of democracy, even within contexts that exhibit more of these negative characteristics and abdications that one would wish, I have, over the last 20 years or so, developed a number of frameworks and interrogative prompts intended to enable, support and extend different initiatives involving a more overt and valued reciprocity between young people and adults in schools. Most recently, drawing inspiration from the pioneering contributions of writers like Shelley Arnstein (Arnstein, 1969), Roger Hart (Hart, 1997), Harry Shier (Shier, 2001) and others my own typology (Fielding, 2011, 2012) offers a differentiating tool which is not only grounded in the complexities and specificities of school based contexts but is also committed to the need to name, explore and extend participatory democracy as a legitimate and increasingly urgent aspiration. The typology – *Patterns of Partnership: How adults listen to and learn with students in schools* – suggests six forms of interaction between adults and young people within a school and other educational contexts.

Within the context of my wider advocacy of democracy as an animating dynamic in contemporary approaches to education two points are particularly pertinent at this juncture. Firstly, the familiar / real world nature of the examples gestured at here and pursued in more depth in the literature lends support to the contention that it is possible to work towards increasingly meaningful and ultimately more democratically oriented forms of partnership.

Secondly, as I have briefly intimated earlier, in addition to undergirding a collaborative typology such as this with overt reference to power there is also a need to include explicit reference to relationships, to dispositions and orientations to our encounter with each other as persons. When teachers and students begin to work in these new ways they are not just redrawing the boundaries of what is permissible and thereby jointly extending a sense of what is possible: they are also giving each other the desire and the strength to do so through their regard and care for each other; they are coming to 're-see each other' (Weaver, 1989, 83) and in so doing open up new possibilities for intergenerational learning. I have thus underscored this relational imperative through the two framing columns of very different values – 'the instrumental dimension' typified by high performance schooling through market accountability and the 'fellowship dimension' typified by person-centred education for democratic fellowship.

| *Instrumental* *dimension* | Patterns of partnership *How adults listen to and learn with students in school* | *Fellowship* *dimension* |
|---|---|---|

| | *Students as data source* staff utilise information about student progress and well-being | |
| High performance schooling *through* market accountability | *Students as active respondents* staff invite student dialogue and discussion to deepen learning / professional decisions | Person centred education *for* democratic fellowship |
| | *Students as co-enquirers* staff take a lead role with high-profile, active student support | |
| | *Students as knowledge creators* students take lead roles with active staff support | |
| | *Students as joint authors* students and staff decide on a joint course of action together | |
| | *Intergenerational learning as lived democracy* shared commitment to / responsibility for the common good | |

In each of these ways of working the power relations and the interpersonal relations are different, thus not only enabling or prohibiting the contributions of one side of the partnership, but also influencing the potential synergy of the joint work, and thereby affecting the possibility of both adults and young people being able to listen to and learn with and from each other.

Each Pattern of Partnership operates at multiple levels, e.g. one-to-one, small group, class, team or department, whole-school and school / community and it is the range, depth and multiplicity of levels of partnership that fires the developmental synergy of the school as an emerging democratic learning community.

## Partnership in Action

Examples of Pattern 1 – *Students as Data Source* – might be a teacher paying particular attention to performance data of her students when preparing a lesson / a team of teachers sharing examples of student work / a whole school student survey. Examples of Pattern 2 – *Students as Active Respondents* – might be inviting students to adapt assessment criteria for a current piece of work / a team agenda based in part on student evaluations / the increasingly thoughtful and sophisticated involvement of students in the appointment of new members of staff. Examples of Pattern 3 – *Students as Co-enquirers* – might be involving students in a teacher-led piece of classroom-based action research / supporting and learning from an on-going departmental team of students involved with evaluation of units of work / the now well-established Students as Learning Partners scheme in which schools enable teachers to enlist the support of students in observing their practice. Examples of Pattern 4 – *Students as Knowledge Creators* – might be the development of Student-Led Reviews in which young people take major responsibility for the preparation, organisation and leadership of an annual review of their work / a Student Council researching the effectiveness or otherwise of their playground buddying scheme / a piece of action research investigating the cause of low-level bullying in class.

The distinction between Pattern 5 – *Students a Joint Authors* – and Pattern 6 – *Intergenerational Learning as Lived Democracy* – is more one of emphasis and orienting values than one of method. Both involve a genuinely shared, fully collaborative partnership between students and staff that is overtly and appreciatively reciprocal. Examples of Pattern 5 – *Students a Joint Authors* – might be co-construction of a lesson or a class visit / student involvement in developing a series of 'Research Lessons' (sometimes called Lesson Study) / a joint student and staff Learning Walk within the school or across schools focusing on an agreed area of practice. In Pattern 5 the egalitarian reciprocity of the partnership is paramount. Not only does it provide an energising dynamic, the degree to which it is a mutually and joyfully attentive undertaking is likely to affect its subsequent success. In Pattern 6 – *Intergenerational Learning as Lived Democracy* – those other-regarding orientations become explicit commitments to the furtherance of the common good. They also entail a receptivity and mutual attentiveness between generations as, for example, in an action research project in which young people identified and responded to loneliness amongst old people in their community / follow-up work to a successful visit, where a class, their teacher and museum staff co-plan a subsequent visit for younger students as an engaging learning experience for their younger peers / the work of a Student Action team identifying and researching a safety issue in their community – e.g. drug needles in a local park or the need for a safe crossing point at a busy road near the school – taking it to the school and local community and following through on subsequent action.

The difference that values and principles make to these kinds of partnerships can be seen by contrasting a couple of examples as seen through the lens of 'the instrumental dimension' typified by high performance schooling through market accountability and then through the lens of the 'fellowship dimension' typified by person-centred education for democratic fellowship.

A high-performance schooling perspective, typical of contemporary a neo-liberal, results-driven orientation might approach Pattern 1 *Students as Data Source* by a teacher paying particular attention to performance data of her students, checking them against required levels, requiring extra lunchtime and/or after-school sessions, contacting parents and form tutors and making additional materials and tasks available. In contrast, a democratic fellowship orientation might encourage a teacher to go beyond test data and draw on her emerging knowledge and understanding of the student's range of involvement in multiple areas of the curriculum, in a variety of school and non-school situations, and on her developing knowledge and appreciation of the young person as a person in both formal and informal contexts.

A high-performance schooling example of Pattern 4 – *Students as Knowledge Creators* might be the development of Student-Led Reviews that involve adult learning coaches, small groups of students inducted into the language and expectations of exam requirement, and the creation of opportunities, spaces and cultural expectations that cherish high performance. A person-centred, democratic fellowship example of Student-Led Reviews might be small groups of students taking shared responsibility in the mutually-supportive preparation of multi-faceted evidence of achievement, not just in academic matters, but also in developing grounded aspirational realities that contribute towards the individual's answer to the wider, deeper question 'How do I live a good life?'

## Schools for Democracy

My hope is that the *Patterns of Partnership* framework offers a way of illustrating how the beginnings of more democratic ways of living and learning together are possible in schools, even within current contexts which for many of us are distorted by the greed and insidious dishonesty of trans-national neo-liberalism. In the hope that it will assist our opposition and stiffen our resolve still further I offer, very briefly, a second framework, *Schools for Democracy*, which suggests a wider institutional and social schema to which *Patterns of Partnership* contributes and by which it is sustained.

### a) Education in and for radical democracy

My suggestion here is that schools develop a proclaimed, not just an intended, democratic vitality. If democracy matters it must be seen to matter. Its aspirations require the dignity and eloquence of articulation; its legitimacy requires enacted practical arrangements and humane dispositions that embody its living reality. Context and circumstance will, of course, determine how those commitments are stated and shared and it may well be that much of the work is named with circumspection. Notwithstanding the cautions that practical realities demand, we need to find ways of naming the authenticity, tenacity and grounded reality of our democratic obligations and aspirations.

## b)  *Radical structures and spaces*

We know from our work on student voice how important it is to sustain and develop structures and spaces that legitimate and enable the perspectives and contributions of young people. Here I am further arguing that these structures and spaces insist on a permanent and proper provisionality. We need to encourage a restless democratic energy, a residual unease with hierarchy. We need to develop transparent structures that encourage ways of working which transcend boundaries and invite new combinations and possibilities. We need to attend to the spatiality of democracy, to interpersonal and architectural spaces that encourage a multiplicity of different forms of formal and informal engagement with a multiplicity of persons.

## c)  *Radical roles*

Roles are important, but, as I have argued earlier, their justification is derivative: they are the servants of certain kinds of human flourishing. A commitment to democracy entails the kind of variety and energy gestured at in my Patterns of Partnership typology, to Roberto Unger's celebration of 'Role defiance and role jumbling' amongst staff, amongst students and also between staff and students.

## d)  *Radical relationships*

I have for many years argued that radical democratic relationships are not just important, but foundationally important.

Politics and education are the means to certain kinds of human flourishing and the forms of flourishing they seek to establish must themselves inform the structures, processes and activities we develop to bring them about. We need to encounter each other as persons, not just as role occupants.

In a sense, what I and others have called 'democratic fellowship' is what democracy is <u>for</u>. Not only does it name a form of human encounter that acknowledges our stature as members of a democratic community whose reciprocal rights and responsibilities require an active, respectful enactment. It also names fundamental dispositions towards each other as persons. Rights are necessary and important: they are an essential bulwark against the tyrannies of both majority and elite. But they can only ever provide the basis of a procedural and respectful co-existence. For democracy to flourish, for it to grow into a more demanding, more joyful, more fulfilling way of being-in-the-world its organisational manifestations must be both expressive and generative of democratic fellowship. They must be expressive of, if not care, then a generosity of disposition that has within it the seeds of a deeper, more welcoming mutuality.

We not only need to nurture a new understanding, sense of possibility, and felt respect between adults and young people. We also need to nurture and celebrate a greater sense of shared delight, care and reciprocal responsibility.

## e) Personal and communal narrative

I feel very strongly that we need to develop multiple spaces and opportunities for young people and adults to make meaning of their work, separately and together, both personally and as a community. Such spaces and processes are crucial because they return us to purposes, to a quest for meaning that transcends the treadmill of endless acquisition and the impoverishment of self-regard.

Crucially important, too, are communal narratives and the narratives of history. Schools must author, tell, retell, revisit and further develop their own narratives which name their aspirations and achievements. Vitally important, and predictably marginalised by the intended amnesia of neo-liberalism, are the radical histories and traditions of democratic education from which we learn and to which we contribute as best we can.

*f)  Radical curriculum, critical pedagogy and enabling assessment*

We must develop a formal and informal curriculum which equips young people and adults with the desire and capacity to seriously interrogate what is given and co-construct a knowledge that assists in leading good and joyful lives together. Starting with the cultures, concerns and hopes of the communities that the school serves we must include integrated approaches to knowledge with students and staff working in small communities of enquiry.

We must support a critical pedagogy that develops a reciprocity of engagement and involvement not only with the immediate community, but with other communities and ways of being, at a local, regional, national and international level. This must be partnered with enabling forms of assessment at both national and local levels that have the flexibility to respond to the particularities of context. This is likely to include high levels of peer and teacher involvement through assessment-for-learning approaches and additional community and family involvement through public, portfolio-based presentations.

*g)  Insistent affirmation of possibility*

Our work must be informed by a generosity of presumption that requires us to keep options open and counters the confinement of customary or casual expectation. There will be no ability grouping, emulation will replace competition, and intrinsic motivation and communal recognition will replace the paraphernalia of marks and prizes.

*h)  Engaging the local*

Education is seen as a lifelong process and the school becomes a site of community renewal and responsibility in which young and old explore what it means to live good lives together. School and community are seen as reciprocal resources for broadly and more narrowly conceived notions of learning.

*i) Accountability as shared responsibility*

Democratic accountability is better understood and enacted as a form of 'shared responsibility' – i.e. an accountability that is morally and politically situated, not merely technically and procedurally 'delivered'. We must develop new forms of accountability better suited to a more engaged understanding of democratic living. Young people can and should be involved in such process, a good example being at Bishops Park College, Clacton, an 11–16 school in England where, towards the end of its radical phase of development, it developed a Research Forum out of which emerged a framework of aspirations and practices that formed the basis of the College's accountability framework (see Fielding *et al.*, 2006).

*j) Regional, national and global solidarities*

Crucially important in any approaches that seek to develop new ways of being-in-the-world, new ways of living and learning together are regional, national and global solidarities. These are made real through reciprocal ideological, material and interpersonal support through values-driven networks and alliances, which draw on and contribute to the dynamic of radical social movements.

## Tripwires of Integrity

One of the most difficult challenges we face at the present time is how we remain true to our beliefs in education in and for a form of democracy that is radical, inclusive and worthy of pioneers like the great Catalan radical educator, Francisco Ferrer (Ferrer, 1913); like Alex Bloom in my own country (Fielding, 2005, 2014 [a] and [b]); like Lawrence Kohlberg in the USA (Kohlberg, 1980) and like other brave pioneers from many countries around the world.

    When teachers are under so much pressure to conform to the performance-driven betrayals of neo-liberal forms of schooling how might they create small spaces of hope in their daily work, link arms with others who share their commitments and together develop alternatives that offer a quite different vision of the future to the one that dominates so many countries at the present time?

My suggestion is that we develop what might be called 'Tripwires of Integrity' (see Fielding, 2016), so-called mainly because I see them as practical reminders of the purposes to which we aspire; practices which, despite or, indeed, because of the relentlessness of the pressures we encounter in our work, require us to draw breath and ask ourselves and each other questions which are conjointly and reciprocally educational and instrumental. Of the many that we could reflect on I offer two in a spirit of friendship and solidarity. The first concerns individual and communal narrative and the second concerns the deeper, longer narratives of history that have the capacity to inspire us to reject the bullying lies of 'the dictatorship of no alternative' (Unger, 2004) and sustain us in our future endeavours.

We need to encourage and develop ways in which our processes of reflection and renewal can connect with our own narratives, with those threads of learning and encounter that weave together the tapestry of meaning in our life's work. We need to develop spaces and practices like Self-Managed Learning Groups in which teachers come together in a small group of four or five and explore issues of importance to each member. Each teacher has about twenty minutes to present an issue she is concerned about or keen to develop in some way. The role of the group is not to supply answers, but to ask clarifying questions to help the teacher think things through and develop a future course of action on which she then reports back to the group next time it meets, usually about two or three months later. What is key here, is not just the process, but the fact that in introducing the issue that concerns her, the teacher locates it within her own professional narrative, within her own set of values and aspirations about what really matters to her.

At whole school level, externally they might include the membership of local, regional, national and international groups and alliances that are visibly and joyfully driven by a particular set of values. Internally, they might include practices like those developed by the great UK pioneer of radical democratic public education, Alex Bloom, who sustained and developed the moral, educational and democratic integrity of his work, in part by use of what he called 'Our Pattern', a document which in five short paragraphs sketched out a living set of aspirations that were constantly returned to and adapted in the course of the school's development as one of the most remarkable examples of radical democratic progressive education the UK has ever seen (see Fielding 2014[b]).

Lastly, and crucially, our individual and institutional narratives are themselves bound up with the longer narratives of history, of multiple histories that have contested, bravely and resolutely, former hegemonies whose exclusions invariably circumscribed an inconvenient past or denied its relevance to the myopic imperatives of the present.

Now, more than for a long time, it is important to "mobilize the past against a reckless present" (Blackburn 1993, 7). The pasts to which we choose to give our allegiance contain not only a timeless integrity, but also a sense of hope, a sense of possibility that invites our allegiance and beckons towards a better future than the present allows or understands.

### *'Democracy is not only something to fight for, it is something to fight with'*

I conclude with two exhortations. The first was written three quarters of a century ago in the early years of the Second World War. Its simple reminder is profound and enduring. It insists we remember democracy's immanent transformative power, not just its compelling vision of future possibility. It argues that "Democracy is not only something to fight for, it is something to fight with" (Williams 1941, V–VI).

The companion exhortation, written thirty years later by the pioneering UK feminist, Sheila Rowbotham, re-enforces the continuing urgency of our task: "[S]ome change have to start now else there is no beginning for us." (Rowbotham 1979, 140).

Kyriaki Messiou
*University of Southampton*

# The Voices of Students: Silenced Voices and Strategies to Make Them Heard in Schools

'Student voice' has gained prominence over the last twenty years, especially since the UN Convention on the Rights of the Child in 1989. The term student voice can have varied meanings. Thomson argues that voice means "Having a say, as well as referring to language, emotional components as well as non-verbal means that are used to express opinions" (Thomson, 2008b, p. 4). In addition, Cook-Sather argues that "over the last 15 years, a way of thinking has reemerged that strives to reposition school students in educational research and reform." (Cook-Sather, 2006, p. 359).

However, Fine (1991 cited in Anderson and Herr, 1994) argues that schools engage in an active process of silencing students, through their policies and practices, in order to smooth over social and economic contradictions. Similarly, more recent research has argued about the dangers of student voice being done in a tokenistic way (e.g. Fielding, 2001, 2004; Messiou and Hope, 2015). At the same time, though there is lot of emphasis in research on student voice, recent literature views have drawn attention to gaps in knowledge that need to be addressed. Gonzalez, Hernandez-Saca and Artiles (2017) in their review of 49 studies published in peer-refereed journals between 1990 and 2010 in the US about student voice, highlight that the largest majority of research has focused on high school students (69.4 % of the 49 studies), with 0% at the primary grade, 2 % at intermediate and 8.2 % at middle-school grade. At the same time, they found that only 20.4 % looked at learning and teaching. Therefore, there is a need for student voice to extend beyond asking students their views about their school uniform or where to go on a school trip, for example. In addition, Robinson (2014), focusing on studies carried out since 2007 in the UK, concludes that more research is needed that focuses on children's experiences of primary schooling. In addition, she notes that most studies used surveys, with few studies involving interviews. Therefore, it seems that the need for more engaging methodologies to capture the views of students about their schooling requires further exploration. This chapter will focus on different ways that can be used in order to engage with the views of students in schools, either by researchers, by student co-researchers or by practitioners in schools.

The key questions that will be addressed in this chapter is:

– How can we engage with students' voices in schools?
– In which ways do different ways of engaging with the views of students facilitate democratic processes in schools?

## Engaging with students' voices: An inclusive process

The idea of engaging with the views of students in schools is closely linked to the principles of inclusive education. Inclusive education has been described as an ongoing process that aims to reduce barriers to participation and learning for all learners in schools (Ainscow, 1999, Booth and Ainscow 2002; Slee 2011; Ainscow 2014; Messiou 2017). Barton defines inclusion as being "about listening to unfamiliar voices, being open, empowering all members and about celebrating 'difference' in dignified ways. Inclusive experience is about learning to live with one another" (Barton, 1997, p. 233). Such notions of inclusion directly relate to democratic processes. Fielding using Dewey's work defines democracy as "primarily a mode of associated living, a conjoint communicated experience." (Fielding, 2016, p. 115). In this paper, the focus will be on this conjoint communicated experience and how this can be brought about through an engagement with the views of students. As I have argued elsewhere, listening to students' voices is a manifestation of being inclusive (Messiou, 2006).

Thomson argues that:

> "Voice' is inherently concerned with questions of power and knowledge, with how decisions are made, who is included and excluded and who is advantaged and disadvantaged as a result. Weak forms of 'voice' generally support the status quo or aim for modest reforms. The strongly democratic use of 'voice' equates to a call for a public sphere in which there is dialogue, reciprocity, recognition and respect. Reaching that utopian state is understood as a struggle to be heard, listened to and taken seriously". (Thomson, 2011, p. 21)

Therefore, it can be argued that the notion of voice is complex. The forms of voice that I am interested in are the ones that facilitate dialogues amongst adults and students, either in research or in work in schools.

## Research with children and young people

Some authors (e.g. Fraser, 2004; Punch, 2002a; Punch 2002b) argue that research that involves children and young people is different from research with adults, especially because of the power relationships that exist between adults and children and young people. Morrow and Richards (1996) have described these disparities in power and status between adults and children as the biggest ethical challenge for researchers who involve children in their research. They argue that: using methods which are non-invasive, non-confrontational and participatory, and which encourage children to interpret their own data, might be one step forward in diminishing the ethical problems of imbalanced relationships between researcher and researched at the point of data collection and interpretation.

On the other hand, Christensen and James (2001), argue that methods are not different when doing research with children compared to when doing research with adults, but what might be different is the use of certain techniques which might be more appropriate when working with children and young people. The focus of this chapter is on such techniques that can be used in order to facilitate conversations with students in schools. These can be used by teachers or other practitioners in schools, by student co-researchers, or by researchers working along- side children and young people. In addition, the techniques that I am describing below can be used with all children and young people. One crucial feature of my work over a number of years, is that of focusing on all rather than focusing on some (Messiou, 2003; Messiou, 2017). These ideas relate to the notion of inclusive education as a process that facilitates active involvement and participation of all (Mittler, 2000). In addition, though many researchers argue that there are groups of learn- ers that might be silenced in schools, such as those defined as having special educational needs, travellers and gypsies etc. (e.g, Derrington and Kendall, 2003; Lawson, 2010), I am also arguing that there are students in schools that are not given the opportunity to be heard simply because they do not belong in any group that has received special atten- tion such as the ones mentioned above. Therefore, my effort is to focus on all through a range of techniques described below:

*Message in a bottle*

This is a technique used by Davies (2000) to investigate children's un- derstanding of democratic processes in primary schools. Students in schools are asked to write a message, stating something that they are not happy with at school and would like to change. The technique can be used in a number of different ways. If this is used by teachers with a whole class, the students usually write their message. Whereas if the activity is used by researchers. as part of individual interviews with stu- dents, they can be given the option of either saying to the researcher or writing down their message, taking into account the differences among children and the fact that some of the children might have difficulties with writing. Of course, even in a whole class context the teacher can go around and ask children to say to her/him their message and they can write it down for them, but this might not allow them to truly express what they want to say since others might be able to hear. Obviously, if the activity is used in individual interviews the researcher is in a posi- tion to know who the child/young person who wrote or said the message is. However, if this technique is used by teachers, it is up to each school to decide whether the students will write their names on the message or not. Issues of confidentiality and anonymity are important here. If the activity is done anonymously, then there is a danger of not being in a position to identify the concerns of particular students and, therefore, act on them. However, there might be students who if they know that they can be identified they might not freely express their views. In my view, students should be given the option of identifying who they are, if the wish to do this, but should be assured that, if they decide to disclose their identity, whatever they say will remain confidential.

*Post it notes*

Similar to the above technique post it notes can be used with whole classes where students are asked to write on a post it note a statement based on what the teacher or the researcher wants to find out about. For example, students can be asked to write down what helps them with their learning, what makes it difficult for them, what is good about group work, or what makes it difficult for them during group work. Each student writes their own post it note, either anonymously or with their names on the post it note, and then these can either be picked up by the teacher or the researcher to be analysed, or they can be put on the walls in the classroom for students to go around and have a look and facilitate a discussion around the specific area of focus. A variation of this activity would be to ask students to draw a picture expressing their views, if they do not want to write a statement.

*Diamond nine*

This is an activity that we used both in primary and secondary schools in various countries and in different ways (Fox and Messiou, 2004; Messiou and Hope, 2015). This activity can be used with a whole class, where students are asked to work in groups of four usually, or can be used as part of focus group interviews where a researcher is facilitating discussion. It is an interactive group-based activity involved giving students 15 cards with certain statements that could focus on areas that we choose to focus on. For example, the statements could be related to learning (e.g. "Learning should be fun", "Learning should be about preparing students to get a good job", "Learning is about working with others" etc.) or related to participation (e.g. "Participation means taking decisions" etc.). Then students are asked to choose nine cards and put them in the shape of a diamond, having at the top the one they believed to be the most important and at the bottom the one they thought was the least important. What is powerful in this activity is that it can facilitate intensive discussions amongst the students on the one hand, in order to come to a discussion about which card goes where, and on the other hand it allows students to see that their thoughts might be different from one another. Where this activity was used as part of focus group interviews the conversations can be transcribed and analysed later.

*Power maps and star charts*

Power map is another activity suggested by Davies (2000) for understanding democratic processes and where decisions in schools are made. This activity can be used with a whole class or with small groups of students. Students are asked to work in groups of four, drawing a rough map of their school and indicating where they think decisions are made. On some occasions we have provided students with ready-made maps of the school. However, in most occasions students are asked to draw their own map and then highlight the places where decisions are made, as well as the people who are involved in these decisions. This activity has the power to promote discussions amongst students about how decisions are made in schools and who I involved in the decision making. It is a way for finding out how decision making in schools is perceived by students themselves. In one school, we had a group of students highlighting that the decisions are made in the headteachers' office, whereas in other schools it was clear that students felt more involved in decision making in school.

A variation of the power map activity, designed by a group of secondary school students (co-researchers) that I worked with was that of the star chart. The student co-researchers drew a line and the two ends were seen as two extremes (i.e. I am involved in decision making at school versus I am not involved in decision making at school). Then star stickers were given to students of each class in the school and asked them over a period of one week to indicate what they felt by placing a star on the line.

In some classes, most of the students placed their stars very near to the end that indicated that they felt involved in decision making in the school. In others, there were stars that were placed near the other end indicating that they did not feel involved in decision making in the school. Even though this activity does not provide data in relation to individual students' perspectives, it does provide with an overview of how students feel about their involvement in decision making in school.

*Scenarios and role-play*

This activity is based on an idea from McNamara and Moreton (1995) but was adapted for the purposes of my own work (Messiou, 2003). Students are asked to work in groups of four. Each group is given one incident which can be developed by teachers or researchers. For example, the following incident was developed from observations in the playground or in classrooms (Messiou, 2008).

At playtime a group of children are talking in the playground. They make jokes, they tease each other and they seem to be having a good time. Close to them there is a child from the same classroom, standing, listening and looking at this group of children. The group of friends walks while they are talking, and the other child is following them but without being a member of the group. Children in the group seem to ignore that child as if it is not there. At some point a teacher comes and asks a child from the group to go and find one of their classmates. As soon as the teacher leaves, the child whom the teacher asked to go and find the classmate turns towards that child who is outside the group and says 'Go and find [name of the pupil]'. The child immediately runs to find the pupil that the teacher was looking for.

When developing scenarios, the real names of the students involved should not be mentioned and care should be taken so as individuals cannot be identified by other students. The focus of the above incident was focusing on marginalisation in schools, but scenarios can focus on other areas, such as that of democratic processes.

After the group receives their scenarios they are asked to carry out a role play based on what has happened and then discuss in their groups the following questions:

Questions
*   How does the child involved in the above incident feel?
*   What else could this child do during the particular incident?
*   How could the others in the group have behaved?

At the end of the discussion they are also asked to consider what should happen next through role play. In this way, students are encouraged to think about what is happening in schools and how they can contribute positively towards their own experiences as well as towards their class-mates' experiences in schools.

*Visual images*

Visual images include a range of approaches, such as the photo voice approach, the use of drawings and blob trees. A number of researchers have used such approaches (e.g. Burke, 2008; Kaplan, 2008; Kaplan and Howes, 2004; Thomson, 2008a). Thomson (2008b) distinguishes be-tween two approaches of using visual images in research. The first one relates to the use of visual artefacts by researchers to explore how these were produced and their uses, as well as how participants interpret them. For example, in a study in a primary school my colleagues and I used 'blob trees' (an image of a tree with children figures with different fa-cial expressions) and children had to choose representative figures which aligned with their perceived place in the classroom from a range of both happy and sad figures (see Adderley *et al.*, 2015). Then they had to ex-plain their choices. In other words, the image was used to explore chil-dren's perceptions in relation to where they perceived themselves to be in the classroom. The second approach, according to Thomson (2008a), refers to the production of visual artefacts as part of the research process. For example, both the photo voice approach as well as the production of drawings relate to this second approach. Asking students to draw pictures or to take photographs can be used to explore various topics related to school life, such as exploring children's feelings about what is happening in schools (e.g. where they feel safe and where they do not feel safe, what activities help them with their learning or what makes it difficult for their learning).

## Discussion

All of the above strategies can be seen as the starting point for promoting inclusion and democratic processes. For example, each of these activities can be used in schools but without achieving any changes, neither facilitating moves towards inclusion or democratic processes. What is of most importance is what follows after each of these activities. For example, if we take the "Message in a bottle of activity", if students are asked to write messages that nobody in the end reads or act upon, then this undermines the purpose of the activity and the idea of listening to students' voices. Roberts (2000) argues that listening to children, hearing children, and acting on what they say are three very different activities. What I am arguing here is the importance of acting on what children and young people say. This does not necessarily mean that everything that the students will suggest is possible to be implemented. For example, in using the "Message in a bottle" activity in various contexts, I have found that a common suggestion by students is to have a swimming pool in their school. Such comments should not be seen as unrealistic. Instead, they should be seen as opportunities for deeper discussions with students about what is possible and what is not, as well as being seen as opportunities to understand better the students and what matters most to them. I, therefore, see techniques such as the above as important facilitators for "opening doors" to important conversations that we should have with children and young people in schools. Ultimately, such conversations will lead to changes in each context, in order to develop more inclusive practices and more democratic processes in schools. In this respect, I suggest a framework (Figure 1), for promoting inclusion in schools (Messiou, 2012). The framework involves four interconnected processes as can be seen below:

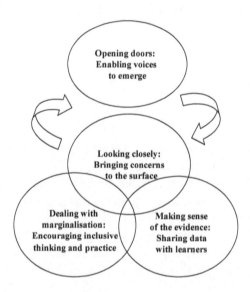

*Figure 1: A framework for promoting inclusion*

The framework can be used in schools by researchers, practitioners or by students who take the role of co-researchers or researchers. The first step can stand on stands on its own, whereas the three following steps are overlapping. Specifically, the process is as follows:

*Step 1: Opening doors: Enabling voices to emerge.* In this first step, various techniques are used that allow voices and issues that might lead to marginalisation of students in the schools to emerge. What I have dealt with in this chapter is this first step, where various techniques that can be used as standalone activities have been described. The focus of the framework is marginalisation, however, the process can apply to any issue that will be brought up by students.

*Step 2:* *Looking closely: Bringing concerns to the surface.* This step involves the close examination of the information gained during the previous step in order to identify those who are experiencing forms of marginalisation in school, as well as issues that might lead to marginalisation. The focus of the framework is on marginalisation and inclusion, and therefore, the focus is on those issues. However, in the context of this chapter, this step could be used in order to look closely at any issues that emerge from the views of students and how these can be addressed.

*Step 3:* *Making sense of the evidence: Sharing data with learners.* This step focuses attention directly on issues of marginalisation that have emerged through the previous step, or any other issues as mentioned above. This step involves dialogue between practitioners, students and researchers. Through this process of collaboration and sharing of information deeper understandings are achieved. This relates closely to the ideas of democratic processes. For example, the scenarios and role play activities are a good example of gaining better understandings by engaging with the views of various participants.

*Step 4:* *Dealing with marginalisation: Encouraging inclusive thinking and practice.*

This last step can be seen as overlapping with the previous one. By sharing data, and issues that have emerged through data collection with students, they are most likely to start making suggestions about how to address some of these issues. Issues of marginalisation are addressed in order to determine actions to be taken in the light of the evidence that has been analysed. Again, this involves collaboration between students, practitioners and researchers. As highlighted above, the focus does not have to be on marginalisation but it can be on any issue that might emerge from students' voices that would allow promotion of inclusion and democratic processes.

The framework highlights even further the need to move away from using standalone strategies to engage with the views of students. Each of these strategies could be used as a standalone activity, however, they are not likely to achieve significant changes neither been seen as facilitating democratic processes unless they become part of the overall approaches used in schools. The suggested framework can act as a facilitator in relation to promoting a culture of listening in schools.

However, such ways of working in schools are challenging not least since they require a change in mindset and a change in educational relationships within institutions (Cook-Sather, 2002). For example, if we look at the power map activity, this can bring up students' perceptions that might be challenging for a school to accept. The issue of the feedback from students being challenging for a school has been discussed in a number of studies (e.g. Ainscow and Messiou, in press; Cunninghame et al, 2009; Kaplan, 2008). Therefore, schools must be prepared that when allowing students' silenced voices to come to the surface the process might not always be straightforward. However, there is evidence that such approaches can have positive effects in relation to the growth of agency, belonging and competence for students (Mitra, 2003; 2004; Mitra and Serriere, 2012), as well as promote stronger relationships between students and teachers (Fielding and Bragg, 2003; Fielding, 2004; Hope 2012).

## Conclusion

Strategies such as the ones described in this chapter are only the starting point. In a truly democratic environment, strategies such as the above should not be used on ad hoc basis, but should be embedded within the school's work. Thomas (2013) suggests that inclusive education should explore the different ways in which schools enable the creation of community, as well how they enable students believing in themselves as members of the community. Strategies such as the ones described here can be used to explore whether students feel that their school does promote a sense of community on the one hand, and at the same time empower students by allowing them to be heard. Most importantly, if those voices are acted upon then the creation of powerful communities can be achieved.

JORDI COLLET-SABÉ
*University of Vic-Central University of Catalonia*

# Democracy and Participation of Families and Community in Schools

The question as to how much inequality democracy as a political system can sustain is, in our view, one of the crucial issues we face today. The increase in inequality and the consequent shift of democracy into plutocracy is, without doubt, one of the key elements in understanding phenomena like the victories of Donald Trump in the US, Brexit in the UK or the huge increase in vote for Marie Le Pen in France on the right-wing end of the political spectrum or the new left-wing movements fuelled by anger like Podemos in Spain, Mélenchon in France, Bernie Sanders in the US or Jeremy Corbyn in the UK. We fully share the analysis of Nancy Fraser[1] when she points to the 'progressive neoliberalism' of the Obama administration or of the (supposedly) socialist governments of Spain and France among many others, as the great cause of the surge in the new populist movements of both the right and the left. As Fraser explains in relation to the US:

> In every case, voters are saying "No!" to the lethal combination of austerity, free trade, predatory debt, and precarious, ill-paid work that characterize financialized capitalism today. Their votes are a response to the structural crisis of this form of capitalism, which first came into full view with the near meltdown of the global financial order in 2008.

It is not in vain that world-renowned authors like Piketty, Wilkinson and Pickett or Atkinson warned years ago that equality is the cornerstone upon which the whole edifice of (representative) democracy rests. If democracy loses the game against neoliberalism, which even in its

---

1    <https://www.dissentmagazine.org/online_articles/progressive-neoliberalism-reactionary-populism-nancy-fraser>

kinder (progressive) guise silences the voice of the citizens, undermines the quality of life of the majority of the population, makes the work and lives of most people precarious and leaves them at the mercy of an exploiting market and a state that is increasingly weakened, what way out remains for the middle and working classes? And families at risk of social exclusion? Why would they support a political system, formal democracy, that excludes them, silences them, impoverishes them and leaves them by the wayside? For us, this analysis is corroborated by the World Values Survey 2016 that warns that people under 30 value democracy less than adults do, and according to the historical series of this survey, as time passes, young people value less the importance of living in a democracy (Foa and Mounk 2016).

So how much inequality can democracy support? Or, to put it differently, up to what point will people from democratic countries continue to support a political system that the national and international elites have left with very little effective power? Or as Bauman (2013) asked, when the distance between those that govern formally and those that have real power becomes greater by the day, what real and practical meaning does (representative) democracy as a political system have? As Branko Milanovic of the Inequality project (2016) clearly demonstrates, the less democracy serves to generate good life conditions for individuals, families and collectives, the more support among the population grows for the idea of a plutocracy, of government by elites that are 'strong and stable'. If the current 'low-intensity representative democracy' understands 'progress' in terms of liberal and individual meritocracy where 'the same' few win, instead of a call for collective equity where everybody has a voice and that promotes redistribution, recognition and participation especially of the weakest, then we are already living in a plutocracy (Fraser, 2012). That is to say, in a government of the rich, powerful and famous 1% that have already amassed over 50% of the world's wealth (Oxfam, 2016[2]).

Given this complex scenario, we can conclude that the binomial democracy-equality is the key to understanding many of today's challenges. One idea, already evident to Dewey, is that "democracy is more

---

2    <https://www.oxfam.org/sites/www.oxfam.org/files/file_attachments/bp210-economy-one-percent-tax-havens-180116-en_0.pdf>

than a form of government: it is above all an experience of life lived together, a way of life based on the equality of its members" (Dewey, 1978, p. 8). Democracy and equality are two sides of the same coin that, if decoupled, creates monsters like those that were suffered throughout the 20th century and those that we are suffering today.

With this context and the great challenges that it presents, in this chapter we wish to examine the role of the school in such a scenario. Since Dewey (1916) we have been aware of the key role of education as a whole but especially schools, as a place that (should) educate from, in and for an everyday democracy, in conditions of equity. If children and young people, teachers and families, do not live, experience and practice democracy in the many aspects of collective work for a shared end, with true equal opportunities for all members of the school, debate and the confrontation of ideas, consensual conflict management, direct involvement – or through delegates or representatives – in collective affairs etc., this becomes synonymous with a vote every four years in adult life. But despite the evident importance of the school as a place for creating experiences and lessons of/in/for democracy and equity as the foundations of a more just society, today the new world consensus promoted by organisations like the OECD, the World Bank or the increasing philanthrocapitalism (Ball *et al.*, 2017; Olmedo, 2017) is going in the opposite direction. According to this new mainstream, educational centres should not focus on becoming equitable and democratic but rather on, individually, their pupils gaining excellent results in the different tests and, in this way, obtain good places in the rankings and promote a competitive economy. In the words of Clarke and Phelan

> Education has been captured by a 'discursive duopoly' of instrumentalism, involving the pervasive view that the main purpose of education is to serve the needs of the economy, and consensualism, involving the valorization of agreement regarding this purpose. (Clarke and Phelan, 2015, p. 1).

Against this, there are schools, teachers, families, movements and research that propose the opposite: that it is precisely today that we need more than ever, for all the reasons we have outlined, that schools become places for the experience of equality and democracy. And not just this. We agree with Fielding and Moss when they propose that schools should become a place for inventing, constructing and implementing "equal and democratic pre-figurative practices" (Fielding and Moss, 2011, p. 167) that do not just reproduce already existing dynamics. Rather, they should go beyond them and be capable of producing new "experiences of life lived together" (Dewey, 1978, p. 8) in accordance with the concrete reality of each centre. These equal and democratic prefigurative practices can only exist, as several authors (Apple and Beane, 2007; Edelstein, 2011; Prieto *et al.*, 2017 etc.) have pointed out, by being practiced on an everyday basis involving all members of the educational community: children, teachers, families and community. From our research we can affirm that this capacity of the school to become a place for practising, learning and building equity and democracy for all, is only possible from this perspective that intertwines children, teachers, families and community (Collet *et al.*, 2014, Collet and Tort, 2015; Beneyto and Collet, 2017; Collet, 2017 (JEP); Feu *et al.*, 2016a and 2016b; Prieto *et al.*, 2017). But at the same time, also based on our research data, we can affirm that in order to build democratic and equitable schools, not just any model of participation of families and community in the schools is applicable.

## School, families and community: A critical look from democracy

Along with authors like Bernard Lahire (1995), Carol Vincent (2000) and Crozier and Davies (2007), we believe that too often the idea of a school open to the participation of families and the community has been conceived and practised under the influence of two significant biases that, in our view, have made it difficult to construct schools that are truly democratic and equitable for everyone. The first bias is related to understanding 'participation' only, or fundamentally, within the parameters of the local middle class. This involves normativising and normalising 'one' good way for families and the community to participate in the school and, at the same time, label as 'negative' many other forms practised, above all, by families with a working class and/or migrant background. As Vincent and Ball point out, the participation of families and the community is always "classed, gendered and raced" (Vincent and

Ball, 2007, p. 1062), and therefore we cannot base their participation in schools on a generic and abstract model. If teachers do so, they are taking as a universal a concrete *model* of participation, that of the local middle class, and in doing so they are invalidating many other forms of participation that remain outside what is considered 'normal', positive, expected and tolerated. In the words of Crozier and Davies (2007), we need to be aware of the underlying perspective with which the school analyses and judges what forms of participation of the families and the community are legitimate or not. If teachers do not ask themselves this question, the most likely outcome is that all those families that do not participate in the forms, the languages and the manner of the local middle class will be seen as 'hard to reach parents'. That is to say, in families that are seen by teachers as those that: are not interested in education (not in the correct way), that fail to participate (well), that do not come to school (as and when they should), that delegate the education of their children to the school, and so on (Collet and Tort, 2011; Collet *et al.*, 2014). And who are therefore a problem for the school and not part of the democratic and equitable solution.

The second bias relates to all those forms of participation of families and the community in the school that ignore relations of power. Thus, we feel that even researchers like Driessen *et al.* (2005), Lee and Bowen (2006) or Hornby and Lafaele (2011), when they analyse difficulties and obstacles in the connection between teachers and families, do not take the dimension of power sufficiently into account and point to the families and their characteristics and circumstances as the barriers to good participation. In doing this, these ingenuous examinations forget that participation, like democracy and equality, bears no relation to abstract identity essences but rather to frames of concrete relations. Frames that, in our view, avoid the unequal relations of power in schools. Thus, the question 'who gives the orders and how?' seems to disappear and is it forgotten: a) that the relations of power between teachers and families are structurally unequal in schools since it is the teachers who frame how parental participation is structured and governed; b) that some families are close to the 'school culture' while others are much more set apart from it and who, without specific intervention, do not participate in the habitual and normalised channels of participation; c) that if teachers do not open the door to different forms of participation of the parents, many of them cannot participate even if they wish to (Lareau, 2003; Monceau, 2011, Collet *et al.*, 2014; Prieto *et al.*, 2017).

We believe, therefore, that the key question when it comes to analysing a centre and to proposing what a democratic and equitable school would be like with respect to the participation of all the families and the community is: how is the government of the school conceived and carried out? In our view, whether a democratic and equitable participation of families is possible or not depends on how the school is governed. More specifically, the way the school is governed with respect to the families and pupils, meaning *how* the relations between teachers and families are produced in areas like entering and leaving the school, the school governing body, parents association, festive celebrations, work commissions, meetings at the beginning of the school year, interviews with parents, bulletin boards, web page, physical and virtual communication, how discipline is maintained, norms and punishments and so on; all of these are the analytical key for responding to the question as to what extent a school is (or is not) democratic and equitable. And at the same time it provides the key questions and dimensions when it comes to building more democratic and equitable schools. In relation to this, the next section, based on the results of our research, examines what a school needs to be like if it is to be no longer 'hard to reach' (Crozier and Davies, 2007), but rather quite the opposite, for the different and unequal families and the community.

## How can a school be governed so that it becomes democratic and equitable in the participation of all families and the community?

*How has the participation of families and the community in schools been governed until now?*

Authors like Annette Lareau (2003), Diane Reay (2005), Carol Vincent (1996, 2000, 2012) and Gill Crozier (1999, 2007) problematized the question of participation of families in schools with great skill. On the one hand, Lareau showed how some families and the school possessed the same model of socialisation, with the same objectives, methods and ways. Middle class families practised a "concerted cultivation" (Lareau, 2003, p. 31) that fit perfectly with the model of school socialisation and, at the same time, this proximity enabled a 'collaborative participation' between teachers and families that shared social class and culture. But on the other hand, many other families, of working class and/or migrant background, experienced a gulf between their own practices of socialisation (accomplishment of natural growth) and those of the school (concerted cultivation). They also felt far removed from the forms of family participation (characterised by concerted cultivation) that the school proposed and that were considered natural and taken for granted. Likewise, Vincent (1996, 2000) criticised the fact that schools proposed two forms of participation for families (as consumers and supporters) for which, first, only middle class families were suitable, and which, second, failed to produce either more or better participation of all the families. With respect to building, through the government of the school, families as consumers "research analysis shows that it does not necessarily result in greater parental involvement with the school" (Vincent, 2000, p. 3). This involves the participation of families "undertaking particular activities and practices suggested by the school as appropriate and useful tasks" (Vincent, 2000, p. 5). In both cases, consumers or supporters, the model of participation that is built narrows at the same time what parental participation (consumers or supporters) means and, above all, who can access it and who is left out.

Finally, Crozier (2008, 2016) highlights how all the barriers to parental participation mentioned are often attributed to, in a clear exercise of symbolic violence, deficits of the families that are not 'good parents' (Bourdieu, 1992). The difficulty of achieving a high participation of all the families in the school is often presented by teachers (and by the local middle class families) as a problem of the 'other families'. As Gilles Monceau points out, using his research into schools in the *banlieues* of Paris (2011), even in schools with great diversity, those parents that are family representatives and participate in the habitual official channels are from local middle class families ('the families'). And within this dynamic, the 'other families' with a working class and / or migrant background and their linguistic deficits, incapable of understanding the school logic and lacking awareness of the ways of the school, are seen as the cause of their 'non-participation in the school'. This view of the 'other families' based on their deficits and incapacities can even include to those families that share social class with the teachers but not ethnic group (i.e. black middle classes) (Rollock *et al.*, 2015). This way of looking that considers the parental deficits of 'the other families' as the cause and obstacle to not participating in the school, apart from being morally unjust, fails to take into account the structural elements that narrow, condition and demarcate what participating means (or does not mean) and what the correct (or incorrect) ways of participating in the school are. In other words, the reality is that the school, governed by local middle class teachers together with 'the families' with whom they share the same habitus, takes for granted that there is *one* good model of parental participation. And with this perspective, schools push away and discredit other ways of being and relating in the school. But the final result is that it is the 'other families', who have not been included, recognised or accepted in their forms of participation and connection to the school, that become 'hard to reach' (symbolic violence). With Feu *et al.* (2016) we can come to see that also within 'the families', those of middle class background, there are significant differences in their relation with the school. Some middle class families, due to income, knowledge and proximity to the school forms and languages, participate very fully in every sphere, while others, despite sharing the same social class as the teachers, are less involved. We therefore need to provide nuance to the overly simplistic idea that there are 'the other families' and 'the families'. Within both groups there are different degrees of proximity in relation to the school. In fact, this argument brings us to the notion, expressed in previous research (Feito, 2011; Feu *et al.*, 2016b; Collet, 2017), that even the participation of families closest to the school is, in Catalonia and Spain and in their majority, superficial. Despite the clear inequality between different families in their relation to the school, it is fair to say that even those families that are closest to teachers (parents association, school governing body and so on) are allowed, in general, only a rather superficial participation. They are given very few opportunities, places and powers that go beyond expressing their opinion (school governing board) or organising activities that are peripheral to the school (parents association). We therefore need to see both aspects: a framework that is structurally not very democratic that allows the families and pupils to participate on a very superficial level; and at the same time a notable inequality in the superficial participation between the different families (and pupils).

In the UK, the research of Andrew Wilkins (2016) and Antonio Olmedo (2017) confirms that today, basing the participation of families on the consumer and supporter models has not improved parental participation in the school, neither its equity, its diversity, its quality nor its extent. Quite the contrary. English schools are today less democratic that they were 20 years ago. And one of the key reasons for this is the narrowing of the participation of families to the roles of 'consumers' or 'professional supporters' in the setting of the school governing bodies. This limitation occurs in the three ways that we have already pointed to. First, because fewer types, models, channels and forms of participation are offered, which ends up being reduced to these two. Second, because these positions of consumers and/or professional supporters are increasingly occupied by fewer families that need to have a greater income in order to be able to do so, which results in an increase of homogeneity in the profiles of fathers and mothers that 'are allowed' to participate, and the exclusion from this model of the participation of many families. And third since, as we have said, the dominant discourse ends up pointing to the deficits, incapacities and lack of awareness of the 'other families' as the cause and obstacle to their non-participation in the school. This fails to take into account the structural elements that take for granted that the local middle class way of educating and participating in the school is the natural, obvious, correct and only way.

Something similar occurs with respect to the connections between the school and the community. Despite the diversity of contexts that make it difficult to understand community or family in the same way in the UK, US, France or Catalonia, we can say that it is very common in these different countries for schools to relate with 'equals' at the level of community: museums, libraries, civic centres and so on. But the relation of the school with neighbour associations, movements for popular education, associations of immigrants, soup kitchens, informal groups of diverse mother/fathers and so on, however, is not so frequent. The difficulties of relating with community groups and entities that are not made up of the local middle class are habitually explained by teachers with the same deficit arguments that are often used with respect to the 'other families' (Collet *et al*, 2014; Monceau, 2011). In response to the above dynamics, we will now have a look at other perspectives that might contribute to the creation of a more equitable and democratic parental participation.

*Ideas and proposals for governing schools and producing a democratic and equitable participation of all families and the community*

There have been many proposals on what kind of relations between teachers and families are required in order for a school to be equitable and democratic. Cunningham and Davis (1985) took a first step to overcome the expert and transplant models of relations between families and professionals. Twenty-two years later, Davis and Meltzer revisited the subject and proposed the 'Family Partnership Model' as a tool that might enable schools, by transforming themselves into a service, to become useful for all families – especially by "giving significant attention to the general outcome of enabling or empowering parents" (Meltzer, 2007, p. 7). Along these lines, Appleton and Minchcom (1991) proposed the empowerment model, a model of relations between teachers and parents that promotes parental power and control, and that placed families as partners of the school. In this model, the teacher is required to actively promote the parent's sense of control over decision-making. In 1996, Naomi Dale proposed 'the negotiating model', which recognised that the contributions of both professionals and families are of value and that what was required was an established framework to enable different perspectives, expectations, opinions and practices to work together. As we have already mentioned, Vincent (1996, 2000) proposed the model of parent as participant or citizen as "an exemplar of relations between citizens and state institutions" (Vincent, 2000, p. 7). This model proposes that families get involved in the governance of the school as well as in the education of their own children through mechanisms like parent governors, statutorily-based parents' groups or membership of local/national educational pressure groups.

In our view, the above Anglo-Saxon approaches, and many others, have contributed enormously in highlighting that parental support is by no means homogeneous in its nature since it is classed, gendered and raced. And it has emphasised that this affects differential rates and modes of participation and engagement, as well as the way in which teachers and families build what 'good parenting' or an appropriate parent engagement at school means (or does not mean) (Vincent, 2000, p. 129). But we believe that even in the models of partnership, empowerment, negotiating or participant – citizen, their analyses fail to take into account the central importance, at least in Mediterranean countries, that the school has as an institution. In some way, these Anglo-Saxon approaches see the school as something given, that it is as it is, soon placing their attention on the families and their different and unequal relations with it. But the school, which is precisely the institutional context that produces the (non-natural) category of 'school parent', is, we believe, not taken sufficiently into account. In our action-research on how to improve the relations between teachers and all the families so as to make them more democratic, inclusive and equitable, our priority has been the teachers and how they govern the relations with the families (Collet *et al.*, 2014; Collet i Tort, 2014).

With Foucault (2010), we understand power from a productive perspective. We agree with Barry, Osborne and Rose (1996) or Ball (2013, 2017) that the way people and institutions are conceived (truth) and (micro)governed (government) ends up producing one or another school reality in dimensions like identities of different actors (what is, or is not, a teacher, a parent, a child, a community association), institutional relations and dynamics (more or less democratic), interviews and meetings (more or less participative) and so on (Collet, 2017). Therefore, our proposal for producing relations between teachers and families that contribute to a more democratic and equitable school is not focused on the families but rather on the institution that produces, in a relational manner with the families, one or other form of connection with the parents. And the same can be said of the relation between the teachers, between teachers and pupils, and between the pupils themselves. Using the terms of Tyack and Tobin (1994), we can say that if the grammar of schooling, the structures of power, spaces, times and relations are not modified, new connections and bonds with the families and pupils that are more democratic and equitable are impossible to generate. Even when there are teachers that wish to create them. According to our research, if the structural dimensions of school government (government) and the 'school truth' about what parents are and are not in relation to the school, what they can and cannot do, how they are viewed by teachers and so forth are not transformed, it is impossible to move towards a more democratic school that includes all families and the whole community (Olmedo and Wilkins, 2017). In this we are in full agreement with the approach that Feu i Prieto take in chapter one of their book when they point to the central importance of the dimensions of governance and inhabitancy when it comes to building a democratic and equitable ethos and relations (Feu *et al.*, 2016a and 2016b).

Along these lines, we propose four criteria of school government (government) that, in our view, should be central when it comes to defining the school (truth) and guiding the whole process of building schools that are more democratic and equitable with all the families and the community.

*a) Inclusion.* Ainscow, Booth and Dyson proposed a series of criteria to assess whether or not a school and classroom were inclusive, and to what extent and what dimensions it was necessary to build up in order to move towards the ideal of an inclusive school. According to the authors:

> Inclusion, we believed, referred to [...] the *presence, participation and achievement* of all students' and to achieve this they proposed 'restructuring the cultures, policies and practices in schools so that they respond to the diversity of students in their locality' because 'inclusion and exclusion are linked together such that inclusion involves the active combating of exclusion'. In short, 'inclusion is seen as a never-ending process. Thus an inclusive school is one that is on the move, rather than one that has reached a perfect state. (Ainscow, Booth and Dyson, 2006, p. 25).

Thus the first criteria of school government that we propose is that the whole school needs to guarantee the presence, participation and engagement of all the families. So first, the school, families and community need to engage actively in order to reflect all the diversity of their community (of class, language, ethic group, religion and so on) avoiding above all school segregation (presence). The reality of school segregation has been widely researched with respect to its process and effects on students (Bonal *et al.*, 2013, Benito *et al.*, 2014), but less so with regards to how it impedes the construction of an inclusive school. Second, it is crucial that, once the diversity of the families concerned is included in the school, the latter also builds many different channels, ways and tools that enable their participation in the school. If the families are diverse, then all the forms of school participation have to be designed to attend to this diversity of class, culture and language in such a way that promotes diverse relations and "bridges" with the school. The challenge of teachers is to govern the school so that all the diverse families are included within its normality and normativity, thus making it more democratic. In this sense, therefore, all the diverse families should become normal in a concrete and habitual way in each school, through the construction, by the teachers and 'the families', of channels that enable each family to be able to fully participate in and connect with the school, in diverse ways (democratic engagement) – especially the 'other families'.

*b) Equity.* The second criteria for school government, once the presence, participation and engagement of all the families in the community have been developed structurally (democracy), is equity. When diversity of class, ethic group, language and so on, enters a school context dominated by languages and forms of the local middle class (Bernstein, Bourdieu, Lareau etc.), the latter become inequalities, barriers and obstacles for the 'other families'. To paraphrase Nancy Fraser (2012), while presence, participation and connection promote the recognition of all families, this alone is not enough. We also need to pay attention to how inequalities affect the real, practical and everyday possibilities of participation (barriers). Disadvantaged families are not only diverse, they are also, above all, unequal in resources, opportunities, capacities and expectations, and they are seen and treated as such by 'the families' and teachers (Lahire, 1995; Monceau, 2011). It is therefore necessary, as well as promoting presence, participation and connection with all the families, to work on eliminating the barriers that the inequalities produce and that undermine the real possibilities of a democratic participation of all families (Fraser, 2012). These inequalities and barriers are related to various elements like:

1) The fact that schools, despite being compulsory, are not really free (school materials, excursions, school meals, the parents association's fee and so on), and this generates inequality in access to activities, resources and educational opportunities for some children / families. This means that teachers need to govern the school thinking in *all* the families and their unequal realities, especially the most disadvantaged.

2) The fact that many of the 'other families' are seen and treated as not being interested in the education of their children, in participating in the parents association, in going to meetings or interviews at the school, in the communications that the school sends or delivers to parents and so on. This means that the teachers and the diverse families have to make an effort to question the prejudices that habitually equate the 'other families' with 'bad educators or participants' or with deficits (Lahire, 1995, 2003; Bernstein, 1998; Collet *et al.*, 2014). And to produce practices and relations that can contribute to the construction of another view of capacity, especially of these 'other families'.

3) The fact that the material and symbolic resources are unequal in each children's home means that for some, the home is a continuation of the school reality, while for others a great disruption. This requires that the school questions all those aspects in which the (unequal) families have to take part. For example, extracurricular activities or homework. If not all families have symbolic (linguistic understanding of the homework) or material (having internet and/or a computer at home) resources, then the school needs to think about the type of homework that it gives. And it adapts them to the unequal realities of the families (Beneyto i Collet, 2017).

*c) Empowerment.* Finally, and after these two structural dimensions, we take up the proposal made by Vincent about empowering mothers and fathers as the best way to build a democratic and equitable school. Vincent suggested defining empowerment as school policy, as those actions that "concentrate on developing a participatory ethos within schools so that parents shared decision-making powers with educational professionals" (Vincent, 1996, p. 7). As Bacqué and Biewener (2016) explain in great historical detail, empowerment is an ambiguous term and full of interpretations not just diverse but even contradictory. Despite this we do not feel we should abandon a concept that, with respect to the promotion of democracy and equitable participation of all families and the community in schools, we believe has been and still is highly relevant. To begin with, we can see that, at the very least, this notion has been conceived and practised from three perspectives. 1) Neoliberal: centred on individual self-interest, depoliticised and designed to gain formal equality with respect to the market. 2) Socioliberal: centred on a personal and group agency, and that seeks a more equitable access to all resources by everyone. And 3) Radical: understood as a process off learning (J. Dewey), of consciousness raising (P. Friere) and of self-government (S. Alinksy) that seeks to transform unequal relations of power on the personal, family, collective and political levels. This (self) recognition of knowledge, power and capacities of women and men, families and collectives (L. Gutiérrez, W, Brown), becomes the way to question inequalities in redistribution, recognition and participation in different social areas (Fraser, 2012). As Bacqué and Biewemer (2016) point out, we can understand, from the radical model, that empowerment involves a learning and a democratic and equitable transformation of power: instead of understanding and practising it as *power over* others, empowerment especially from a feminist perspective (N. Fraser, J. Butler), seeks to build it as a process of learning power as a *power to do* things; a *power with* others; and *power over* one's own life. From this radical perspective of empowerment, we believe that government of the relations between teachers and families and community, if they take into account the structural barriers mentioned in the sections above, can become a space for empowering families and so move towards a more democratic and equitable school.

*d) Democratic deepening.* This would involve, on the one hand, not drawing any red lines or lists of taboo subjects on which families can give their opinion. In my view, families should be able to *opine* about everything, making use of the appropriate channels and forms. Because opining and deciding are not the same. I believe that the opinion of pupils and families should always be welcomed, on the condition that this does not imply a power of decision that, in some areas, must logically be the province of teachers. This needs to be nuanced, however, because families and children should be able to decide on many more subjects and areas than they can at the moment. Thus, the proposal of shared government by teachers and families; joint assemblies of teachers, families and pupils; mixed commissions that take binding decisions on academic and organisational topics and so on, are proposals that move, clearly and positively, towards a real, effective and everyday democratization of the school. And with this, a clear improvement of its educational capacity in, by and for a citizenship that is truly critical and democratic. As has been repeated many times, the most important thing for a democratic education are not problems, concepts, school documents or educational projects, but rather practical and concrete experiences.

*Criteria for building school relations – democratic, equitable and empowering families*

In order for this to happen, teachers need to conceive, practice and govern ordinary relations with all the families following three criteria:

*a) First, it is crucial that schools conceive the families and community as intrinsic parts of the school.* Thus, and against what comes up in all our research (Collet and Tort, 2011; 2014), the new 'school truth' is that the families are school, they form an intrinsic, natural and normal part. And they are not, as many Catalan teachers conceive them, an external, intrusive, bothersome and unsettling element. If we want to build a democratic and equitable school, this can only be done when, as the systemic approaches point out, the families and community are recognised by those that hold most power in the school (teachers) as members and an intrinsic part of it with the capacity to act. If, as Dubet (2002) explains, the truth of the school is that of a sacred space in which the profane (families and community) have no right to enter, be there and truly form part of it, any attempt to democratise the school will be severely limited. But if they are an intrinsic part of the school, the families are no longer an 'external' problem for teachers, an intruder in 'my' territory, an exterior agent that delegates education to the school and so on. And they can become a central part of the solution, of the project of constructing a more democratic and equitable school.

*b) Second, it is absolutely crucial that the form of school governance be one in which all the parents and pupils form part of the diverse ways* in which such governance operates (Collet and Tort, 2016). Empowering all the families and pupils to democratise the school and make it more equitable means producing, in an everyday manner, parents with *power to* do things, *with* other families and teachers and *about* the schooling of their children. This should be, in our opinion, a key objective of school governance. And here we propose working from the four dimensions that Feu and Prieto discuss in the first chapter of their book: governance, inhabitancy, otherness and values, and virtues and abilities. To do so, we pose a number of questions that can guide this assessment of current school governance and use them to propose new ways to govern it.

- How are all the diverse and unequal families taken into account in the school's decision making?
- How are information, communication and participation with respect to these families from a perspective of empowerment approached?
- How are they treated as both individual families and a collective of families?
- How are mechanisms, places and forums of debate, deliberation and decision that include all the families and the diverse actors of the community introduced?
- How does the school ensure that diverse and appropriate ways are generated so that everybody can participate?
- How is the self-organisation of families in associations or informal groups promoted, recognised and given a voice in the school?
- How does the school avoid colonisation of formal arenas of participation by the local middle class families (Monceau, 2011)? And so on.

With respect to inhabitancy, some questions could be:

- What are the material difficulties that families experience in relation to the payment of books, school meals, extracurricular activities, excursions, and so on?
- How could the school provide them with support?

- How can all the families and teachers work together collectively to overcome these inequalities?
- How are recently arrived children and families received?
- To what extent is the school a welcoming place both physically and relationally for everybody?

With respect to the third dimension, otherness and values, the teachers and families could ask about the presence or absence of the different family profiles in the parents association, school governing body, work commissions, school celebrations and so on. Other questions can be:

- Are situations of discrimination, bullying, classism, sexism or racism identified and addressed in an everyday manner in the school or among families?
- Is the diversity of families reflected in the school curriculum, the entrance of families into the classroom, the school celebrations and so on?

Finally, with respect to the fourth dimension of virtues and abilities, schools can ask:

- If their underlying values are made explicit?
- If there are areas and moments of debate between teachers, families and community in order to make explicit what kind of school they have, what kind of school they would like to have, and how they should approach the change?
- How an education in, about and for democracy is managed, experientially, at every level of the school (Edlestein, 2011)?

*c) Third, and finally, we can ask what professional identity teachers need to have in order to contribute to building a democratic, equitable and empowering school.* We strongly believe, along with Ball (1995), Collet (2011) and Parker and Meo (2012), that it is necessary to produce a 'broad' professional identity that allows us to go beyond a teacher identity of a transmitter of knowledge. And to understand that the school is a social space, with (unequal) relations of power, and that its orientation and government can contribute to it being either a space that excludes, is hierarchical and legitimates inequality, or one that is democratic, equitable and empowering for all the families. If the dominant teacher identity is restricted, meaning centred only on the unidirectional transmission of knowledge, then proposals for a more democratic, equitable and empowering school make, literally, no sense. That is why it is also very important that the school government orients its professionals towards a broad identity through trainings, through how work among teachers is structured, at the level of timetables and so on. If knowledge, as Freire with his notion of 'banking education' (2004) denounced, is something that the teacher possesses and transmits to pupils unidirectionally, the role of the pupils, of the families and of the community is always passive. The only thing they need to do is to receive the knowledge of the school, assimilate it and reproduce it in the exam in as similar a way possible as the teacher. In contrast, if as Freire argues, knowledge is a collective construction in which the teacher is the mediator, the facilitator through dialogue, then the school is something quite different and the teacher is somebody that teaches and learns in a concrete and contextualised manner with the children, the families and the community.

## Conclusion

The social, economic, political and educational challenges that our societies face today are significant ones. But the way in which our regimes of formal representative democracy are responding, are making them increasingly thin and less thick (Gandin and Apple, 2002). In the face of this process of emptying and formalisation of democracy, the role of schools is crucial for creating a place where children, teachers and families can educate and be educated in, by and on democracy. But for this to happen, especially if we focus on analysing the bonds between teachers and families and community, some things need to be improved. If we wish schools, as Dewey (1915) said, to be a place where people work together to resolve real problems, co-learning from each other, the school's normality needs to be collectively questioned and problematized. This is the key point that we have wished to highlight throughout this chapter. If teachers, as the agents with the greatest power within the school, and 'the families' do not question the class, gender and ethnic biases that the school normality and normativity has on what is and what is not a (good) participation of families, this can never be democratic, equitable and empowering.

In order to build a democratic school, especially in its relations with the families and community, we propose these three axes of work: inclusion, equity and empowerment. This means that all the different families be present in the school (avoiding segregation); that all be recognised and valued participating in different ways; and that this process of diverse participation becomes the source of empowerment for all of them. Further, a democratic school has to take into account the initial family inequalities (material, symbolic, relational and so on) and combat them collectively. In order to build a process that moves towards better and more democratic schools, we also feel it is very important that all families are seen and experienced as a new 'school truth', as an intrinsic part of the school and as key agents of government of the school. Finally, we would like to highlight the need for a broad teacher identity that understands 'being a teacher' as something beyond the mere unidirectional transmission of knowledge. In this chapter we have aimed to present all that we have learnt on a theoretical level and from our data during the last five years in different research on how to improve, from the perspective of democracy, equity and empowerment, the bonds between teachers, all the families and the community.

Òscar Prieto-Flores, Jordi Feu, Carles Serra and Laura Lázaro
*University of Girona*

# Bringing Democratic Governance into Practice: Policy Enactments Responding to Neoliberal Governance in Spanish Public Schools[1]

In the last decades, neoliberal policies have placed emphasis on school competition and New Public Management strategies as mechanisms aiming to improve public school performance and accountability in many countries (Ball, 2007; Ranson, 2008). Representatives of parents play a limited role, carrying out bureaucratic tasks and accountability measures, and are perceived more as consumers rather than citizens (Olmedo and Wilkins, 2014). While this is the hegemonic trend in many countries, other works have focused on how schools can confront dominant neoliberal policy by analysing different cases of schools or city councils (Apple and Beane, 2007, Flecha, 2015; Gandin and Apple, 2002). The aim of this study is to select and analyse what Wright (2010) identifies as *Real Utopias*, that is to say, new forms of emancipatory and workable structures that are an alternative to dominant forms of social organization. We present empirical data from schools that demonstrate the practice of school governance, regardless of the intentions of policy texts promoting neoliberal school management in Catalonia, Spain. To this end, some schools recontextualize policy texts by institutionalizing new microstructures for governance. Practitioners in these schools promote greater opportunity for giving voice to different parent and student constituencies through the creation of new *ad hoc* structures, or by endowing already existing structures with a sense of democracy. When we speak of schools carrying out democratic governance we are referring to those schools that open the process of governing and decision making to

---

1    This chapter is derived from an article published in the Cambridge Journal of Education, doi: 10.1080/0305764X.2017.1288700

parents, students and other school staff beyond the power the State gives to teachers and head-teachers in the Spanish context. To do so, these schools auto-generate governance structures aiming to include these educational agents or new mechanisms that make the pre-existing governing structures such as the *Consejo Escolar* more dynamic and plural. The *Consejo Escolar* is the main governing body in public schools where representatives of parents, teachers and the community are elected for a period of four years. Accordingly, we look at experiences from four public primary schools that have developed especially significant democratic governance experiences. We were able to observe what they have in common and the different existing ways in which policy texts are enacted as an act of resistance to neoliberal managerial logic.

## Neoliberalism and school governance

Neoliberalism is defined as "a theory of political economic practices proposing that human well-being can best be advanced by the maximisation of entrepreneurial freedoms within an institutional framework characterized by private property rights, individual liberty, unencumbered markets and free trade" (Harvey 2007, p. 22). In this regard, the role of the state in creating and maintaining these markets in order to restore class dominance of the wealthiest has been relevant and is presented as an alternative democratic radicalization (Hatcher, 2012). However, Ong (2007) argues that besides this Neoliberalism with a capital "N", conceptualized as a dominant structure condition, we can also perceive neoliberalism not as structure or culture but as global flows of ideas and technologies. This neoliberalism with a small "n" "is not a fixed set of attributes with predetermined outcomes but a logic of governing that migrates and is selectively taken up in diverse political contexts" (Ong 2007, p. 3). For a more accurate conceptualization, Ong and Collier (2005) use the term *global assemblage* to identify how malleable and flexible global technologies are in adapting to situated political regimes when describing neoliberal policy adaptations in several contexts, especially in Asia.

These economic and societal changes, together with the emergence of information and communication technologies, have altered the boundaries of nation-states. States have ceded power and sovereignty upwards, downwards and multilaterally (Castells, 1997). This process of transformation towards greater interdependence between governments and other actors in decision making is affecting the ways governments govern. Similarly, Rhodes (2007) defines *Governance* as the process of governing through interdependence between organizations, with a "broader government", that includes non-state actors, blurs boundaries between public, private and voluntary sectors and has a significant degree of autonomy from the state. Ball and Junemann (2003) also differentiate *Governance* from *Government*. While the former is developed through interactions taking place in diverse and flexible networks, the latter is carried out through hierarchies and bureaucracies. Existing processes of creation and maintenance of these flexible policy networks in advanced capitalist societies are characterized by horizontal interdependence, instead of preservation of the hierarchy of state-centred bureaucracies. These changes have been promoted from a neoliberal proposition arguing that "market forces and partnership-based forms of governance" are inevitable for impeding the failure of the state (Jessop, 2002, 2004). In the last decades, these *heterarchical* "networks" of governance have grown through the creation of new Public-Private Partnerships (PPP) in which the role of businesses, social enterprise and philanthropy in educational delivery and policy is relevant (Jones *et al.*, 2007; Hill and Kumar, 2009; Robertson, Bonal and Dale, 2001). Many of these PPP in education are enhanced by educational experts who work for international organizations. This is especially prevalent in developing countries where the granting of international aid is conditioned by adoption of this education privatization policy (Verger, 2012).

According to Hatcher and Hirtt (1999), these neoliberal dynamics have been introduced in education systems through *exogenous and endogenous neoliberalism*. The first corresponds to the introduction of market or quasi-market logic that entails the defence of parental choice, the cutting of public funding for educational services, and privatization of schooling in educational systems (Ball, 2007). The second refers to the introduction of neoliberal regimes of school administration and accountability promoted by different governments. Along these lines, together with the drive towards decentralization of educational policy and the offer of greater autonomy to schools, *new policy technologies* redefine the roles played by the different actors when schools are held to account. This educational reform introduces a New Public Management and performativity in schools "aligning public sector organizations with the methods, culture and ethical system of the private sector" (Ball, 2003, p. 216). These policy technologies have displaced those of the older regime of professionalism and bureaucracy based on the professional accountability developed by autonomous professional communities in their schools. Ranson (2003) argues that, far from strengthening public accountability, the different understandings of accountability in the enactment of neoliberal governance, namely *consumer, contract, performative* or *corporate*, have strengthened market logic between parents and schools at the expense of the public sphere. Their development has also brought different forms of institutionalization and structuration of school governance depending on the context or territory. For example, in a latter study, Ranson *et al.* (2005) identified the evolution of different forms of school governance that has taken place in different UK regions since the school governance reforms led by the Thatcher government in the 1980s. This policy decentralized and deregulated schools by promoting the introduction of volunteer citizens as governors. It opened the door to inclusion of new agents in the decisions and monitoring of schools, which could be inductees of the state or could respond to local needs of the school. In this analysis, they concluded that the different forms of school governance they identified continued to have difficulties in connecting with parents and especially with the most disadvantaged families. More recently, Wilkins (2015) discusses the way in which increased autonomy of schools and monitoring mechanisms created by the state in the last decades have promoted a series of disciplinary tools and internal and external training tools designed to make school governors comply with the role of control suggested by the State. His research analysed how the assessment of *good governance* is managed. He noted that the government and Ofsted[2] require the governing bodies to act as professional experts and possess skills and knowledge on how to evaluate the performance of schools. He also observed the process by which

---

2    Office for Standards in Education, Children's Services and Skills.

third sector organizations have emerged that provide advice and training to governors, transforming them, not into a counterpoint to government policy, but into accomplices of an administration that promotes and legitimizes the interests of the State, which is that schools be administered under the tenets of corporate accountability and contracts in the same way as businesses (Wilkins, 2015).

In other contexts, this type of implementation has not been developed in the same way or is in an incipient form. In Switzerland, for instance, the processes of decentralization and the granting of greater autonomy to schools have been carried out under the logic of increasing accountability processes and professional leadership of school direction. Hangartner and Svaton (2014) analyzed how policy reforms enacted since the 1990s have given more power and relevance to the role of head-teachers or principals by exploring how managerial rationalities of the New Public Management have influenced school governance. They argue that these policies have been "cutting the competences of the school council boards, questioning their legitimacy and functions and pushing these boards into a liminal status" (2014, p. 294), as occurs in other contexts such as Mexico (Olivo, Alaniz and Reyes, 2011) or Spain, as we will see next.

In order to resist these neoliberal school management assemblages, teachers and other agents are interpreting and developing creative ways to struggle in their everyday spaces. Today, there are teachers who, together with parents, are implementing acts of collective struggle inspired by the discourses and practices of resistance towards a more radical democratic schools (Apple, 2012; Fielding and Moss, 2011). Drawing on Habermas' communicative action, Ranson (2003) argues that democratic governance can take place in schools when accountability functions as a process of internal deliberation where participants reach agreements through communicative narratives. This type of governance can take place "when members of the community of practice (embracing the public as well as the profession) recognize and draw upon the authority of standards, which they can trust for evaluating performance because they have been tested in deliberation. In the pursuit of excellence, internal goods replace extrinsic controls, agency supplants alienated routines" (Ranson, 2003, p. 462). In this article, we will focus specifically on analysing how some schools in Catalonia, Spain shun the neoliberal and managerialist logic of school governance, how they create new democratizing *ad hoc* structures and how they explain their democratic governance. Rather than being perfect and rationalized, these structures stem from the desire and the situated interactions present in different school settings.


## School governance in Spain and Catalonia


In Spain, the current State of the Autonomies was constituted during the transition to democracy (1975–78), after almost forty years of the Franco dictatorship, following negotiations between different actors in Spanish society. Some of these groups and individuals considered the territorial distribution of the *Comunidades Autónomas* (Autonomous Communities) as a political system with regional parliaments and governments halfway towards a federal state. For others, this system has consisted of decentralizing and contextualizing the legislation and policies designed by state institutions. This political situation has been perceived as an incomplete process by some political actors in Catalonia, Basque Country and Galicia where separatist support has grown in recent years. With regard to education policy, legislative competences are shared. However, in this case, only the State legislates on structural issues of great importance while the Autonomous Communities execute the laws enacted by the State, although they also have the authority to legislate on minor and peripheral issues.

Neither Spain nor Catalonia is free from the above-mentioned neoliberal dynamic even though this has its historical and territorial specificity (Serra *et al.*, 2013). Some authors consider the Spanish case to be special, both because of the tension that exists between the policies of the conservative right and those that characterize the new liberal right (Viñao, 2012), and the rapid succession of educational reforms that have been implemented from the end of the fascist dictatorship to the present (Bonal, 2000). However, we can also identify how in Spain the presence of discourses and policy texts of a neoliberal nature have exerted considerable influence beginning with the 1985 Education Act

(LODE[3]). This helped initiate a series of regulations that promoted a quasi-market in education, allowing the funding of private schools. Of significance in the Spanish case are the advances in this neoliberal logic that have been accentuated in recent years by generating greater school autonomy, school choice and accountability. This process has been more pronounced in some Autonomous Communities, such as in Catalonia, than in others (Alegre, Rambla and Valiente, 2009; Olmedo, 2013).

In relation to the governance of schools, according to Feito (2014), there are two regulations that were established by agreement between the main political parties concerning which bodies and procedures should serve as the framework for involving parents and families in schools. This agreement, based on the 1980 and 1985 Education Acts (LOECE[4] and LODE), has endured until the present. The essence of the Spanish legal framework, which replicates the structure of representative democracy in the governing bodies of schools, continues to be the same though. The *Consejo Escolar* (School Governing Board), is where all representatives are elected. Students from primary schools do not have formal representation in this body, only those from secondary schools do. The *Consejo Escolar* discusses and monitors the annual plan of the school and its management, while some of the members take part in the selection of the school principal and other tasks. In many cases, proposals to the *Consejo* are first elaborated and agreed upon by teachers, as the governing role of this body is weak in terms of decision making. For example, one of the most contentious issues surrounding decisions is curricular and instructional. In many cases, these issues are taken up in the *Claustro* (teachers' governing body) and the *Consejo Escolar* is informed of the actions already agreed upon, as the existing belief among some teachers is that these matters should be decided by them alone, and not in tandem with parents (Feito, 2014). This power imbalance limits this body to being a place of consultation and dissemination of information on decisions previously made by teachers in their meetings. However, in recent decades these structures of representative participation have been devalued in favour of granting more power to the head-teacher and her/his team to develop New Public Management

---

3    *Organic Law* 8/1985, of 3 July, regulating the Right to Education.
4    *Organic Law* 5/1980, of 19 June regulating the Schools Statute.

strategies. For example, the 1995 Education Act (LOPEGCD[5]) weak-ened the *Consejos Escolares*, leaving them devoid of competences, and promoting the managerialist figure of the school principal (Olmedo 2008). This model of managerialist direction was expanded and en-hanced by the legislation of the 2002 and 2006 Education Acts (LOCE[6] and LOE[7]), which were promoted by conservative and socialist gov-ernments respectively. These legislations expanded and accentuated the managerial functions in schools and promoted specialized training for principals. Some of these courses train principals in New Public Man-agement strategies of governing schools with private sector methods. More recently, the 2013 Education Act (LOMCE[8]) established the com-pletion of a course in managerial functions imparted by the Ministry of Education, Culture and Sports as a requirement (not as a merit) for becoming a principal. Although from 1985 to 1995 principals governed schools jointly with the *Claustro* (teaching faculty) and the *Consejo Escolar*, subsequent legislative changes after 1995 promoted a greater role for school principals and their directive team.

In many schools, parents' perception of the functions performed by the *Consejo Escolar* is blurred. Only half of the surveyed parents know the role of their representatives in the body (48%) and only one-third know their representatives as family members in this body (38.5%) (Parra *et al.*, 2014). This scarce knowledge is translated into parents' level of participation in School Council elections. The participation rate in Spain for the 2012 elections to each school board was only 12.2% (Consejo Escolar del Estado, 2014).

Specifically in Catalonia, governance of public schools follows along the same lines as the Spanish regulations, while the 2009 Cat-alan Education Act (LEC[9]) increased school autonomy. Although it may seem contradictory, empowering schools with greater autonomy was in fact promoted by the leftist government in power at that time

---

5    *Organic Law* 9/1995, of 20 November, on the Participation, Evaluation and Gov-
     ernance of schools.
6    *Organic Law* 10/2002, of 23 December, on Education Quality.
7    *Organic Law* 2/2006, of 3 May, on Education.
8    *Organic Law* 8/2013, of 9 December, for the Improvement of Education Quality.
9    Law 12/2009, of 10 July, on Education in Catalonia.

in Catalonia as well as by Catalan Pedagogical Renewal Movements[10], which had been defending school autonomy since the democratic transition of the 1970s and maintained this position until the passing of the 2006 National Pact for Education. The aim was to promote the improvement of public school quality relative to the existing level of quality of private schools:

> The *Consell Escolar de Catalunya* [School Council of Catalonia] as well as educational reform movements and other sectors of the education community have persistently called for a significant increase in the autonomy of public schools, understanding that this is an essential tool for improving quality and equity in the education system (Generalitat de Catalunya, 2006, p. 47).

Some professional organizations of teachers, for example, Rosa Sensat, also defended the autonomy of schools in the context of policy influence as an opportunity for promoting new forms of democratic administration:

> For us, autonomy is what fosters recognition of the positive value of singularity, that which is constructed and responds to each specific reality; and consequently, autonomy is linked to participation. Autonomy demands a deepening of democratic governance, in which it will be necessary to recognize the important contribution of families in education (Associació de Mestres Rosa Sensat, 2008).

This demand for school autonomy can turn into a double-edged sword, on the one hand promoting democratic practices, but on the other enhancing managerialization and may give more power to directive teams (which is what the Catalan autonomous government has actively promoted in recent years)[11]. These strategies are explicitly present in the curricula or manifested in the type of institutions that deliver these courses (ESADE business school for example[12]). Other examples of this government ideology are the granting of greater powers to intervene in the definition of

---

10   The Pedagogical Renewal Movements were social movements made up of education professionals whose objective was to improve public schools from a leftist political perspective.

11   As of 2010, the leftist government that promoted the National Education Pact was replaced by a centre-right coalition of Christian Democratic and liberal inspiration.

12   <http://www.edu21.cat/files/continguts/Centres_Educatius_11.pdf>

the teaching staff of schools[13], and making salary increases dependent on teacher performativity[14].

However, as the Spanish and Catalan legal framework gives broad autonomy to schools to organize themselves beyond the above-mentioned structures, in practice, schools enact policy texts by rejecting, selecting out or ignoring parts of these texts (Bowe, Ball and Gold, 1992). In the following cases, they also circumvent those compulsory structures or procedures the State requires them to develop by broadening current governing structures such as the *Consejo Escolar*, or by institutionalizing new governance structures that are substitutive or complementary to the *Consejo*.

## Multi-case study

One of the aims of this research was to identify how primary schools institutionalize new forms of democratic governance by re-contextualizing the existing neoliberal guidelines in Spanish and Catalan education policy. As an analytical strategy to understand policy enactment in schools, the team analyzed the different contexts of the policy cycle (influence, policy text production and practice) where policy is discussed, created and recontextualized (Bowe, Ball and Gold, 1992). After a policy analysis of the Spanish and Catalan legal framework of school governance since the 1980s (with prior debates and texts), the team observed and sought to identify how policy is enacted, not as it was intended but as democratic governance in school contexts, using the multicase study method. This method was used to address the challenges and possibilities that exist for schools in their efforts to practice democratic governance, which could include the participation of all

---

13   Decree 39/2014, of 25 March, regulating the procedures for defining the profile and provisions of teaching places. DOGC, 6591, 1–25.

14   ORDRE ENS/16/2016, of 3 February, amending the Order ENS/330/2014, of 6 November, on teacher promotion procedure by stages. Retrieved on March 5, 2016 from: <http://portaldogc.gencat.cat/utilsEADOP/PDF/7056/1474008.pdf>

parent constituencies. The object of using this method was not to conduct an in-depth examination of the specific nature of each school but to focus analysis especially on the existing commonalities and differences between them (Thomas, 2011). This halfway method of analysis permitted us to grasp the replicability and idiosyncrasy of the microstructures of governance these schools have created. This method provided the possibility to contrast these cases with the ideal types of governance and accountability theorized in the education policy literature (see Ranson, 2003, for example). It also helped us to analyse differences in understandings, dilemmas, intersubjective agreements or dissent that occurred between the actors regarding the need to broaden or to create new *ad hoc* governance structures.

Although our approach was mainly qualitative, we created a purposive and convenience oversample from thirty public schools that emphasized democratic governance as one of the key elements in their *school educational projects*. This micro-policy document states a school's educational objectives, mission and orientation, as well as detailing its pedagogical and organizational structure. From the oversample, we ultimately selected four cases from the results of a semi-structured questionnaire given out to the thirty schools. This technique helped us to target a specific population of interest that is sometimes not easy to identify (Hesse-Bieber, 2010). Through phone calls and informal meetings with informants (principals, teachers or parents) we were able to ensure that, beyond the rhetoric of *involving everyone, and counting on everyone*, these schools were indeed developing practices in democratic governance that were maintained and institutionalized over the years.

The four public schools selected were located in Catalonia in northeastern Spain. Beginning in 2007, and continuing to the present, the economic recession has had a significant impact on Catalan and Spanish society and schools. As in many countries, students' welfare needs have increased and public schools have suffered substantial budget cuts (Freelon, Bertrand and Rogers 2012). This economic recession encompasses a demographic drop in the fertility rate in Catalonia, which at 1.33 was one of the lowest in Europe in 2013 (IDESCAT, 2013). In some areas of Catalonia, student enrolment rate in primary schools remains stable thanks to migration. The immigrant student rate in public schools remained unchanged at 17% from 2007 to 2013 (Departament d'Ensenyament, 2015). However, in other areas many public schools need to create new projects and reach out to families in order to increase their enrolment rates to avoid classroom reductions or school closures. Although the immigrant population is present in the majority of towns in the territory, there is residential segregation of this population in some neighbourhoods. In some public schools in these segregated areas more than 80% of the student body is of immigrant background. Schools selected for this research represent this demographic and geographical diversity in order to draw upon a substantial variety of cases and information for effective study of the same phenomenon in several different settings (Stake, 2006).

Of the four primary schools selected, one is situated in a rural setting where all enrolled students are from white families with different socioeconomic backgrounds. *Themis School*[15] relies on very close relationships between teachers, parents and students because it is a rural school. It only has twenty-three students and shares some teachers with other rural schools nearby. Relationships with parents and the community are based primarily on proximity and trust. The second school, *Aristotle School*, is located in a town and has an enrolment of two hundred seventy students predominantly from lower middle-class families. The number of immigrant students is average for public schools in Catalonia. When the school was built, the school management, with the explicit aim of fostering democratic processes, requested construction of an agora in the centre of the building. This has become the place where discussions are held on collective aspects of the school. One of this school's core projects is promoting the civic education of students through their engagement in assemblies. Of the two schools in urban settings, the first is a segregated school situated in a minority-majority city in a metropolitan area with almost all students coming from low-income families of immigrant background (95%), mainly from Morocco and Gambia. In *Huma School*, a minority-majority school with one hundred fifty students, we were able to observe how a facilitator hired by the centre helped a group of mothers to work on issues that concerned them in their meetings. This was not a strategy to obtain support from mothers to attend to the needs of the schools, rather, central issues

---

15   Fictitious names have been used to maintain anonymity.

were debated in these sessions. The fourth school we chose, *Simourgh School*, has an enrolment of three hundred seventy students and is a *Learning Community School*. It is located in a lower middle-class urban suburb with low levels of migrant resident population. This school has a higher rate of immigrant and ethnic minority students (mainly Romà) than the average (around 40%), due to the school desegregation policy implemented by the city council.

Data gathered from the fieldwork comes from twelve focus groups conducted separately with teachers, students and parents (in order to obtain natural and constructed groups), five in-depth semi-structured interviews with principals and associate principals, and observations carried out throughout the duration of the fieldwork. Guidelines for the focus groups aimed to identify the type of discourses, processes and structures present in these schools concerning existing democratic practices in a variety of school spaces. The focus groups also sought to identify the main points of agreement and dissent on the key factors that sustain their participatory models and help form workable governance structures. We also aimed to identify whether a shared belief existed among teachers that school decision making should involve parents and students to the greatest possible extent, and how they facilitated this participation.

After carrying out the fieldwork, we coded the information into categories that helped us to identify the nature of the democratic practices taking place within the schools. Some of these categories were tools developed in the spheres of (a) Governance, (b) Teacher methods, (c) Curricular contents on civic education, and (d) Other explicit actions promoted to reinforce democracy and involvement. We also took into account whether those who participate in decision-making processes are extending to other people beyond representatives in the governing bodies the law foresees (ii. Symbiotic transformation), or, finally, whether schools developed new *adhoc* structures of decision making not recognized by the law but not in contradiction with it (iii. Interstitial transformation). Lastly, we also took into account when coding whether schools try to involve all parent and student constituencies in decision-making processes (y. Alterity). After the coding process, the team conducted follow-up interviews with the principals and their assistants in order to gather more direct information on how governing structures (paying specific attention to *Consejos Escolares* and other *Adhoc* structures) were managed in the school. This data helped us to finish the triangulation within each school while also providing relevant information to compare and to discern what is common with other schools as well as their particularities (Denzin, 2006).

## Multiple institutional paths in developing democratic school governance

This analysis provides empirical data on how schools either implement specific interpretations of already existing decision-making bodies established by law –*Consejos Escolares*– or create sustainable governance structures that open up participation to include students, parents and school staff other than those who are their representatives. The data also shows how these schools have created different institutional paths for developing democratic governance despite having similar credos in terms of building a democratic community. By school credo, we refer to the set of values and beliefs shared by different agents in a school, specifying how "Education" should be experienced. This credo is usually made explicit in the school educational projects required for every school in Catalonia. In fact, this variety of forms in developing governance exists because of the complexity and creative ways schools bring policy texts into play in their context of practice (Ball, Maguire and Braun, 2012).

In the case of the schools selected, the creation of school educational projects as micro-policy texts represented the institutionalization of the discursive practices present in those schools since the origin of these practices, in some cases ten years ago and in others fifteen years ago. The discourses present in each school regarding participation vary, as well as whether or not those in positions of power (mainly head-teachers, their associates and/or other teachers) have opened the possibility to participate in the generation of the discourse to other agents. These processes were diverse in each case. For example, in *Themis School*, it was the head-teacher who individually established the discourse of democracy because of her own pedagogical creed but also because she wanted to have a good relationship with her neighbours. In the other cases, the reasons differ in function of the various needs of the school and its staff. In the case of *Huma School,* these needs include enrolling more students to avoid the menace of school closure and to increase the participation of minority parents. In the case of *Aristotle School,* the need is to improve communication between parents and reduce parent-teacher conflicts. In reference to *Simourgh School,* the former head-teacher, now retired, fostered a deliberative process with parents and students on how to create a deliberative community. She explicitly aimed to give voice to those excluded by the system, specifically minority and low-income parents and students.

## Extending the participation of the existing governing bodies

*Huma School* uses the *Consejo* as most schools do but expands participation in this body to include fifth and sixth grade students, although these grades are not considered by law to have student representatives. The school principal highlights this situation also compels them to carry out an adequate follow-up of the meetings and a shared decision-making process.

> Interviewer: Do they actively participate in the *Consejo Escolar?* [referring to parents]
>
> María: Yes, they participate actively in the *Consejo Escolar*; there are representatives of parents and students and they attend regularly. It is also good for us that there are students because this compels us to hold very pedagogical School Council meetings, such as, for example, when budgets are presented and have to be approved (Teacher at *Aristotle School*).

In the same school, two of the participating parents highlighted the openness of the *Consejo Escolar* gatherings in accepting their proposals, such as the one dealing with changing the method of socialization of academic books to another that is more respectful of cultural diversity. They also remarked on the expectations and role of teachers in opening decision making to the whole community and in delegating shared responsibilities:

Rashida: Over the past two years we have formed an interesting group of parents in terms of the number of mothers and fathers involved, which has made quite a few proposals. For example, how to rethink the socialization of books among many others. […]

Fatoumata: The teachers have a high degree of social awareness and political commitment. They are people who you also find in other forums (Parents at *Huma School*).

These practices gave the opportunity to participate in decision-making processes to individuals who are usually not represented in the governing bodies (primary school students and minority and low-income parents, for example). Nevertheless, the degree of these effects varies among the schools. Some are more contradictory than others concerning "who can where" and "who decides what". For example, in *Aristotle School* students do not participate in the *Consejo Escolar* but teachers say they try to bring their voices and demands when needed. Civic education values are of key importance in this school, according to the teachers. Students express their agreement on the structures so they can express their opinions and deliberate but teachers tend to have the leading voice in the assemblies:

In class, but especially when we have assemblies. And not so much in the general assembly because the teachers speak more, but somewhat (Student at *Aristotle School*).

With regard to decision making on several issues, teachers in this school agree with the need to broaden and augment decision-making bodies as they have, but they express the opinion that students do not need to participate in certain decisions, such as those related to time schedules, as affirmed below:

Yes, because there are issues that are better left to adults. They can intervene in the majority of topics but there are some in which they cannot. For instance, students cannot have a say on school schedules (Teacher at *Aristotle School*).

## Developing adhoc structures

On the other hand, the cases of *Themis* and *Simourgh* schools go beyond *Consejos Escolares* as governing bodies. They have generated new *governance* structures (the Assembly and the *Gestora*) providing voice and deliberation to a wide range of actors, and ensuring and institutionalizing new paths for governance in the Spanish context. Both schools continue to use the structures mandated by law, but in a different way. The dual structure employed by *Themis School* consists of an operational body (the Assembly) and another mandated by law (the *Consejo*). Meetings of the *Consejo* are merely a bureaucratic performing act, where representatives gather to sign the agreements reached in the Assembly. The sole purpose of these meetings is to ratify decisions already made in parent-teacher assemblies, as expressed next:

> Everyone perceives the *Consejo Escolar* only as a formal meeting that has to be held, and not as a place where decisions are actually made (Parent at *Themis School*).

Decision making and deliberation are transferred to another *ad hoc* structure they call assembly. Meeting are held every three months and the parents' representative is merely another attendee, so the existence of the representative becomes a technocratic formality for complying with legality. This role is expressed in the following quote from the parents' discussion group:

> Joana: The parent representative in the *Consejo Escolar* is just one more person.
>
> Magda: Yes, the exchange of opinions between parents and teachers is important. [...]So, the fact that we have this joint meeting is an added value (Parents at *Themis School*).

Students do not participate in the *Consejo* as foreseen by law. They have their own assemblies and their decisions tend to permeate the parent-teacher assembly. The school principal affirms that having the student assembly and taking their voices into account is a curricular duty to generate citizens as stated in the following quote:

> We don't have assemblies just for the sake of it; we have them because we are convinced that the school belongs to all of them [students]. They must learn to

express their opinions and we have to provide them with the tools to be able to work in assembly (Teacher at *Themis School*).

The case of *Simourgh School* is slightly different. It holds two general assemblies called *Plenario* (Plenary), one at the beginning of the academic course for deciding the main guidelines of action, and another at the end for evaluating the year. However, their main governance body, known as the *Gestora*, is the operational governance structure of the school responsible for bringing into practice the broad decisions reached in the general assembly. Parents, teachers, volunteers, student delegates from to third to sixth grade and anybody else who wants to attend can participate in these meetings. They are held once or twice each trimester with the minutes being emitted after the main meeting, as if these were the minutes of a meeting of the *Consejo*, so as to avoid any possible administrative conflict or confrontation. This would be an example of interstitial transformation of the hegemonic school governing body. In the following quote the principal and her assistant explain how they do not duplicate structures and how they transform a technocratic space reserved for representatives, who have the right to vote (the *Consejo*), into a space where decisions are made by consensus. They avoid voting because it would generate power imbalances between actors, and this situation would go against the *ethos* of the school and of the project they take part in. This inequality in representation and vote is due to the nature of the power differentials established by law.

> Aida: Our approach is called the *Gestora*.
>
> Coral: In reality, it's similar to the *Consejo Escolar* (Teachers at *Simourgh School*).
>
> Aida: What happens is that we expand it. Student representatives –the class delegates– come from the intermediate and upper school cycles, but this is not foreseen for primary school students. Mothers representing each class attend as delegates, but anyone who wishes to do so may attend, not only the representatives. People also come from the mixed committees and there are other individuals as well, because it is open to everyone. This is a decision-making body. The plenary session is for accountability and for presenting proposals, while the *Gestora* is more for managing day-to-day concerns and is more agile.
>
> Coral: Each commission explains their progress and we approve school documents and activities. The nice thing about this *Gestora* is that we've always been able to reach a consensus and we've never had to vote (Teachers at *Simourgh School*).

In all schools, both teachers and parents have identified elements of fragility and incertitude in sustaining these governance structures despite the fact that they are rooted in the schools' credo. These structures require more time and intensity because they need to be developed in addition to the daily tasks that a school requires. Another element would be the arrival of new teachers whose ideas do not converge with these democratic practices and who prefer, and are more comfortable with, a managerial style of school administration. We were also able to observe that the practices developed in these structures are not in clear opposition to the head-teachers and their teams or to the Department of Education. We do not know what might happen in the event of an overt conflict within the school or between the school and the Department. Nor can we predict what would happen if these schools were to perform below what is expected of them on standardized tests. It also remains unclear whether teachers would share decisions with parents and students as they usually do, and whether inspectors would "continue to look the other way", as they have done thus far, or generate institutional pressure to put an end to these structures.

## Discussion and conclusions

While school educational projects were promoted by the Catalan government for the purpose of providing autonomy to schools "to restore the authority" of the head-teachers and to promote New Public Management strategies, the schools we looked at connect these micro-policy texts more with the debates held in the *context of policy influence* about the need to deepen on new forms of democratic administration in schools as some catalan social movements, such as *Rosa Sensat* or *Pedagogical Renewal Movements* among others demanded. Table 1 displays the variety of governance structures created in the four case studies. Two of these case studies reflect what Wright (2010) identifies as *symbiotic transformation* (when processes or strategies extend current governing structures of social empowerment provided by dominant capitalist societies), while the other two what he recognizes as *interstitial transformation* (seeking new forms of social empowerment beyond those established, but not confronting the dominant). On the one hand, the first two schools generate and expand the current *Consejo Escolar* by either bringing the voice of students, expressed in the different assemblies in which they participate, to the *Consejo* (*Aristotle School*), or by enhancing the participation of minority parents and students (*Huma School*). On the other hand, *Themis* and *Simough* Schools are developing new governance structures substituting the *Consejo* aiming to reach all parent and student constituencies but not contradicting dominant structures foreseen in the law.

They carry out these practices and implement these structures against the grain of State and Autonomous Community policy. Their challenges are to be able to maintain these structures of participation over time despite changes in direction and the growing importance that the system attaches to the figure of the principal. Thus, principals and their teams can apply New Public Management strategies more "autonomously", much as they are instructed in training courses given by the state or autonomous governments in accordance with their standards of performativity. This also occurs in parallel with devaluation of the role of governing bodies representing different educational agents (Olmedo, 2008). This trend is similar to what is occurring in Switzerland (Hangartner and Svaton, 2014) and has some parallels to what is taking place in the UK, albeit with certain differences. In the latter case, school governors are trained to act as "inspectors" of the State from within (Wilkins, 2015). However, the cases presented show how despite the pressure and adaptability of neoliberal policies in different contexts, there is floor to generate enclaves of resistance taking advantage of systemic structural holes from where alternative ways of democratic governance may flourish. If these realities can be found in Spain, they may also be developed in other contexts with similar or different forms. We also want to highlight that these stories are not the norm, but rather the exception in the context analysed. As shown, the possibilities for these schools to implement democratic school governance within this system are fraught with complexities. They can develop these micro-policies and be immune to the neoliberal trend, to the extent they do not openly confront the governing bodies established by law. Another fact to take into account is that thus far inspection is not yet as incisive in school governance in Spain and Catalonia as in other contexts, as long as the results of standardized tests do not fall below expected levels.

All four schools successfully managed a process of internal deliberation where participants reach agreements through communicative narratives, identified by Ranson (2003) as democratic governance. These practices of democratic governance, as they undermine the naturalness with which managerialist administration of schools is presented and in turn generate other practices, are bringing to the table a particular act of collective struggle. This does not mean that there is not a plurality of voices, contradictions and ambiguities among teachers and parents when it comes to implementing these practices but they were possible to be created, developed and sustained.

The more extensive the empirical data we gather on how schools develop and maintain democratic school governance, the better we will be able to understand the complexities and difficulties schools and agents have in implementing these practices in the age of neoliberal policy. The paths these schools follow could provide us with cross-national comparative school research that would be useful for theory building as well as for policy (Carnoy, 2006; Carter, 2012). Further multi-level analysis could also be conducted to show contradictions and connections between the effects of national and regional policies in school governance. This can also be connected with European and international policies and treaties aimed at promoting young people's civic participation. In Bhabha's (2014) terms, the heart of the question is how states or schools can fail to protect the right to narrate of those who were silenced or, on the contrary, how they can create spaces for enabling the right of all parent and student constituencies to be heard, recognized and represented.

Núria Simó-Gil and Antoni Tort
*University of Vic-Central University of Catalonia*

# Democracy and Participation in Secondary Schools in Spain

The growing awareness on the part of schools of the need to improve democracy and student participation, particularly in secondary school, is evidenced by the creation of democratizing educational experiences for everybody. The assumption of the social reality present in a wide diversity of students in schools implies a change in the configuration and the functions of the secondary education stage that, in Spain, began to undergo profound changes regarding structure, function and working conditions starting in 1990, when a new education bill modified the configuration of the education system; the Act on the General Organisation of the Education System (LOGSE, 1/1990, 3rd October) substantially reorganized learning stages, schools and syllabae. The fact that secondary schools had since had to cater to 12 and 14 year old students—who up until then were schooled in primary schools by professionals whose experience and qualifications were completely different from those of secondary school teachers—has led to new challenges for secondary schools. Therefore, since the enforcement of the 1990 education bill, the compulsory stage of secondary education encompasses all students aged 12–16. This process is on a par with similar processes in other countries and, as French sociologist François Dubet states, this implies a modification of the institutional program for secondary education, where the learnt trade and discipline defined the teaching profession more than pedagogy and student participation. The changes brought along by the 1990 bill are still looked upon with mistrust and uneasiness by part of the faculty of secondary schools. That is why school life conflicts brought about by parents and students are not just inevitable incidents in a school system that is open to everybody: these conflicts "become extraordinary, they are interpreted as symptoms of a generalized collapse of the institution" (Dubet, 2013, p. 165).

And, ultimately, underlying the discourse of education for everyone, old extractive dynamics survive: different studies (OCDE, 2013) show that educational institutions are unable to compensate background inequalities, as demonstrated by the results of children who come from families with fewer social and cultural resources. This reality leads to a reassessment of the teaching activity and classroom life, though it is not an easy task.

Granting access to compulsory secondary education, by right and duty, to all students from primary school without any prior classification meant an unprecedented challenge to one of the basic rules of thumb of Spanish secondary education: the classification of the students and their distribution in groups according to their capacities. Besides, a new space of meaning and expectations to which the teaching staff and the students could give direction was not created. Quite the opposite. The name was changed—high school institutions became secondary education institutions, but everything else remained the same: teacher training and mentality, spaces, time. However, the students were not the same, nor their needs, backgrounds, expectations, attitudes or their willingness to learn. (Hernández & Sancho, 2004)

The assessment of this issue in the last decades has had, indeed, its highs and lows. It is true that with the advent of democracy in Spain, a new era began, bringing the possibility of wider participation dynamics that sought to improve the mechanisms and management bodies of public institutions, schools among them—or rather, in the forefront. Article 27 of the Spanish Constitution refers to the role of teachers, parents and students in the monitoring and management of educational centres. The first regulations appeared and the laws that established the bases to comply with the constitutional mandate were developed. Parents' Associations and School Boards were implemented and their role regulated as platforms and democratic participatory bodies. Everything seemed to indicate that educational centres were opening up to the different sectors that make up the school and to its surroundings. But in recent years, with the emergence of the Organic Law for the Improvement of the Quality of the Educational System (LOMCE, 8/2013, 9th December), the decision-making capacity which, for better or worse, had been awarded to School Boards[1] has been taken on by the directors and owners of the centres, both in public and private schools, further undermining the role of the educational community when it comes to encouraging participation of students and families or promoting deliberative processes that are central to school life.

All these elements highlight both the need and the difficulties regarding the opening up of the centre towards practices of democratization and empowerment of student participation. In fact, raising questions about student participation in secondary education and considering the improvement of the relationships between the different agents that participate in the school life requires a constant effort and continuous reflection on the organization and operation of the educational centre that is not easy to implement (Freiberg & Stein, 1999). For many years, this has been a concern that lies with individual teachers and, as such, it is driven by the attitude and criteria of each teacher rather than a collective project of the school; but addressing diversity, the right to difference and bridging inequalities demand a more professional, collegial and active teaching approach to meet the needs of secondary school students.

When learners are more diverse and demanding, caring must become less controlling, more responsive to students' varied cultures, more inclusive of their own ideas, perceptions and learning requirements, more ready to involve and not just compensate for the families and communities from which students come in their quest to lift their learning to higher levels. This is the social and emotional mandate for teacher professionalism today (Hargreaves, 2000).

The need to reinstitucionalize secondary school, as a process of improvement and deepening of its democratization, is thus imposed; processes that will enable the transformation of the school culture, understood as a system of shared orientations that hold the unit together and give it a distinctive identity (Hoy *et al.*, 1991). In this case, reinstitutionalization refers to a collective dynamic in the school as a whole that

---

1    It is the participation body of the school community in the centre's government. The school board has representatives from all the groups involved in the educational community: director, faculty, students, administration and service staff, etc. Board members are elected for a period of four years and renewed by halves every two years.

leads to far-reaching and sustainable changes. Talking about democracy in educational centres means the possibility to create and experiment with new forms of subjectivity, relationship, collaboration, and collectivity (De Lissovoy, 2013). We know that this is not always easy. Innovation is usually hampered by the traditional mismatch among the more strictly pedagogical field, the institutional framework and the political context. Therefore, organizations may appear to be progressive but in fact they maintain institutionalized practices that prevent new projects from penetrating into the hard core (the classroom), with the exception of some very experimental contexts. There is a "decoupling" or "loose coupling", a critical factor that accounts for the lack of sustainability of innovations and reforms (Resnick *et al.*, 2010).

In-depth democratization of educational centres is an opportunity to create a new institutional program for secondary education. It is neither a collateral issue nor should it be defined by individual wills or personal inclinations, but rather a crucial challenge in the configuration of a school's educational project that will actually provide better support to secondary students in their academic and personal trajectories.

## Four Areas of Democratic Participation

Living a democratic daily life at school implies overcoming different obstacles to create, maintain and improve processes and structures in educational centres so that young people's actions take centre stage. Placing students at the core of the educational action involves mobilizing changes in secondary schools with two objectives: first, regarding young people from a viewpoint of respect towards oneself and others; and second, transforming the centres into contexts of democratic life (Lawy *et al.*, 2010).

The decisions taken by the teaching team to ensure that the centre becomes a site of democratic experimentation only makes sense if it is oriented towards the agreed goals. Accompanying this process, mobilizing students' ability to make decisions regarding those aspects that affect them, modifying the curriculum in order to share it, adapting spaces to foster new relationships among the people who inhabit the centre and building new ways of working in a teaching team are not easy to undertake or to maintain over time. There are centres that try to do it, and although they do not always succeed, they do move in that direction (Simó *et al.*, 2016). In the hope of highlighting those spaces, we will present four areas of participation in which the democratic quality of some secondary schools can be appreciated[2]:

- Tutoring, assemblies and councils[3]
- Project work beyond the school and *Service Learning* actions
- Appropriation of space and relationships
- Teaching teamwork and the role of the management

## Students in the Foreground: Tutorials, Assemblies and Councils

The schools that undertake the challenge of democratic education place subjectification (Biesta, 2015) as a fundamental objective. The growth of each youth in relation to himself and to others takes shape in the pursuit of what concerns them. Fostering participation spaces that these young people can experience at school involves performing actions that lie at the heart of the curriculum; paying attention to what young people have to tell us means being able to look at what they show and insinuate as a whole since, what is at stake here, even in understanding the

---

2    We got to know those secondary schools during the course of the *Demoskole* Project.
     *Proyecto Demoskole: Democracia, participación, y educación inclusiva en los centros educativos*. Universitat de Girona (UdG) i Universitat de Vic – Universitat Central de Catalunya (UVic-UCC). Plan Nacional I+D. Ministerio de Ciencia e Innovación. (EDU 2012-39556-C02-01 y 02). 2013–2016.
3    The council is the communication body between the students and the governing bodies of the school, which channels student participation in the school life. The council is made up of delegates and sub-delegates elected by each class and by the representatives of the students in the school board.

relationship of young people with knowledge, has to do with each of their lives as a whole, not just with cognitive or school matters. The relationship with knowledge, the wish to learn and the relationships between being and knowing cannot be understood by looking only at the connections young people make with school matters, or their response to the demands of the educational system. At some point in their paths, when young people are broadening their horizons and wondering what their lives can be, secondary education must also wonder about its capacity to accommodate dimensions of development and personal growth of youths at times of delicate decisions and transformations (Hernández, 2006). Thus, individual and group tutoring become spaces where the educational relationship that each adult builds with each of these youths, as well as among them, takes place.

From the students' perspective, individual tutoring is a well-valued space for support and reflection that each student shares with a teacher who provides individualized monitoring of their academic and personal development. This kind of relationship with each teacher is key for consolidating the environment of the school. For the students interviewed, the role of the tutor is pivotal in establishing a wide sense of trust with his or her group and a climate of dialogue in the classroom:

Researcher: But are tutoring sessions a space for debate?

Student 1: Well, in our case, we would say no.

Student 2: It also depends on the tutor. [...] but M. and I have a tutor who trusts us. We can talk to her about anything and she will try to help us. She is always very close to us, especially in our studies.

In addition, these tutoring groups are an excellent test laboratory to initiate participatory processes where the teacher's role is key to encouraging students to express their own opinions, and in which they are required to understand the viewpoints of others and establish dialogues in order to further their understanding of a problem. Students expressed the need to find more spaces, during school hours, where they can express their opinions and discuss them in an open and spontaneous dialogue, and not only in planned learning activities. In short, students themselves demand more spaces where they can be able to express themselves and be listened to.

In Class Assemblies and Student Councils young students give their views on aspects that directly affect them. Students value the opportunities for participation and decision making regarding their academic life that the school offers them. They are aware of the fact that there is margin for shared participation, but they also stress the limits of participation. As stated by Thornberg and Elvstrand (2012), students express their participation in everyday life in terms of process and relationships rather than results, since they realize that they can decide on some issues but not on others. Being fully aware of these limitations, students value the chance to make some decisions that concern them and directly affect them in Assemblies and Councils. The result of these practices impacts on their coexistence and the decisions that the students take, as well as on school climate, as stated by a student:

> Student 2: For us to give opinion, we are given a topic that has been a problem or something, and we have an assembly and we all give our opinion and then that goes to the Student Council or, I don't know, we make a proposal or something and then they take it to the Student Council and they check if it's OK or not.

Turning Assemblies and Student Councils into real decision-making spaces for youths is only possible in contexts where adults respect the students' voices and the school has the organizational will to include these spaces in a global pedagogical project, beyond isolated educational initiatives or circumstances.

## Rethinking the Curriculum with the Community: Project Work and Service Learning

Schools that take on the challenge of democratic education question the educational sense of the curriculum by offering spaces for participation in which young people can become co-researchers (Fielding, 2012). Formulating the educational sense of projects from the viewpoint of democratic education means dealing with organizational, structural and institutional changes, thus posing many questions to the teaching teams instead of offering easy and immediate answers.

Organizing project work implies, first and foremost: rethinking what relevant school contents are and adapting old school time and space structures; that the teacher be a companion in the learning process; and that information and communication technology become an essential tool in this process. From this perspective, project work is not a matter of methodological innovation but is based on a political approach that aims at a deep-seated change in the conception of academic knowledge.

The organization of academic knowledge in an integrated way through project work guides student participation towards a community perspective. It creates opportunities in which young people can listen and be listened to and can make decisions in spaces of shared responsibility that not only affect their individual and group growth, but can also entail possible improvements for the community. The service learning activity seeks to ensure that students experience and be at the forefront of civic engagement activities, learn in the active exercise of citizenship and put into play their knowledge and capacities to serve the community. Using service learning methodology, the acquisition of skills in the classroom (10 hours) and competence development are combined with social action (10 hours minimum), responding to a previously detected need in either a local or distant environment. One of the strengths of this activity lies in the wide range of services being carried out simultaneously, including aid in schooling, intergenerational exchange, environment, heritage, sustainability, digital literacy, etc.

This diversity adds organizational complexity to the project but fosters student autonomy, encouraging them to make their own decisions about the project they wish to develop. The students interviewed mentioned that they could choose a specific community service that everyone would like to take part in, and each group analysed the needs and defined their own goals with the community partner. As a consequence, there is a mutuality to this kind of project: while it clearly impacts on the community, it also needs it to develop the project.

## Greater Presence of Students in the School Environment and Educational Relationships

Schools that have a more democratic will are committed to organizing both spaces and working times according to a coherent educational sense oriented towards student participation. In this line, we find, for example, two-hour blocks that enable different means of participation and establishing relationships with flexible and heterogeneous student groups. In fact, this breaks away from the formula 1 teacher / 1 classroom with 25–30 students / 1 hour of class in different educational activities, such as project work, cooperative group work or support brigades[4] at the school, opting instead for classes of 20 students organized in five groups of four students each, plus two teachers per classroom for some class sessions. In these sessions, research, debate and development of ideas among members of each subgroup prevail, as well as the joint agreement on results that in many cases offer answers to problems that the community is trying to solve. These learning spaces become articulating axes of different horizontal relationships between students and teachers through which young people express a shared sense of belonging in the school and a feeling of personalized support that helps them grow individually. They feel that they are listened to and are confident in making decisions, despite the fact that these educational situations pose new challenges:

> Student 1: I remember that at first we complained about cooperative groups, I guess because we weren't used to that, there were always problems, and just once in a while you were in a group that you liked, but now, well, I don't know about the others, but at least I think in general you begin to like all the groups because you learn to adapt, because with co-evaluation we can give grades, when we do group work we can grade our group mates for the work they've done.

---

4    In Support Brigades, students are responsible for participating and taking decisions regarding improvements in different areas of school life (e.g. decoration, computer maintenance, providing academic support to other students, etc.). They are an open and dynamic experience that encourages students' active participation, involvement and sense of responsibility.

In the centres with greater democratic participation, students stated that the teachers are close, they feel that they are available for whatever they may need: "here the relationship is closer and we are more like friends" (GD_CC_A2:2). Students say that there is a good climate that is directly related to the opportunities young people have to participate and voice their opinion (Leitch & Mitchell, 2007). This can be seen in intangible or anecdotal aspects, for instance that the teachers' room is in fact a space where young people are constantly coming and going, that the director's office is actually the same teachers' room, or that students start to work on their own initiative when the teacher is not in the classroom. In short, students from the centres with greater democratizing participation know that the way in which the educational activity is organized in these schools is unique. However, students also highlight that the spaces and times for participation and debate are subject to the school's schedule, which consists of fixed times that are strictly structured around the subjects included in the curriculum.

Giving voice to students has consequences at the level of school organization, and must therefore lead the centre to reflect on what it prioritizes over the course of a school day as well as on how to balance the need for flexible times and spaces while ensuring a proper quantity, quality and distribution of time dedicated to instruction and studying. Indeed, school culture or "school grammar" (Tyack & Tobin, 1994) implies a set or rules, structures, practices, codes and organizational forms of government that define the concept of space and time, transmissions, grading, teaching… A "hard core" that the educational centre has maintained over time and that society in general and some of its actors still perceive as the mold of what 'true school' is. Delving into the democratization of school thus demands addressing the characteristics of its organizational arrangements and parameters, and once again students themselves express that school practices are hierarchical:

> Student: There are powers that we can't deal with here at school because if we want to change subjects or if we want to change the schedule, we can't change that, but we can change, for example, tutoring activities, or ask for, for example, here in the schoolyard there was nothing before and now it's full of sand; with proposals we made, they have brought tables, soccer goals, ping-pong tables, a volleyball court, those are things that we had asked for and they have listened. And [these requests] are voted on by students themselves in workshops.

Student: We have a kind of little service, which is service, I don't know if it's 20 students from the whole school that on Fridays get together and make a list of things that can be fixed, that can be improved.

All in all, committing to the students' voices and enforcing young people's right to be heard implies setting in motion processes of change in educational centres that impact on the school's day-to-day life.

## Rethinking the Teaching Participation in Schools

The centres that take up the challenge of democratic education need to develop a great degree of complicity with the people who are part of the educational community, first of all, among the teaching team when the time comes to share and promote the education project. This is the means for the teaching body to be in a position to experience student participation as a collective and not an individual challenge, and to take this responsibility as part of the teaching task. Needless to say, a certain stability and duration certainly facilitates the continuity of the initiated processes of change. The size of a centre is revealed as a significant element when it comes to thinking, methodologically, how to address the question of the centre's democratization. We have observed that in schools that have one or two lines (one or two classes per grade) it is easier to implement projects that generate changes in the practices than in schools with three or more lines. In recent years, organizational complexity, schedule, the number of teachers, groups, lines, spaces, etc. have undoubtedly been major obstacles to changes in vision and practices, unless there are strong coordination and decentralization capabilities in terms of stages, seminars, cycles or teaching teams.

With regard to the leadership of the project, the role of the management is key to giving it institutional coverage on the one hand, and adding momentum, effectiveness and pedagogical depth to the process and the proposed actions on the other. If the school management does not prioritize student participation, with the endorsement of the teaching staff, the project cannot move forward. In this regard, the institutional configuration of each centre, its ownership (public, private, chartered, etc.) must also be taken into account. The burden of time and working conditions is also a factor to bear in mind. In this situation, the management teams become keys to democratically sharing democratic experience. This task demands listening and negotiating skills in the exchange of interests—particularly towards the voices of those teachers that might be sceptical about the project—trying to find collective solutions to individual situations. This requires spaces for debate and time to reach agreements:

> Teacher 1: If you offer participation, it's obviously longer, more expensive, there's more debate, but it's all enriching and educational. If you don't want debate, don't ask for participation, the same goes for the teaching staff. The management team could decide everything, but it's not the case, we agree on and make decisions about many things.

Improving democratizing practices at school requires determination on the part of the teaching team to promote this way of working and learning, and reaching agreements to include the most participatory activities during school hours and in the curriculum. For the teaching team, working in this direction implies facing new opportunities in which to take risks to innovate, exercising complicity and cohesion, learning new methodologies and forms of assessment, gaining insight into the working methods of work colleagues and trusting that you learn from and with others, as well as questioning whether the decisions taken have been the most appropriate ones.

In these situations, the management team has the responsibility to lead the process, communicate it and learn to value the personal efforts of each actor involved, with the common goal of creating relevant learning environments. For students, the visibilization of this leadership is also essential, and they request a management that is close to their activities and participation spaces.

Organizational and academic flexibility is crucial to progress and overcome obstacles along the way, to improve the quality of educational processes and results in a climate of respect and trust that configures the culture of the school and which poses challenges to new uncertainties every time the school makes new decisions. In this context, new dilemmas arise, such as deliberation and representation in centres that grow, thus making participatory democracy more difficult, as stated by a teacher who works for one of the schools that has taken participation to the highest degree of development:

> Teacher 2: We also participate, less than some people would like to and less than when we started, because when we started the school was very, very participatory, really assembly-based… that is, there was a management team because there had to be one, but we decided everything together. Now, of course, we are bigger, the current management team has a different approach, which is also more practical because there are many open fronts in the day-to-day and sometimes you, it's never ending, there are many hours of discussion, many hours of… so in the end you say 'we don't have time, you decide'.

And in all, in this democratizing process, the teaching team faces the complexity of the profession. According to Connell (2009), sustainability, emotional management and collective work are essential for moving towards the improvement of the participatory processes that define the collaborative culture of the schools.

Good teaching must be *sustainable*; and that can only be planned when we see teaching as a practicable labour process. Further, teaching involves a great deal of emotion work. Classroom life involves a flow of emotions, both on the part of the teachers and the pupils, ranging from simple likes and dislikes to enthusiasm, anxiety, boredom, joy, fear and hope. Any teacher has to manage this flow, and make it productive for the pupils' learning and survivable for herself or himself. Also, recognition of the collective labour of teachers is essential for a better understanding of good teaching (Connell, 2009).

As Leitch and Mitchell state, we also need to include the students' voices in this process. Given that cultural change is a slow process, it seems reasonable to postulate that there is a connection between the health or toxicity of a school's culture, as perceived by students, and the potential for student rights and student voice to be cultivated therein (Leitch & Mitchell, 2007).

## Moving Forward on Participation as a Strategy for Democratic Life

Democracy and participation—one of its fundamental instruments—in educational centres allow children and young people to exercise their rights as citizens, which contributes to the construction of a more democratic society; this fosters their personal development, and provides them with substantial knowledge and practical skills. In those schools that generate more spaces for teachers and students to experience democratic processes, these are articulated through learning activities and methodologies such as cooperative groups, project work or service learning, and mentoring and class assemblies play a prominent role; in these schools, spaces for student debate, opinion and decision making are frequent, common and regular, thus generating many and varied situations where decisions are valued from different points of view. There is a better bonding with the group, an overall improvement regarding reflection on rights in balance with shared and agreed responsibilities, as well as a commitment to community participation. At the same time, taking students—with their criteria and opinions—into account turns them into competent citizens instead of passive recipients of services aimed at them, but not thought out for them (Checkoway, 2011).

At the same time, deepening democracy at schools necessarily involves opening up to other community agents, favouring the creation of public meeting points based precisely on the actions and democratic practices carried out in the school. The idea is to generate relational spaces and spheres in which teachers and students experience democratic processes through strategies such as those that we have briefly commented on. These must be areas where debate, opinion and assumption of co-responsibility by students are relevant; areas in which new situations are generated where decisions are respected and valued by the different agents of the community.

This democratic approach goes hand in hand with the collaborative culture of the teaching team as an integral part of the teaching practices. Bearing in mind that the life and work of teachers are influenced by their personal and social background, the management team is responsible for bringing forth the discourses and representations that teachers build around their professional identity and their positive or negative experiences towards the commitment to educational challenges (Day & Gu, 2014). Complicity in the educational relationships with students—the central figures in secondary schools—presents a way of working that subverts traditional and standardized power relationships through participation. In these cases, student participation broadens the decision-making areas already in place and, as a result, students have higher degrees of freedom and responsibility when exercising decision making about school matters. Accordingly, genuine student participation (Simovska, 2004, 2007) requires a transfer of power from teachers to students when it comes to taking decisions that affect the boys and girls in secondary schools.

We would also want to point out that, beyond what is established by regulations, it is important to make the most of all communication channels, both formal and informal, without them substituting one another. Together with the rules governing educational centres, the ways of organizing academic and curricular activities—as well as school life in general—are planned according to high standards of ethics, awareness and reflection on the part of the different sectors involved, knowing that, in an educational centre, human relations are put into play among people of different ages that occupy different positions within a framework that, by definition, is hierarchical. In short, democratic education involves welcoming, negotiating and deciding on agreements regarding a way of living in a community that is nurtured by the multiple social and economic conditions, lifestyles, biographical trajectories, aspirations and hopes of those individuals that are part of a school.

There is something that is not formally included in the legislation and which would roughly translate as 'institutional warmth'; it does not equate to very many meetings, but to spaces and times that foster personal exchanges that, however brief, might be intense. The experience of democracy on the part of students does not depend solely on the participation bodies that schools have in place, but rather on relationships and the existing school climate. Close, human relationships with the teaching staff, as well as participation spaces and activities, are the key condition for well-being in the centre and for the development of democratic practices. Actually, participation spaces are valued as the places where participation is enabled and where people feel they are an integral part of the institution. In fact, if such spaces are not enabled, students demand them.

Improving times and spaces for listening and understanding is an important matter, not only in terms of formal structures and pre-established norms, but also in informal spaces and relationships. As proposed by Biesta *et al.* (2009), young people should feel what it means to 'live citizenship'. Experiencing citizenship in secondary schools implies the construction of a facilitating context for transversal democratic values, with a view to improving educational centres and the willingness to extend them to their closest community.

JORDI FEU, ÒSCAR PRIETO-FLORES, XAVIER CASADEMONT &
LAURA LÁZARO
*Unviversity of Girona*

# Three Models of Initial Teacher Training in Social, Citizenship and Democratic Competences in Europe

Civic knowledge is a key element in achieving more and better citizen and civic participation of individuals. Some studies even suggest that the presence of this type of knowledge among students could be a predictor of citizens' future electoral participation (Torney-Purta, Lehman, Oswald & Schultz, 2001, Kerr *et al.*, 2009). Moreover, civic knowledge must be transmitted, at least in part, in the classrooms of primary and secondary education. For this reason, and connecting with European recommendations, the importance of teacher training is recognized as part of the strategy to promote education for democratic citizenship and human rights education (Council of Europe, 2010). These recommendations include good planning and adequate availability of resources in the training of education professionals, and instruct member states to implement policies to conduct research aimed at improving the effectiveness of teachers in this area of competence.

This chapter is the result of a study conducted by a team of researchers from the universities of Girona, Vic and Ramon Llull (Catalonia) during the years 2014 and 2017, whose objective was to develop a comprehensive plan for the promotion of democratic and participative attitudes, practices and culture among university students studying to become teachers (research funded by AGAUR [Agency for Management of University and Research Grants], an agency of the Generalitat de Catalunya, the autonomous government of Catalonia). This chapter, which develops the first objective of the research mentioned, focuses on a comparative analysis of the training model in the field of democracy, participation and civics in the three European countries that, according to the latest international study assessing civic and citizenship competencies (ICCS, 2009) [International Civic and Citizenship Education Study], have the highest democratic standards. These countries are, in order: Finland, Denmark and Sweden.

The analysis that follows comes from in-depth interviews that were conducted with both leaders in the field of higher education of future teachers in the three countries and, in the case of Denmark and Sweden, with practicing teachers in specific schools. It should also be noted that the analysis was carried out taking into account two simultaneous parameters in order to realize a multifaceted and comprehensive treatment of democracy. The first parameter is strictly theoretical in nature and is related to the approach of democracy in schools proposed in the first chapter of this book; the second parameter, with a more organizational dimension, has to do with what we consider to be key issues—the curriculum taught in teaching studies, the organization and design of the training practices of future teachers, the organization of the centres and the ethical, social-community and professional commitment of teachers.

The content of this chapter is fundamentally structured in two sections, the first being the most extensive and substantive. This section, entitled *Teacher training curriculum*, sets out to analyze the curricular treatment of training in social, civic and citizenship education in the countries under study, and is made up of three parts: the first focuses on presenting the general approach to training in relation to the subject that concerns us; the second part analyzes in a specific and detailed manner the training in areas of otherness and habitance in the curriculum in the field of primary education as well as in higher education; the objective of the third part is to analyze how governance is also considered in the curricular approach of both higher education centres and in primary education.

The last section contains some conclusions and recommendations aimed at improving the curricular proposal in the field of democracy and the training of future teachers. Please note that the conclusions, apart from presenting the most important ideas that appeared throughout the chapter, are used to make a brief comparative analysis of what has been observed in the area of training in the countries analyzed and the Catalan educational reality and, more occasionally, also that of Spain.

## Teacher training curriculum

Broadly speaking, the basic structure of the studies that comprise initial teacher training in the three countries under study in this chapter—an aspect that gives some idea of how to situate the activities and curricular content related to social and citizenship competency and to the knowledge and practices of educational democracy—poses two training perspectives. One, the more comprehensive, holistic, competential and transversal perspective, promotes citizenship learning and knowledge on civics, ethics, rights, systems of political participation, school and educational democracy, etc., distributed in all subjects, modules and educational experiences of the degree; and the other, which is based on the idea that this knowledge must be developed as a subject or content explicitly in specialization sessions. The first perspective is adopted by all cases; the second, on the contrary, occurs almost exclusively in one case.

All the people interviewed have established important relationships between the high level of awareness of citizens, students and educational institutions regarding democratic education, and the historical, social and cultural importance that these issues have in the social and cultural foundation of the country and in the social welfare systems of Nordic countries.

### *Perspectives of training in social, civic and citizenship education*

The case of Denmark is perhaps the one that best suits the dual perspective, transversal-competential and at the same time *subject oriented*, of social, civic and citizen education. These contents are not only a transversal or cross-curricular subject; they are also formalized in a course with a minimum of 10 ECTS credits, which in some educational institutions can reach 15 or 20. The course has a rather curious name: "Christianity studies, life, enlightenment and citizenship education", and is usually taught during the first year of studies. The religious part of the subject combines in a non-confessional way the contents of the Christian religion in relation to other religions, European culture and the management of the multiplicity of religions and faiths among students.

The other two parts of the subject are devoted to ethics and existential questions, on the one hand, and to citizenship, democratic education and human rights, on the other. The aim of this course is to offer a forum to discuss current social challenges in relation to these three dimensions (religion, ethics and democratic citizenship). The opinion of one of the professors of Danish teacher training we interviewed is critical in that she considers that the subject does not allow in-depth examination of all aspects and that the latest educational reform of 2013 has had a reducing effect on the subject—the 17 ECTS that were compulsory for all institutions have been reduced to 10 in most of them.

From another standpoint, one of the interviewed Danish school teachers, while attributing to this subject the most important part of common higher education of teachers in citizenship, brands it as excessively Eurocentric claiming that when dealing with religious aspects it centres too much on Christianity and that no effort has been made to find a more generic name that can represent all religions on an equal basis.

Apart from this subject, which has its own entity within the teacher education system, Danish higher education institutions (colleges) also offer educational specializations to teach the subject of Social Sciences in secondary education. This training is situated in the specialization of Social Studies, and is only taken by students who choose this specialization. The subject of Social Sciences in secondary education is taken by students aged 14 and 15, is a subject in itself, with an exam, and is common to all students. From here, more in-depth studies in higher education on subjects related to civics, citizenship, etc. depend on the specializations offered by each institution and the fact that the student chooses these specializations over others. For example, the D2 institution has two offers related to the topic at hand, which are the specialization in human rights and the international specialization "Didactics of dialogue and reconciliation" focusing more on conflict resolution and conflict transformation.

It should be noted that the specialization in human rights of this subject was designed jointly with the Danish Institute of Human Rights, which, according to the interviewee, has a firm commitment to schools and often collaborates in educational projects and with the development of human rights education aimed at teachers and children. This coincides with what another Danish university professor explains about the empirical studies conducted by this institute to examine the way the subject of human rights is taught and learned in Danish schools. These studies conclude that the teaching of human rights in Danish schools and initial teacher training is done from a highly theoretical perspective and does not explore in depth the application of knowledge in the social field and, therefore, is not reflected in acts.

In conclusion, this same interviewee affirms that Danish students are generally strong in competencies related to citizenship and democratic education and that the university is working to increase the amount of time devoted to these subjects through the optional specializations. This opinion coincides with that expressed by the teacher referred to above. According to this individual, students are well trained in questions of democratic citizenship and, above all, in matters of otherness, in particular with regard to cultural issues and ethnic minorities, thanks precisely to the subject we have referred to.

Regarding whether the training during practice teaching in these schools offered any specific activity or training in citizenship, civics or democracy to university students, the teacher confirmed that such training does not exist, but argues that, in fact, the education system is based on values arising from the concept of democratic citizenship.

However, she acknowledges that the emphasis on these issues during the counselling sessions with teaching practice tutors depends on the interest that the individual tutor has. In fact, one of the teachers interviewed considers that their colleagues in the profession do not specifically address issues of social and citizenship competency. Despite this opinion, Danish schools seem to have a wide range of subjects and content related to the topic at hand.

In contrast, we find that Finland and Sweden conform much more to the transversal-competential perspective in articulating the curriculum in higher education institutions in relation to what we call social and citizenship competence. In these two countries, there are no prescribed subjects in their own right dealing which knowledge and practices related solely to one or several topics of civic and citizenship education, although, in practice, some institutions offer them as short courses adjacent to the core program of studies.

In Finland, there is a great amount of university autonomy in programming content and subjects. It follows, then, that every department devoted to teacher training has a different curriculum. In addition, university faculty members also have a great deal of freedom in terms of emphasizing (or not) certain content within their subjects. Nevertheless, the development of content on citizenship, civic education, etc. is part of the national curriculum. This means that all institutions and university teachers have to address this, although they do so in an autonomous and differentiated way. Issues related to citizenship, civic education, etc. are dealt with throughout the higher education cycle, but as part of discussions on educational issues, not as pre-established curricular content. As explained by a Finnish university professor who teaches teacher education courses, there are five phenomena that must be worked on: *interaction, society, chance, learning* and *guidance*, which include all content related to citizenship. During higher education, therefore, content is not treated as a specific part of a curriculum but as part of the reflection on the five phenomena. Moreover, it is not treated in a more specific way because it is assumed that the basic contents of these subjects have already been worked on at a sufficient level in secondary education. The basic idea is for there to be a process of research on these five phenomena. This perspective on research is very present in Finland, reflected both in the interview with the representative of the higher education institution and in the interview with the primary school teacher.

The Finnish teacher we interviewed also made mention of the treatment of social and civic competence and professional ethics during the practice teaching and the continuous training of teachers. As mentioned, these issues appear constantly in higher education and in student teaching in schools.

In reference to the curriculum in primary and secondary education, there is a subject programmed for 11-year-old students called History and Civic Education. Later, from ages 13 to 15, they have another subject called Civic Education, although the teacher points to the open and transversal nature of these contents in the national curriculum.

In the case of Sweden, the curricular perspective of higher education in relation to our subject of study is clearly transversal, and there is no curricular trajectory to be followed to become a teacher or educator in civic education, citizen education or similar subjects. The university professor we interviewed also spoke of some types of continuing education, including *seminars, workshops* and *presentations*, which are offered in each institution on an autonomous basis, so that although in her university they are quite frequent, she does not know if this is the case in other centres of higher education. For example, she teaches a four-session course called "Democracy and the democratic values system". In her opinion, the presence of this extra training depends largely on the commitment of each university to this subject and on whether there are individuals interested in these issues. However, she points out that the values of democracy and democratic tenets prevail and are an important part of the foundation of all universities.

In relation to the specific content of this transversal training, the teacher highlighted the following dimensions and topics that, in general, are clearly more emphasized in higher education in Sweden: the development of students' opinions is a priority, in accordance with the development of the skills required to guide discussions and debates in the classroom. In fact, she emphasized that Swedish education is particularly accustomed to setting up debates in the classroom; therefore, it is a methodology fully accepted by all teachers. Other dimensions worked on are the development of interpersonal skills, democratic values, equality of opportunity between men and women, cultural differences and minorities, environmental issues, and empathy and recognition of the dignity of others. Addressing the area of relational work, the interviewee explained that in Swedish universities much work is done in groups and projects are worked on jointly, which promotes the development of interpersonal relationships and the taking of shared and individual responsibility within the group, among other aspects.

In general, she argued that in Sweden content is touched on very superficially and that this is partly due to this transversal perspective of the curriculum on civic and citizenship education. The problem, she says, is that each teacher sees their students for very few hours, so, although they try to integrate content in all classes, an in-depth treatment is difficult. In the case of the course that she herself teaches, she has so few hours that she must make a very restricted selection of content.

Beyond content, the methodological perspective, in line with what we saw in Finland, interprets the educational reality and context based on research, however, not precisely on the results of the research, but rather the detailed analysis of all possible factors that influence a particular educational context.

The assessment of this curriculum by the interviewee is that students may be sufficiently prepared in the areas that are covered but that, in general, they are unprepared to successfully carry out this methodological perspective of interpretive and critical research of educational reality and contexts.

*Training in areas of otherness and habitance in the curriculum and in the general framework of primary and higher education*

Training on issues of otherness and habitance in higher education occurs through the formal curriculum of subjects, modules or programs, but also through the learning that teacher education students can access in the framework of their practice teaching in schools. In order to know what curricular and practical training they have in these settings, throughout the interviews we asked them about the formal curriculum of the universities and colleges and inquired about the topics discussed in the classroom. They were also asked about the institutional importance that is given to these areas and about the practices of otherness and habitance that exist in general in primary schools in each country and that, therefore, are likely to be present in practice teaching.

In the case of Finland, it was emphasized that the prominence of issues surrounding the treatment of otherness has increased in recent years. Within the framework of educational practice, the interviewee explained that the phenomenon of cultural heterogeneity in the classrooms is relatively new, and that there is still a need for practice-oriented knowledge. As explained to us, this topic has begun to be addressed from a theoretical perspective, but this is not enough. There needs to be greater interaction between agents of the educational process and more contact with the real world. In this connection, the primary and secondary school teacher pointed out that the regulation of equity is one of the few things that are determined by law in Finland. For example, freedom of confession is respected to the point that each child must be able to receive classes from the religion they feel involved with, even if there is only one child who needs to receive classes from a particular faith. She also points out that the issue of otherness regarding cultural differences is becoming increasingly prominent because of the refugee crisis in Europe and the reality of refugees in Finnish schools, and she defends the fact that in the Finnish system everyone has the obligation to assume the same duties and enjoy the same rights. The interviewee also says that Finland still has a good public system of social protection and that, except in particular cases, most families and individuals can make use of it and do so in a very acceptable way.

Congruently, it seems that Finnish society is very sensitive to issues related to gender and alternatives to traditional family models. In this context, we were told that textbooks containing orthodox descriptions of the family model have caused a stir in public opinion. In fact, she herself as a writer of textbooks says that she has to be very careful to present all people and life models in an equal way in the contents of English books.

In Denmark, the policy of integration of all children, regardless of their abilities, is implemented in the school itself. Only in very exceptional cases will a student be isolated for physical or mental reasons. This, according to the professor interviewed, is because the social protection system is excellent and educational spaces are adapted for special needs. This description is consistent with what the teacher tells us about a blind student in her class who was integrated into the school because he was accompanied by a support person throughout the day. In general, as she explained, there are always resources to maintain students integrated in school for as long as possible.

However, in the opinion of another university professor, issues related to habitance are touched on in teacher training, but too superficially. She explains that economic factors and their relationship with learning have traditionally been addressed, and continue to be addressed, in the framework of higher education, although now this is done with less intensity than before. She also claims that there is concern for the environment and aesthetics as important elements of schools, and that the economic differences between regions of the country are being studied as a factor to be taken into account. In general, however, this professor considers that the aspects of habitance do not constitute an area that is addressed in depth in the framework of teacher training.

This same professor also expressed her opinion on the political influence that families can have in municipalities, and concerning the quality of their requests and the adaptations of municipalities to their needs, a topic that converges with the dimension of otherness. The interviewee explains that there is much difference between families, and that not all of them have the same culture and participatory skills within the framework of the municipality. In some cases this is due to language problems, but she recognizes that there are families of second and third generation immigrants who also participate very little. She attributes this to a cultural background that does not include the idea that they can participate and influence through structures of democratic participation. This, she believes, is one of the challenges that Denmark faces today. The same opinion is shared by the primary school teacher who emphasizes how the arrival of refugee children is a challenge at present. This teacher also emphasizes that he believes that recognition of the socio-cultural otherness of children from other cultures is not a requirement handed down from the school or educational system, but rather a personal choice of each teacher. In his opinion, it is the most commonly shared values of Danish society that make teachers active and respectful regarding issues concerning the treatment of otherness.

In Sweden, in relation to otherness, the interviewee informs us that this country has a specific regulation that urges all teachers and teaching students to overcome discrimination and rights violations. This legislation establishes seven groups susceptible to discrimination, and includes discrimination for reasons of gender and sex, as well as age-related discrimination. Another law directly prescribes the need to fight against the violation of rights, and of integrity itself, not only for questions of belonging to a particular group but also because of feeling that one's integrity has been violated. In these cases, the regulations establish that it is necessary to investigate where the feelings of violation of the integrity of each person come from and determine whether they respond to facts; thus, it is not possible, in the context of the Swedish educational system, to pass over or relativize issues of this type. S1 appreciates this sensitivity shown by Swedish regulations to give equal importance to different types of violations of rights and integrity, not only in matters related to belonging to a particular group, but with respect to any difference or otherness that could lead to discrimination.

Throughout the interview there was also talk about the concept of habitance and the treatment of this subject in the Swedish educational framework, and in particular, in the initial teacher training. According to the university professor, the concept used in Sweden is that of work environment, which is divided into two areas: ergonomics, which is the physical dimension, and aesthetics. Issues related to the amenity of spaces to adapt physically and to convey an aesthetically cosy and welcoming atmosphere are addressed both in primary school and in higher education institutions. Concurrently, though, one of the university professors interviewed emphasized that educational research in Sweden is also interested in social or relational welfare, stemming from the growing discomfort of teachers and students due mainly to stress. As she said on several occasions throughout the interview, this is a current topic of concern in Sweden. Specifically, with regard to the welfare of teachers, she emphasized that they feel pressured on all sides: by students, public opinion, political representatives and the educational institutions themselves, with structures managed in an increasingly vertical, top-down way.

*Training and experiences of participation (governance) in the curriculum and in the general framework of primary and higher education*

In the preceding sections we have already looked at a part of the teacher training curriculum in relation to social, civic, citizenship and democratic knowledge and competencies. This is the part that is programmed and then developed in classes and training activities. As we have seen, the interviews were designed not only to find out about the content that is programmed and taught in training spaces, but also to inquire about the content of the curriculum that emerges from participatory practices in the institutions of higher education and early childhood and primary education, and therefore, also the training experiences that take place during practice teaching. This other, perhaps less explicit, curriculum that arises from the experiences that teaching students can have during their higher education and also during their practice in schools is, we believe, as important as the rest of knowledge that emerges in the bachelor's degree subjects and modules, in the sense that it provides students with a participatory culture and a certain culture of institutional governance.

Next, you will find two sections; the first contains a description of the participatory practices and the state of the participatory question in higher institutions, and the second, a description of these same practices and situations in primary schools.

## *Participation and democracy in higher education institutions*

Finland, in general, has a culture with a high degree of autonomy in schools and universities. This seems to go hand in hand with the autonomy that is granted to higher education students when it comes to considering participatory spaces and their participation in the day-to-day functioning of the educational process. At the university, students have their own participatory organizations; for example, all students are part of their department's study groups. In each department, there is a student group for each basic activity of the department (research, pedagogical development, interaction with society, etc.), in which the head of the department also participates. These groups can, and indeed do, make meaningful proposals that may involve changes within the educational institution. For example, in the latest curricular reform based on phenomena, already discussed above, the university institution organizes work groups composed of university professors and teaching students.

In relation to the presence of community organizations in the university and the level of participation of the university community in these types of spaces of social participation, it is considered that there is an important presence of community organizations but that ties with the community, in general, are not particularly strong. Relationships usually occur with organizations having close links to the university or with the reference school or the school located closest to the university and, in many cases, the relationship is quite circumstantial. On the other hand, from time to time students or a teacher contact individually with an organization to organize a talk or listen to experts on a specific topic.

Sweden is intensifying an increasingly top-down governance model of higher education institutions. Aside from this more global vision, the theoretical perspective regarding student participation is that the learning of knowledge should not be detached from experience. However, according to one of the interviewed professors, it is understood that freedom to participate must go hand in hand with responsibility and, therefore, knowledge.

With regard to structures of participation, the only structure that exists as such is the Student Council, supported and promoted by the university institution and that, as it stands, has a great deal of power within the university. Student representatives are democratically elected and, in general, the purpose of this student body is to collect questions and complaints from students. Institutional recognition of this council is so great that student representatives are often invited to the most powerful governing bodies of the university.

This great influence, however, does not always generate virtuous circles designed to improve the situation; rather, there are often cross-accusations between the student and faculty communities. According to the professor interviewed, the form of expression of students' opinions often consists of closing ranks against a specific person, with which they achieve the scapegoating of a single individual by a group, so that the whole situation becomes a form of bullying.

By contrast, university professors have their own forms of participation and they are often asked for their opinion within the framework of the institution. However, they are often trying to exert influence on a system that is governed too vertically for their voices to be heard in a significant way. As S1 explains, decisions appear to be made in advance and all the participatory acts seem to be merely "playing to the gallery".

We could say that the conclusion reached by the interviewee is that participatory experiences, whether of students or teachers, are not necessarily democratic or based on democratic principles solely because they exist in some form (for example, because of having of certain bodies and regulations or specific institutional acts). Many factors can make these experiences become undemocratic or turn them into a pantomime without participatory authenticity.

In Denmark, the overall feeling is that there has been a loss of influence of students and professors in universities. Again, we see the idea that progressive educational reforms have been increasingly concentrating power in the institution and less in its agents. For instance, it was mentioned that not many years ago, teaching students could negotiate the inclusion of contents in subjects, or they could decide directly, along with the directors of the colleges, on the inclusion of subjects in their programs of studies, which is now impossible because the curricula are closed and the modules are fixed in advance. Instead, what is maintained is the participatory nature of classrooms in the higher institutions. Thus, the Danish culture of discussion and dialogue in the classroom remains alive.

Concerning the specific governing and participation bodies, the university also has a powerful and influential Student Council according to a professor interviewed. It is made up of students from different degrees, who also participate in the main governing body of the university.

On the other hand, some of the existing collective organizations within the university institution that have been mentioned, although not working from a political standpoint, do, however, illustrate in some way the state of participation at their university. As stated, in recent times there has been an increase in participation in terms of community, which seems to be propitiated within the subjects, based on projects, and promoted by recent regulatory reforms, especially in the field of community participation and collaboration. These new regulations have promoted a social and community opening, from both universities and schools, to their neighbourhoods and cultural contexts.

*Participation and democracy in schools*

Next, we present a series of practices and assumptions that are followed in schools and in the Finnish, Swedish, and Danish school systems. It must be considered that these practices and assumptions, and participatory, democratic and educational culture in social, civic and citizenship competencies have been described from the perspective of the individuals who have acted as informants in each of these countries.

In Finland, the interviews with the university professor and the school teacher offer markedly divergent versions when assessing participation and the presence of a democratic environment in schools. The first interview shows that, despite the efforts of higher education institutions to improve the democratic participation of teaching students in higher education, and despite the relative success of doing so, this does not translate to schools. According to the interviewee, teachers are reluctant to give children their confidence, and this ends up hampering students' participation. He emphasized that the Finnish school culture, despite being innovative and tending to establish a relational climate of informality in schools, limits the participation of children. This culture, based on the idea of "children's inability" to participate in certain activities, would be the barrier that prevents teaching students from making their own participatory experience permeable, that is, the participatory experience they have had in higher education. As explained, Finnish teachers have historically tended to conceive of themselves as models for students, models of perfection, to express it in some way. This idea represents a very high level of pressure for teachers on the one hand, and on the other, it tends to generate the vision that students must place themselves in a position of imitation of the model. This reproductive position does not contribute to generating a construction of their own, situated and deliberated from the model of citizenship by students, but rather, limits them to the correct application of "rules of the good citizen". Finally, he also argues that the type of model that prevails in the imaginary of teachers corresponds to a model of citizenship from hundreds of years ago rather than to the current political and social model in Finland. He continues to argue that the national curriculum is so open that it requires a high degree of interpretation and application, and this is, according to the interviewee, very positive, because it serves as an inspiration for schools and cities to develop their version—more concrete and contextualized—of this model.

The design of mechanisms of participation occurs in a very autonomous way in each school, similar to the design of the curriculum. The city, the university and the school itself are responsible for establishing the guidelines of operation based on a very basic design established by the national curriculum. For instance, there is the School Board, but this body is no longer mandatory by law, so many schools no longer incorporate it.

The teacher points out that there is a participatory body encompassing the whole centre that is similar to what the School Board would be. It meets monthly and is comprised of representatives of all stakeholders. Participants include parents, the director of the centre, members of the team of teachers, two practicum students, one or two members of the university (at the request of the university) and students from the upper levels of secondary education (16 to 18 years old), who are elected each year. The basic functions of this body are to evaluate, support and develop the educational task of the centre. It must also approve the curriculum—after having drafted the model—and decide on timetables and vacations, the rules of the school and the rules of the participatory body of students. This body does not have the power to choose the director of the centre, who is elected only with the votes of the whole team of teachers, for periods of six years. It neither decides on funding issues nor has responsibility for managing the money that, in this case, comes from the university (since they are part of the network of practice schools linked to the university). Economic management is handled by the directive team of the school, which twice a semester presents the statement of accounts, budgetary proposals and expenses to the group of teachers (however, it seems this is not presented to the governing body of the school).

The task of economic management carried out by the directive team must necessarily guarantee these services and benefits: that the educational needs of all students as well as special educational needs be met, and that all students have a free lunch. Once these needs are covered, the rest of the available money is managed according to the school project, necessities, etc. It is significant that, as an aspect of initial teacher training, student trainees participating in this body are called twice a semester to give their opinions on the operation of the practicum in the school. We also point out, as an aspect that could be negative for participation, the fact that parents and students do not seem to have information or decision-making capacity regarding the funding and intended use of the school budget.

The team of teachers meets weekly to discuss pedagogical topics, school rules and curriculum. The interviewee FP1 calls them *teacher meetings*. Similarly, she uses the term *student meetings* to describe the participatory student body. This body is made up of one student from each class, from the lowest to the highest courses, who is elected in their class for a triennial period. A teacher is also present, who ensures the proper functioning of the body. Meetings are held weekly to discuss the needs of students and to make demands in this regard. Some examples of topics that can be addressed in these meetings are changes in school regulations, the need for a new playground area, and so on. It is the task of each member of this body to transmit the discussions and agreements reached to their respective classes.

Finally, we discuss the participation of parents in schools in Finland. Apart from parent representatives in the main governing body of the school (School Board), when it exists, there are other forms of family participation. One of these is the meetings that teachers organize every semester with the class parents. Once a year, students also attend these meetings to comment on their performance. Moreover, the individual communication (parents / tutors) is very fluent and open. The teacher emphasizes, however, that at times communication between teachers and parents is infrequent, due to the large number of students she teaches (150, in the case of the teacher interviewed). Nevertheless, the interviewee believes that this fact does not cause mistrust on the part of parents, who, she says, let her do her job. On the contrary, it seems that Finnish parents have confidence in the professionalism and excellent work of teachers. In opposition to this idea and to the idea that the school is already very open to families, this teacher mentioned that the new national curriculum specifically emphasizes the need for teachers to encourage greater presence of parents in schools in order for them to have a better idea of what teachers are doing. This, according to her, is unnecessary precisely because, in her view, the school is already very open to families.

In the case of Sweden, to improve the skills of democratic participation and to promote equal opportunities in school, much importance is given to the fact that school organization is well structured, so that all agents clearly know their responsibilities. In this connection, the professor interviewed mentioned that the educational or participatory methodology in itself is not as important as the capacity of the organizational structure to adapt to the context, to grant equal opportunities and responsibilities to the agents of the school community. With regard to student participation, she believes that in Sweden there is concern for ensuring that students participate in their schools. It is her opinion that this participation has been increasing; however, this has sometimes been accompanied by the problem that the degree of self-assurance of students to participate is greater than their knowledge. She links this to the "commodification" of educational institutions, which considers the student as a client and, therefore, as a person whose attitude is to demand a service that is tailor-made for them.

In Sweden, there is a strong culture of parental participation in school, and the flow of information from schools to families is fluid, with schools being quite willing to have families participate. In fact, she states that, in her view, the influence of parents is too great, to the extent that this is currently a topic of public debate.

In general, despite these issues, the Swedish school is sensitive to the issue of democracy and often speaks of the democratic foundation of the school, and of values and virtues as a "way of being" in a democratic context. In general, as the interviewee says, values are a strong point of the educational system and are addressed in classrooms, though often too superficially, as facts or concepts that are taken as a given instead of as concepts that require appropriate analysis and contextualization.

In the case of Denmark, student participation in school is practiced through an exclusive participatory body—the student councils that exist in all schools. The competencies of these student councils have more to do with the organization of the school than with pedagogy or substantive issues in the educational system, such as timetables or the subjects that are taught. However, in organizational matters, such as infrastructure, playground or school activities, which go beyond the classes themselves, students have the capacity to talk with the school, both to make proposals and to analyze these issues. In addition to this, one teacher explained that some schools hold classroom councils that take place on a weekly basis with all of the students in a class. These sessions last 45 minutes and deal with issues such as interpersonal relationships in class or topics that students want to address or decide on. On some occasions, a vote is held to decide on everyday classroom issues, always with the presence of the teacher, unless the students themselves ask to be alone.

Regarding classroom dynamics in early childhood education and primary schools, this teacher affirms that the dialogical nature of the learning methodology in higher education institutions is maintained in primary and early childhood education institutions. In his opinion, this methodology is part of a very profound cultural trait, engrained in Danish schools since the Second World War.

Furthermore, the question of parents' participation in school is a topic that is worked on during higher education and that is important in the Danish school tradition, which attaches great importance to the fact that families must have stable and democratic structures of participation in schools. Danish parents have a national association that is influential in the design of regulations, and in addition, school legislation stipulates that everything that happens at school must be done in cooperation with families. To this end, there is a Council of Parents, which is quite influential in school decisions. One of the teachers interviewed gave the example of timetables, which were recently changed by the director of his school at the petition of the Council of Parents.

## Conclusions and recommendations

By way of conclusion, a synthesis of the issues addressed in this article is presented, as well as some "recommendations" exemplified as good practices that, from our point of view, can provide ideas for improving teacher training in the area of social and citizenship competencies.

In the curricular aspect, with regard to study paths and qualifications, none of the educational models studied have a specific itinerary of subjects, number of credits, or specific training geared towards becoming a teacher of subjects related to civic education, citizenship, etc. Indeed, there are trajectories to become a teacher in the area of social sciences, but this area includes much more content than that which concerns us here.

With regard to the curricular perspectives focused on our subject of study, we can state that an exclusively transversal perspective and a mixed perspective (transversal and subject oriented) coexist. The second perspective is more favourable when the subjects or modules where content on democracy and citizenship must be included are already overloaded by other content or have little classroom time. In these cases, content on citizenship is included, but cannot be dealt with in depth.

Some of the individuals interviewed positively assess the fact that the content and didactic material of subjects addressing citizenship, human rights and civics, etc. are developed jointly with organizations engaged in the defence of human rights. This leads us to recommend that the individuals and educational institutions responsible for generating the basic school curriculum and materials do so in conjunction with institutions dedicated to the defence and analysis of democratic values and human rights, and with research centres and institutes working in related fields.

Regarding methodology, it has been seen that the dialogical perspective and group work is one of the strengths in all three models of basic and higher education. The dialogical commitment is justified in different ways: to enhance relational work, empathy and mutual recognition, to develop the discursive and communicative capacity of students and to support the research perspective, which is one of the strong points of the three educational models we analyzed. Nevertheless, it has also been detected that dialogism alone is insufficient if the skills related to the analysis of contents are not worked on and if there is no prior in-depth knowledge of the contents. In this direction, then, our recommendation would be for secondary education to guarantee a strong foundation of social and citizenship competencies so that higher education may go into greater depth in the research perspective and the development of capacities to analyze these contents.

The treatment of otherness in schools is quite similar to that of Catalan schools. The compensatory perspective is identical. In addition, we have not detected a special sensitivity to encourage the participation of immigrant families in school, nor to promote content and curricular materials that recognize the diversity of cultures in the country.

As for the treatment of socioeconomic problems with families, we can highlight the local and decentralized management of social protection in Finland and Denmark. It is possible that this decentralized management will be beneficial to address problems if it generates greater flexibility of the protection system in terms of adapting to the particular needs of each local context. It remains to be seen if more decentralized models, like the Finnish one, are effective, and reflect on whether the Catalan model is too centralized and if this may be a source of problems.

Considering student participation in higher education institutions, we have seen that all three countries have a more significant participatory culture than Catalonia. In particular, we could highlight existence of strong student councils legitimized by the university and social community, which have a real voice and act significantly not only within the university institution, but also in the social plan, legislation and public opinion. However, there have also been certain participatory method-ologies of student organizations that are built on pressures and threats against individuals by groups with great media influence. With this in mind, we recommend the need for participatory bodies and spaces for student participation that are both strong and legitimized, as well as the construction of cultures of dialogue and responsible communica-tion between the different agents of the educational institutions so that extremes are not reached, like those mentioned above. Promoting deci-sions that are consensual and the result of deliberations among equals by all involved parties is one of the basic objectives of democratic par-ticipation. The techniques of ridicule, public cruelty or unilateralism of demands are often the result of, on the one hand, the lack of a dialogi-cal and democratic culture of the institution itself and, in consequence, of its members, and on the other, the abuse of power in the spheres with the most decision-making power manifested in vetoing or limiting the voice of a majority or a specific group. Therefore, we recommend training in democratic participation not only for students, but also for teachers and those responsible for determining participation policies in universities, so that all stakeholders can contribute together to generate the necessary democratic *ethos*, that is, a climate of trust that allows respectful dialogue to be established.

Further, we would like to stress the need for participation to be gen-uine and meaningful. Throughout the interviews, we detected a problem that also exists in the Catalan educational institutions: there are regula-tions and participation bodies that do not have any type of negotiation or decision-making capacity, and which are used to consult or gather opinions, to inform the educational community or even to vote, but that do not generate decisions that are carried out in a strict sense or that can produce significant changes in the institutions.

Regarding student participation in relation to decisions concerning educational content, we have observed that one of the elements that hinders participatory and decision-making capacity is the fact that the curriculum is too closed, that subjects and programming are too stipu-lated, and timetables and training spaces too restricted. We consider that it would be advisable to open up the curricula, both in terms of content and timetable, in order to allow the entry of continuous and non-formal training in university education. The seminars and workshops, and the inclusion of other types of activities and contents in the curriculum, whether on the initiative of students, teachers, primary schools or social organizations, is an important point to keep in mind if we believe that a significant part of civic and citizenship education occurs through self-training and training within the framework of the social group that we have around us.

With regard to community ties between universities and schools and their social environments, we have seen that in Denmark and Finland there is renewed interest in opening universities and schools outward. The case of Denmark illustrates the fact that sometimes a regulation that governs this aspect in primary school can help develop the network of community relations of schools. In the case of Catalonia, we know that much remains to be done in this area. Educational regulations, in general, have always called for the educational community to be considered something that goes far beyond the school community, yet this has not met with much success in the effort to articulate a real network of communication between social agents. General regulations promote and prescribe actions and dynamics, as we know, but this is worthless in the absence of decrees that regulate and finance specific actions, or convene at the local and regional level, or in any other way articulate actions throughout the territory. In short, we can offer a negative recommendation and state that it is not advisable to wait for the dynamics of interaction between institutions, often acquired by tradition and maintained by inertia, to change without the contribution of the necessary revitalization of administrations with a desire for transformation of these dynamics.

In connection with the training of competent teachers to stimulate participation and to project participatory culture to children, we have found that, in general, the training and opportunities of teaching students to participate during their higher education is not sufficient to achieve a transfer of these abilities to children in school. This may be due to two basic ideas: one is the idea that girls and boys are not capable of carrying out tasks autonomously or of understanding certain participatory situations, while the other set of ideas are largely identity-related. Considering the analysis of the interviews that were conducted, it is possible that a great many teachers think of themselves as teachers in a traditional sense, or more explicitly, as the sole sources of knowledge, which is unilaterally imparted by them. In consequence, they represent models of attitude, behaviour and knowledge that situate the position of the child at the antipodes of this relationship, that is, as a passive subject with little capacity to act or decide on their own. In this connection, we feel that reflective work on the part of teaching students would be advisable. This would enable them to come to know their own beliefs about educational relationships, to understand the models they have had in their own experiences as students and to and transform their expectations as teachers.

In terms of participation of children in the participatory bodies of schools, we do not see a substantial difference with respect to the Catalan and Spanish models. In general, the student councils would be equivalent to our delegate councils, with a very similar system of consultation and information within a fully representative model of democracy. With reference to school boards, in all countries (perhaps with less intensity in Denmark) we also see a representative model in which children, in general, have little to say and much less to decide. However, we can draw some conclusions from the interview with the Swedish informant S1: according to the interviewee, the methodology to promote the participation of children and the entire school community in Sweden involves having a highly organized school structure, in which each agent is given a participatory role in the school. In some way, this idea is found among the foundations of the model of distributed leadership, according to which the organizational model must have the structural capacity to distribute responsibilities among community agents, so that the power of action and decision is distributed horizontally throughout the school. In view of this, we recommend that, as far as possible, responsibilities be distributed among all the agents of the centres, in order to give everyone the opportunity to participate in a genuine and decisive way in the operation of the school.

Another thing is the participation of children in the classroom. As we have seen, in all three countries an important dialogical culture was detected in classrooms as well as a methodological perspective that is very committed to research, not only in the classrooms of the youngest students but also in university classrooms. We can affirm that this practice is far from what has occurred in Catalan classrooms and continues at present. However, we firmly believe that the research perspective is gaining ground in practice and is increasingly legitimized by teachers in Catalonia. In spite of the great dialogism of Nordic classrooms, we have also seen that decisions, ultimately, are usually made by the adult group, both in and out of the classroom. This leads us to think that the more educationally advanced countries also face challenges in enhancing genuine participation of children.

# Epilogue

Democracy and participation in education is, as Kincheloe points out (2008), a fundamental issue that, no matter how much it is studied this will never be enough. This is because the full democratization of society and the institutions that make it up—the educational ones too—is an ideal that we must fight constantly and tirelessly to move towards and approach. This approach, as Easton says (2005) is not linear: the vicissitudes of the political system of the "advanced" countries, the struggle in the economic system, the tensions produced in the social system, and above all the way in which all these conflicts are resolved, can make it just as likely for us to move forward as backward. The permanent reflection on the state of democracy in our world, the attentive gaze on social pressures to make it either progress or move backwards, and the continuous study of this issue is a good antidote against any attempt at de-democratization and the curtailing of rights.

Democracy and participation in education, as has been shown in the different chapters that make up this publication, is a subject of paramount importance because the context does not favour it. The pressure to comply with the curriculum, the restricting of a large part of the educational methodologies, the hyper-institutionalization of the educational process, academicism and the acceleration of all of these aspects, condemns both democracy and participation to a slow and difficult path. This difficulty is exacerbated in the stage of secondary education because democracy and participation are often reduced to the minimum expression and practiced only in a formal (and quite unnatural) way in institutional spaces (Fernández, 2014). In any case, and appealing to the theses of authors such as Escudero Muñoz (2009) among others, if you want to build citizenship in the broadest and most profound sense of the term, it is absolutely necessary to do everything and more so that democracy, as Dewey (1916) said, shall be "a mode of associated living, of conjoint complicated experience" that leaves a significant mark on the minds and behaviour of people.

Despite these difficulties, however, and as noted in this publication, another democracy is possible. A democracy that goes beyond rhetoric, which fights half-truths and lies, gives voice to people and collectives, which questions hegemony and obstructionist dynamics. We must fight to implement a "real", "radical" democracy (as M. Fielding calls it), more effective and committed both politically and socially.

One of the important assets of this publication is that it makes clear that in certain situations and contexts, the democracy that we have just called for is a tangible and objectivable reality. This opens a door to hope because it shows that utopia can become a reality.

Whether this utopia is real depends on many factors and, as shown in this publication, requires a critical and propositive analysis of reality, the capacity to offer alternatives, the ability to speak and listen to each other, the ambitious yet adaptable perspective of the objectives we want to achieve, the capacity to know how to say "no" to any form of discrimination, the unwavering determination to stop the mechanisms that generate inequality, the empowerment of individuals and collectives, the resolute struggle for emancipation, the distribution of power, horizontal relationships, the integration of all people (especially those that are easily left out and who we often do not even realize are not there), the promotion of values including solidarity, cooperation and mutual assistance, among many other aspects. The enhancement of democracy in education is also achieved by being flexible so that heterodox educational structures with a social perspective can arise in the system, thus reducing the level of bureaucratization of the centres, etc.

With the idea of contributing to enlarge this utopia, this dream, this social and political necessity, we want to close this publication by presenting a series of measures in the form of a decalogue that, with humility and discretion, we are convinced will make this easier. These are measures, as the reader will appreciate, that are theoretical and practical, generic and specific and that, in any case, are sufficiently transversal to be applied in different national contexts and in all stages of the educational system. With this contribution, our desire is simply to modestly contribute to making this path easier.

*Decalogue to improve democratic participation in education*

1.  It is important that schools that want to experience a democratic experience first confront the controversy of the term itself, then opt for a concrete and, above all, workable definition. Democracy, although we all will agree to define it etymologically as the government of the people, in wanting to objectify it we will find several possibilities that will shape, and very much so, its practical orientation.

2.  It is important that the definition the centres end up adopting is the most shared among the educational community in order to avoid misunderstandings, disappointments and frustrations. To assume that everyone understands democratic practice as the same thing is a mistake that too often occurs and yet we ignore.

3.  It is true that democracy in general and democratic culture in particular is learned by exercising it and living it, but it is no less true that theoretical reflection—whether it is from history, sociology, political science or law—helps us to have an intellectual background that undoubtedly questions practice. We consider it beneficial for children to have a clear referential framework of how the concept that concerns us here has been constructed up to the present moment; to know the political, economic and social forces that have fostered it or slowed it; how democratic processes and participation have been achieved or annihilated; and for them to be aware of the social, economic, political and educational consequences of democratic gains and reversals when they occur, etc.

4.  Democracy in any educational centre pivots on the structuring of governing bodies, decision-making and debate on collective or common interest aspects in which several people participate. In relation to what has been said in points 1 and 2 of this decalogue, the community will have to decide who attends these bodies, how and when they are elected and, in another order of things, it will be necessary to determine whether decisions are made by deliberation or by voting. All of this helps us to put democracy in practice and to know what kind of democracy we are talking about. Apart from that, we urge centres to not only discuss the organization of the government (quite ironclad incidentally, as established in the legislation) but also broaden the democratic facet by integrating

aspects related to *habitance* and *otherness*. As pointed out by the DEMOSKOLE research group (Feu, J., Prieto-Flores, O., 2013), we believe that democracy is strengthened and expanded to the extent that as many actions as possible are engaged in so that the educational community can truly participate and feel comfortable in the centre (habitance), and because diversity in its maximum expression (otherness) is recognized, visualized and positivized.

5.  The materialization of democratic practice in primary and secondary schools also involves the conscious and intense experience of certain values, the application of educational methodologies in the classroom and the teaching of a democratic curriculum. The embodiment of values such as freedom, responsibility, justice, respect, temperance, knowing how to listen and knowing how to speak, etc. is central to the task that we address here. Active and cooperative methodologies, those that encourage creativity and critical thinking are also helpful, as well as the imparting of non-dogmatic scientific knowledge that provides information and forms the backbone of analytical processes for all members of the educational community, and particularly among students.

6.  We believe that the creation of a sense of belonging and of community is essential for the establishment of a fully democratic system. If some members of the educational community do not feel part of..., if they do not establish ties—even minimal ones—what is the point of asking people to participate? We consider that this question, to which the current educational discourse has devoted much attention—although in most cases this is pure rhetoric—is essential and complex to address.

7.  For the educational community to participate, it is not enough to feel part of a collective, not even if this feels very comfortable. If we want quality and influential participation, the centre must be transparent and make sure that everyone, especially those who participate in decision-making bodies, is well informed far enough in advance to be able to express their opinion, assess, propose and decide reasonably and with arguments.

8.  Given the functioning, results and involvement of the various strata of the educational community (especially students and families) in formal participatory bodies (established by the educational

administration) and, on the other hand, considering the new forms of participation, association and structuring of the collective interests of young people, we recommend that centres create new bodies for participation and decision-making. We are talking about bodies tailored to each centre, suited to their particularities, and emanating from the debate, imagination and interest of the community. We recommend creating parallel bodies that are more flexible and open, more participatory and deliberative, and more decisive.

9. Considering the broad consensus in demanding democratization of schools and the enormous difficulties that exist in implementing this, it is necessary for each centre to identify, to the extent of its possibilities, the obstructive factors. We are of the opinion that the structural brakes hampering the democratizing process of the educational system are basically two: the prevailing grammar of schooling (Tyack and Cuban, 1995, 2001) and the hegemonic school culture (Viñao, 2002). In consequence, we believe that it is necessary to radically change the structures, rules, practices, rituals, interactions, organization of work, organization of time and space, etc. that give meaning to the education system in general and to the school in particular. Perhaps this recommendation seems like an unattainable utopia. We, however, consider that—surely not without great difficulty—it is feasible, because apart from the cases exemplified in this publication we have knowledge of free and reformed schools that have done so or are in the process of doing so. Rethinking the grammar of schooling and the culture of the centre entails, in essence, conceiving and distributing power in a different way than we are accustomed to.

10. Finally, it is unlikely that we will have democratic schools unless effective and efficient work is done during initial training. That is why it is so necessary and urgent to focus on the training of teachers and secondary school professionals as well as university faculty. Theoretical training is required that invites contextualized reflection, training that provides stimulating and feasible ideas, strategies and practices that contribute to democratizing work in the classroom and at the centre.

# Bibliography

Adderley, R.J., Hope, M. A, Hughes, G.C., Jones, L., Messiou, K. & Shaw, P.A. (2015). Exploring inclusive practices in primary schools: focusing on children's voices, *European Journal of Special Needs Education*, *30*(1), pp. 106–121.

Agulló, M. V. (2014). La democracia republicana: problemas y límites de un modelo alternativo a la democracia liberal. *Revista Española de Investigaciones Sociológicas*, 146, 217–238.

Ainscow, M. & Messiou, K. (2018). Engaging with the views of students to promote inclusion in education, *Journal of Educational Change, 19*(1), 1–17.

Ainscow, M. (2014). "From Special Education to Effective Schools for All." In *The Sage Handbook of Special Education*. 2nd revised ed., edited by L. Florian, pp. 171–185. London: Sage.

Ainscow, M.; Booth, T.; Dyson, A. (2006). *Improving schools, developing inclusion*. London, Routledge.

Ainscow, M., T. Booth and A. Dyson (2004). Understanding and developing inclusive practices in schools: a collaborative action research network. *International Journal of Inclusive Education*, *8*(2), pp. 125–139.

Ainscow, M. (1999). *Understanding the Development of Inclusive Schools*. London: Falmer Press.

Alegre, M.A., Rambla, X. & Valiente, O. (2009). *L'elecció de centre escolar a Catalunya. Elements per a un debat* [School Choice in Catalonia. Elements for a Debate]. Barcelona: Fundació Jaume Bofill, Col. Finestra Oberta 53.

Álvarez, E. (2004). Participación en la escuela: visión crítica y propuestas para su mejora. *Aula Abierta*, 83, pp. 53–76.

Anderson, G. L. & Herr, K. (1994). The micro politics of student voices: Moving from diversity of bodies to diversity of voices in schools. In Marshall, C. (Ed.) *The New Politics of Race and Gender*. London: RoutledgeFalmer.

Apple, M.W. (2013). *Can Education Change Society?* New York: Routledge.

Apple, M.W. and Beane, J.A. (2007). *Democratic Schools: Lessons in Powerful Education.* Portsmouth, NH: Heinemann.

Appleton, P.L. & Minchom, P.E. (1991). Models of parent partnership and child development centres, *Child: Care, Health and Development,* 17, 27–38.

Árnason, Vilhjálmur, Nordal, S. & Ásgteirsdóttir, K. (2010b). The main conclusion of the working group on ethics. Reykjavík: Rannsóknarnefnd Alþingis. <https://www.rna.is/media/skjol/WorkingGroupOnEthics_Summary.pdf>.

Árnason, Vilhjálmur, Nordal, S., Ástgeirsdóttir, K. (2010a). *Siðferði og starfshættir í tengslum við fall íslensku bankanna 2008.* Reykjavík: Rannsóknarnefnd Alþingis. <http://www.rna.is/eldri-nefndir/addragandi-og-orsakir-falls-islensku-bankanna-2008/skyrsla-nefndarinnar/english/>.

Arnstein, S. (1969) 'A ladder of citizenship participation in the USA' *Journal of the American Institute of Planners* 35 (4), pp. 216–224

Associació de Mestres Rosa Sensat. (2008). *Document de l'AM Rosa Sensat sobre les bases per a la Llei d'Educació de Catalunya.* Retrieved on October 25, 2015 from: <http://rosasensat.org/arxius/documents/Bases_LEC_Rosa_Sensat.pdf>.

Bacqué, H.; Biewemer (2016). *El empoderamiento.* Barcelona, Gedisa.

Ball, S.J., (2017). *Foucault as educator.* Cham, Springer.

Ball, S.J., Junemann, C., Santori, D. (2017). *Edu.net: Globalisation and education policy mobility.* London, Routledge.

Ball, S.J., (2013). *Foucault, Power and Education.* London: Routledge.

Ball, S.J., Maguire, M. & Braun, A. (2012). *How schools do policy: Policy enactments in secondary schools.* Abingdon: Routledge.

Ball, S.J., (2007). *Education plc: Understanding Private Sector Participation in Public Sector Education.* Abingdon: Routledge.

Ball, S.J., (2003). The Teacher's Soul and the Terrors of Performativity. *Journal of Education Policy, 18*(2), 215–228.

Ball, S.J., and Junemann, C. (2003). *Networks, New Governance and Education.* Bristol: The Policy Press/University of Bristol.

Ball, S.J. (1995). "Intellectuals or technicians? The urgent role of theory in educational studies", *British Journal of Educational Studies* 43(3), pp. 255–271.

Barber, B. (1987) *Strong Democracy*. Berkeley, University of California Press.

Barbosa, M. (2000). Educar per a una ciutadania democràtica a les escoles: una discussió de models. *Temps d'Educació*, 24, pp. 359–373.

Barton, L. (1997) Inclusive education: Romantic, subversive or realistic? *International Journal of Inclusive Education*, 1, 3, pp. 231–242.

Bauman, Z. (2013). *¿Does the Richness of the Few Benefit Us All?*. Polity: Cambridge. Barry, A.; Osborne, T.; Rose, N. (Eds.) *Foucault and political reason*. The university of Chicago press: Chicago.

Beneyto, M.; Collet, J. (2017). Análisis de la actual formación docente en competencias TIC. Profesorado, revista de currículum i formación del profesorado (forthcoming).

Benito, R. Alegre, M.A.; González, I. (2014). School educational project as a criterion of school choice: discourses and practices in the city of Barcelona, *Journal of Education Policy* 29 (3), pp. 397–420.

Bensaïd, D. (2011). Permanent Scandal. In *Democracy in what state?* New York: Columbia University Press.

Bernays, E. L. (1928). *Propaganda*, New York: Horace liveright.

Bernburg, Jón Gunnar. (2016). *Economic crisis and mass protest: The pots and pans revolution in Iceland*. Burlington: Ashgate.

Bernstein, B. (1998). *Pedagogía, control simbólico e identidad*. Madrid, Morata.

Bernstein, R. (2010). *Filosofia y Democracia: John Dewey*. Barcelona: Herder.

Bertran, M. (2005). *Relacions entre famílies immigrades i institucions educatives en l'etapa de zero a sis anys*. Barcelona: Fundació Jaume Bofill.

Bessette, J. M. (1980). Deliberative Democracy: The Majority Principle in Republican Government. In *How Democratic Is the Constitution*, ed. R. Goldwin and W. Shambra. Washington, D.C.: AEI Press.

Bhabha, H. (2014). The Right to Narrate. *Harvard Design Magazine, 38*. Retrieved on March 3, 2016 from <http://www.harvarddesignmagazine.org/issues/38/the-right-to-narrate>.

Biesta, G.; R. Lawy and N. Kelly (2009). Understanding young people's citizenship learning in everyday life: The role of contexts, relationships and dispositions. *Education, Citizenship and Social Justice*, 4(1), pp. 5–24.

Biesta, Gert (2015). What is Education For? On Good Education, Teacher Judgement, and Educational Professionalism. *European Journal of Education*, 50 (1), 76–87.

Biesta, Gert, Lawy, Robert, & Kelly, Narcie (2009). Understanding young people's citizenship learning in everyday life: The role of contexts, relationships and dispositions. *Education, Citizenship and Social Justice*, 4(1), p. 5–24.

Birch, S. (2012). Co-op schools: Is the future of education co-operation? *The Guardian,* July 26; <https://www.theguardian.com/social-enterprise-network/2012/jul/26/co-op-schools-future-education>. Downloaded 22/01/2018.

Birrell, Ian. (2015) Iceland has jailed 26 bankers, why won't we? *Independent*, November 15, 2015. <http://www.independent.co.uk/voices/iceland-has-jailed-26-bankers-why-wont-we-a6735411.html>.

Blackburn, R. (1993) 'Edward Thompson and the New Left', *New Left Review* No 201, September / October, pp. 3–9.

Blanqui, A. (2006). Lettre à Maillard (6 juin 1852). In *Maintenant, il faut des armes*. París: La Fabrique.

Blattberg, C. (2003). Patriotic, Not Deliberative, Democracy. *Critical Review of International Social and Political Philosophy*, 6(1), pp. 155–174.

Bloom, A. (1952) 'Learning Through Living', *In:* M. Alderton Pink (ed) *Moral Foundations of Citizenship* London, London University Press, pp. 135–143.

Bobbio, N. (1986). *El futuro de la democracia*. Mexico: Fondo de Cultura Económica.

Bonal, X. (dir.) (2013). *Municipis contra la segregació escolar*. Barcelona, Fundació Jaume Bofill.

Bonal, X. (2000). Interests Groups and the State in Contemporary Spanish Education Policy. *Journal of Education Policy*, *15*(2), 201–216.

Booth, T., and M. Ainscow. 2002. Index for Inclusion. 2nd ed. Bristol: Centre for Studies on Inclusive Education.

Bourdieu, P. (1992). *An invitation to reflexive sociology.* Chicago, UCP.

Bouton, T. (2007). *Taming Democracy. "The People," the Founders, and the Troubled Ending of the American Revolution,* Oxford, New York: Oxford University Press.

Bowe, R., Ball, S., & Gold, A. (1992). *Reforming Education and Changing Schools.* London: Routledge.

Brady, H. E.; S. Verba & K. Lehman (1995). "Beyond SES: A Resource Model of Political Participation". *The American Political Science Review,* 89 (2), pp. 271–294.

Brown, W. (2011). We Are All Democrats Now. In *Democracy in what state?* New York: Columbia University Press.

Bruner, Jerome. (1960). *Process of education.* Cambridge, MA: Harvard University Press.

Burke, C. (2008) 'Play in focus': children's visual voice in participative research. In Thomson, P. (Ed.) *Doing Visual Research with Children and Young People.* London: Routledge.

Carbonell, F. (2000). *Educació i immigració: els reptes educatius de la diversitat cultural i l'exclusió social.* Barcelona: Mediterrània.

Carnoy, M. (2006). Rethinking the Comparative and the International. *Comparative Education Review,* 50(4), 551–570.

Carter, P.L. (2012). *Stubborn roots. Race, Culture and Inequality in U.S. and in South African Schools.* New York: Oxford University Press.

Castells, M. (1997). *The Power of Identity: The Information Age: Economy, Society and Culture. Vol. II.* Oxford: Blackwell.

Checkoway, Barry (2011). What is youth participation? *Children and Youth Services Review,* 33(2), pp. 340–345.

Christensen, P. and James, A. (2001) Introduction: Researching children and childhood: cultures of communication. In Christensen, P. and James, A. (Eds) *Research with Children: Perspectives and Practices.* London: RoutledgeFalmer.

Clarke, M. (2018). Democracy and education: In spite of it all in Special edition eds Matthew Clark, Linda Hammersley-Smith, and John Schostak, *Power & Education.*

Clarke, M.; Phelan, A.M. (2015). "The power of negative thinking in and for teacher education" *Power and education* 7 (3), pp. 257–271.

Collet, J. (2011). "Educación: ¿arte, burocracia o artesanía? Por una nueva metáfora de la teoría y la práctica educativa" *Pedagogia i treball social* 1, pp. 27–50.

Collet, J. (2017). "I do not like what I am becoming but...": transforming the identity of head teachers in Catalonia. *Journal of Education Policy* 32 (2), 141–158.

Collet, J.; Besalú, X.; Feu, J.; Tort, A. (2014) "Escuelas, familias y resultados académicos. Un nuevo modelo de anàlisis de las relaciones entre docentes y progenitores para el éxito académico de todo el alumnado" *Profesorado. Revista de currículum y formación de profesorado* 18 (2), 7–33.

Collet, J.; Tort, A. (2011). Famílies, escoles i èxit escolar. Barcelona, Fundació Jaume Bofill.

Collet, J.; Tort, A. (2015). "What do famílies of the 'professional and managerial class' educate their children for?" *British Journal of Sociology of Education* 36 (2), 234–249.

Collet, J.; Tort, A. (coords.) (2014). Millors vincles, millors resultats? Barcelona, Fudació Jaume Bofill.

Collet, J.; Tort, A. (coords.) (2016). *La gobernanza escolar democrática*. Madrid: Morata.

Connell, Raewyn (2009). Good teachers on dangerous ground: towards a new view of teacher quality and professionalism, *Critical Studies in Education*, 50(3), 213–229.

Consejo Escolar del Estado (2014). *La participación de las familias en la educación escolar*. Madrid: Ministerio de Educación, Cultura y Deporte.

Cook-Sather, A. (2006) Sound, Presence, and Power: "Student Voice" in Educational Research and Reform, *Curriculum Inquiry*, 36(4), 359–390.

Cook-Sather, A. (2002). Authorizing Students' Perspectives: Toward Trust, Dialogue, and Change in Education. *Educational Researcher* 31 (4), 3–14.

Crozier, G. (1999). "Parental involvement: who wants it?" *International Studies in Sociology of Education,* 9 (3), 219–238.

Crozier, G.; Davies, J. (2007). "Hard to reach parents or hard to reach schools? A discussion of home–school relations, with particular reference to Bangladeshi and Pakistani parents" *British education-al research journal* 33(3), 295–313.

Cunningham, C.; Davis, H. (1985). *Working with Parents: Frameworks for Collaboration*. Buckingham: Open University Press.

Cunninghame, C. Aslam, P. F. Kirby, J. Oldham, and S. Newton (1999). *Report on the Whitley Abbey Community School Project.* Smethwick: Save the Children.

Dale, N. (1996). *Working with Families of Children with Special Needs.* London; Routledge.

Dave Grace and Associates (2014). Measuring the Size and Scope of the Cooperative Economy: Results of the 2014 Global Census on Co-operatives, April, For the United Nation's Secretariat. Online at: <https://www.un.org/esa/socdev/documents/2014/coopsegm/grace.pdf> Downloaded 22/01/2016.

Davidge, G. (2017). *Rethinking Education through Critical psychology. Cooperative schools, social justice and voice*, London and New York: Routledge.

Davidge, G., Facer, K., & Schostak, J. F. (2015). Co-operatives, democracy and education: a critical reflection. In Tom Woodin (Ed), *Co-operation, Learning and Co-operative values Contemporary Issues in Education*. Routledge.

Davies, L. (2000) Researching democratic understanding in primary school. *Research in Education*, 61, pp. 39–48.

Davis, H.; Meltzer, L. (2007). *Working with parents in partnership.* London, department for education and Skills.

Day, Christopher; Gu Qing (2013). *Resilient Teachers, Resilient schools: Building and sustaining quality in testing times*. London, Routledge.

De Lissovoy Noah (2013). Inventing democracy: Teaching and togetherness. In A. A. Abdi & P. R. Carr (Eds.) *Educating for democratic consciousness: Counterhegemonic possibilities*. Lang, New York, NY, 219–231.

Delgado, M. ed. (2003). *Inmigración y cultura. Ciudad e inmigración II*. Barcelona: Centre de Cultura Contemporània de Barcelona.

Denzin, N. (2006). *Sociological Methods: A Sourcebook*. New Brunswick, NJ: Transaction Publishers.

Departament d'Ensenyament (2015). *Dades d'Ensenyament. Alumnat, professorat, centres i grups. Curs 2012–2013*. Barcelona: General-itat de Catalunya. Retrieved on March 24ᵗʰ from: <http://ensen-yament.gencat.cat/ca/departament/estadistiques/>.

Derrington, C. and Kendall, S. (2003) The experiences and perceptions of Gypsy Traveller pupils in English secondary schools. In Shevlin, M. and Rose, R. (Eds) *Encouraging Voices: Respecting the Insights of Young People Who Have Been Marginalised*. Dublin: National Disability Authority.

Dewey, J. (1978). *The Challenge of Democracy to Education. The Later Works Vol. 11*. Carbondale: Southern Illinois University Press.

Dewey, J. (1938). *Experience and Education*, New York, Collier.

Dewey, J. (1927). *The Public and its Problems*, Athens: Swallow Press, Ohio University Press.

Dewey, J. (1922). "Review of Public Opinion, by Walter Lippmann", in *The Middle Works, 1899–1924*, vol. 13: 1921–1922, ed. Jo Ann Boydston. Carbondale and Edwardsville: South Illinois University Press, 1983.

Dewey, J. (1915). *Democracy and Education. The Middle Works. Vol. 8*. Carbondale: Southern Illinois University Press.

Dewey, J. (1916). *Democracy and Education*. New York, The Freedom Press.

Dewey, John. (1899/1915). *The School and Society*. Chicago IL: The University of Chicago Press.

Dodds, Annelise. (2013). *Comparative public policy*. New York: Pal-grave Macmillan.

Driessen, G.; Smit, F. & Sleegers, P. (2005). "Parental involvement and educational achievement". *British educational research journal*, 31 (4), pp. 509–532.

Dubet, F. (2002). *Le déclin de l'institution*. París: Seuil.

Duca, L. (2016). Donald Trump is Gaslighting America, *Teen Vogue*, December 10; <https://www.teenvogue.com/story/donald-trump-is-gaslighting-america>. Downloaded 20/01/2018.

Dýrfjörð, Kristín, & Magnúsdóttir B. R. (2016). Privatization of the early childhood education in Iceland. *Research in Comparative and International Education, 11*(1), 80–97.

Easton, L. B. (2005). Democracy in Schools: Truly a Matter of Voice. *English Journal*, 94 (5), p. 52–56.

Edelstein, W. (2011). "Education for Democracy: reasons and strategies". *European Journal of Education*, 46(1), pp. 127–137.

Edelstein, Wolfgang. (1984). Um samfélagsfræði [On sociology]. *Morgunblaðið*, February 8.

Edelstein, Wolfgang. (1988/2013). Markmið og bygging samfélagsfræðinnar [Purpose and structure of social studies]. In Guttormsson, L. (Ed.), Sögukennsluskammdegið: Rimman um sögukennslu og samfélagsfræði 1983–1984 [The long nights of history teaching: The battle over teaching of history and social studies in 1983–1984]. Reykjavík: University of Iceland Press.

Enochsson, A. (s.d.). *ICT in Initial Teacher Training. Sweden*. Recuperat de <https://www.oecd.org/edu/ceri/45046846.pdf>.

Escudero Muñoz, J.M. (2009) «La formación del profesorado de Educación Secundaria: contenidos y aprendizajes docentes». *Revista de Educación*, 350, p. 79–103.

European Agency. (2016a). *Sweden – Teacher training – basic and specialist teacher training*. Retrieved from <https://www.european-agency.org/country-information/sweden/national-overview/teacher-training-basic-and-specialist-teacher-training>.

European Agency. (2016b). *Policy into practice examples – Sweden*. Retrieved from <https://www.european-agency.org/agency-projects/Teacher-Education-for-Inclusion/country-info/sweden/policy-into-practice-examples>.

EuropeanAgency.(2016c).*Structureandcontentofinitialteachereducation courses – Finland*. Retrieved from <https://www.europcan-agency.org/agency-projects/Teacher-Education-for-Inclusion/country-info/finland/structure-and-content-of-initial-teacher-education-courses>.

Feito, R. (2014). Trenta años de Consejos Escolares. La Participación de los Padres y e las Madres en el Control y Gestión de los Centros Sostenidos con Fondos Públicos en España. *Profesorado. Revista de Currículum y Formación del Profesorado, 18*(2), 51–67.

Feito, R. (2011). *Los retos de la participación escolar*. Madrid, Morata.

Feito, R. (2010). "Escuela y democracia". *Política y sociedad*, 47(2), 47–61.

Feito, R. (2009). "Éxito escolar para todos". *Revista Iberoamericana de Educación*, 50, 131–151.

Ferrer, F. (1913) *The Origins and Ideals of the Modern School* London, Watts.

Feu, J.; Simó, N.; Serra, C.; Canimas, J. (2016a). "Dimensiones, características e indicadores para una escuela democràtica" *Estudios pedagógicos* 42 (3).

Feu, J.; Simó, N. & Serra, C. (2016b). "Elementos clave para una gobernanza democrática de la escuela. Dimensiones e indicadores" A: Collet, J.; Tort, A. (coords.) La gobernanza escolar democrática. Madrid: Morata.

Feu, J., Prieto, O. i Simó, N. (2016). ¿Qué es una escuela verdaderamente democrática?. *Cuadernos de Pedagogía*, 465, 90–97.

Feu, J., Simó, N., Serra, C., Canimas, J. i Lázaro, L. (2015). *Democracia y educación: Una propuesta de clarificación teórica para el análisis de las prácticas democráticas en el ámbito de la educación formal*. [Internal report].

Feu, J., Simó, N., Serra, C. i Canimas, J. (2014). *Hacia una gobernanza escolar democrática y de lo común: más allá de los modelos neoliberal (Gran Bretaña) y neoconservador (España)*. Seminari internacional, Vic, 30 i 31 d'octubre de 2014.

Fielding, M. (2016). 'Why and how schools might live democracy "as an inclusive human order"' *In* S. Higgins and F. Coffield (eds) *John Dewey's Democracy and Education: A British Tribute* London, UCL IoE Press, 114–130.

Fielding, M. (2014)(a) 'Bringing Freedom to Education' – Colin Ward, Alex Bloom and the possibility of radical democratic schools *In:* C. Burke and K. Jones (eds) *Education, Childhood and Anarchism: Talking Colin Ward* Abingdon, Routledge, 86–98.

Fielding, M. (2014)(b) Radical democratic education as response to two World Wars and a contribution to world peace – the inspirational work of Alex Bloom *Forum* 56 (3), 513–528.

Fielding, M. (2012). Beyond student voice: Patterns of partnership and the demands of deep democracy. *Revista de Educación*, 359, 45–65.

Fielding, M., & Moss, P. (2011). *Radical Education and the Common School*. London: Routledge.

Fielding, M. (2011) Patterns of partnership: student voice, intergenerational learning and democratic fellowship, *In* N. Mockler and J. Sachs (eds) *Rethinking educational practice through reflexive research: Essays in honour of Susan Groundwater-Smith* Dordrecht, Springer, 61–75.

Fielding, M. (2009). Public Space and Educational Leadership: Reclaiming and Renewing Our Radical Traditions. *Educational Management Administration Leadership*; 37, 497–521.

Fielding, M., Elliott, J., Robinson, C., and Samuels, J. (2006) *Less is More? The development of a schools-within-schools approach to education on a human scale at Bishops Park College, Clacton, Essex* Final Report to Department for Education and Skills Innovation Unit.

Fielding, M. (2005) Alex Bloom: Pioneer of radical state education *Forum* 47 (2 & 3), 119–134.

Fielding, M. (Guest Editor) (2005). Reclaiming the Radical Tradition in State *Education, Forum*, 47, 2 & 3, pp. 43–232.

Fielding, M. (2004) Transformative Approaches to Student Voice: Theoretical Underpinnings, Recalcitrant Realities, *British Educational Research Journal* 30 (2), 295–311.

Fielding, M., and Bragg, S. (2003). *Students as Researchers, Making a Difference*. Cambridge: Pearson.

Fielding, M. (2001) Students as radical agents of change, *Journal of Educational Change*, 2 (2), 123–141.

Fielding, M. (1999). Radical Collegiality: Affirming Teaching as an Inclusive Professional Practice *Australian Educational Researcher* 26 (2) August, 1–34.

Flecha, R. (2015). *Successful Educational Actions for Inclusion and Social Cohesion in Europe*. Dordecht: Springer.

Flores d'Arcais, P. (2005). *El sobirà i el dissident. La democràcia considerada seriosament*. Lleida: Pagès.

Flutter, J. (2007). Teacher development and pupil voice. *Curriculum Journal*, 18(3), pp. 343–354.

Foa, R.S.; Mounk, Y. (2016). "The Danger of Deconsolidation: The Democratic Disconnect" *Journal of democracy* 27 (3), pp. 5–17.

Foucault, M. (2010). *The Government of the Self and Others: Lectures at the College de France 1982–1983*. Basingstoke: Palgrave Macmillan.

Fox, S., & K. Messiou. (2004). Manchester Inclusion Standard: Pupil Voice Toolkit. Manchester: Manchester City Council.

Fraser, N. (2012). *On justice. Lessons from Pató, Rawls and Ishiguro.* Barcelona, CCCB.

Fraser, V. (2004). Situating empirical research. In Fraser, V., Lewis, V., Ding, S., Kellett, M. and Robinson, C. (Eds) *Doing Research with Children and Young People.* London: SAGE.

Freelon, R., Bertrand, M. & Rogers, J. (2012). Overburdened & Underfunded: California Public Schools Amidst the Great Recession. *Multidisciplinary Journal of Educational Research, 2*(2), pp. 152–176.

Freiberg, H. Jerome (Ed.) (1999). *School Climate: Measuring, Improving and Sustaining Healthy Environments.* Routledge Falmer Press, Londres.

Freire, P. (2004). *Pedagogy of the oppressed.* New York: Continuum.

Galston, W. A. (1991). *Liberal Purposes. Goods, Virtues, and Diversity in the Liberal State.* Cambridge: Cambridge University Press.

Gandin, L.A. and Apple, M.W. (2002). Challenging neo-liberalism, building democracy: Creating the citizen school in Porto Alegre, Brazil. *Journal of Education Policy, 17*(2), pp. 259–279.

Gandin, L.A.; Apple, M. (2002). "Thin versus thick democracy in education: Porto alegre and the creation of alternatives to neo-liberalism", *International Studies in Sociology of Education, 12*(2), 99–116.

Garreta, J. (2009). "Escuela y familias inmigradas. Relaciones complejas". *Revista Complutense de Educación,* 20(2), pp. 275–291.

Garreta, J. (2008). *La participación de las familias en la escuela pública. Las asociaciones de madres y padres del alumnado.* Madrid: CEAPA.

Generalitat de Catalunya. (2006). *Pacte Nacional per a l'Educació.* Retrieved on October 25, 2015 from: <http://www.gencat.cat/educacio/butlleti/PNE_06.pdf>.

Giner, S. (1998). "Las razones del republicanismo". *Claves de Razón Práctica,* 81, pp. 2–13.

Giroux, H. (2005). *Estudios culturales, pedagogía crítica y democracia radical.* Madrid: Popular.

Gonzalez, T.E. Hernandez-Saca, D. I. & Artiles, A.J. (2017) In search of voice: theory and methods in K-12 student voice research in the US, 1990–2010, *Educational Review*, 69:4, pp. 451–473.

Grímsson, Ólafur Ragnar. (2006). Icelandic Ventures. Lecture by President Ólafur Ragnar Grímsson, delivered in a series of lectures presented by the Icelandic Historians' Society, January 10. The text is available at: <http://wayback.vefsafn.is/wayback/20060303154653/><http://www.forseti.is/media/files/06.01.10.Sagnfrfel.utras.enska.pdf>.

Guarro, A. (2005). La transformación democrática de la cultura escolar: una respuesta justa a las necesidades del alumnado de zonas desfavorecidas. *Profesorado. Revista de Currículum y Formación del Profesorado*, 9 (1), pp. 1–48.

Guarro, A. (2002). *Currículum y democracia. Por un cambio de la cultura escolar*. Barcelona: Octaedro.

Gutmann, A. & Thompson, D. (1996). *Democracy and Disagreement*. Cambridge, MA: Belknap Press.

Guttormsson, Loftur. (1990). The development of popular religious literacy in the seventeenth and eighteenth centuries. *Scandinavian Journal of History, 15*, pp. 7–35.

Guttormsson, Loftur. (2013). *Sögukennsluskammdegið: Rimman um sögukennslu og samfélagsfræði 1983–1984*. [The long nights of history teaching: The battle over teaching of history and social studies in 1983–1984]. Reykjavík: University of Iceland Press.

Gylfason, Thorvaldur. (2013). Democracy on ice: A post-mortem of the Icelandic constitution. *OpenDemocracy*, June 19th 2013. <https://www.opendemocracy.net/can-europe-make-it/thorvaldur-gylfason/democracy-on-ice-post-mortem-of-icelandic-constitution>.

Habermas, J. (1998). [1992] Política deliberativa: un concepto procedimental de democracia. In *Facticidad y validez*. Madrid: Trotta.

Habermas, J. (1998). Three normative models of democracy. In *The Inclusion of the Other: Studies in Political Theory*. Cambridge, MA: MIT Press.

Halldórsdóttir, Brynja E., Jónsson, Ó. P. & Magnúsdóttir, B. R. (2016). Education for democracy, citizenship and social justice: The case of Iceland. In A. Peterson, R. Hattam, M. Zwmbylas & J. Arthur (editors.), *The Palgrave international handbook of education for citizenship and social justice*. London: Palgrave Macmillan.

Hangartner, J. and Svaton, C.J. (2014). Competition between Public Supervision and Professional Management: an Ethnographic Study of School Governance Reforms in Switzerland. *Ethnography and Education, 9*(3), pp. 284–297.

Hannesdóttir, Sigrún K. (2013). Creating an educational paradigm shift in the face of economic crisis: An interview with Katrín Jakobsdóttir, Minister of Education, Science and Culture in Iceland. *The Delta Kappa Gamma Bulletin, 79*(4), pp. 7–12.

Hannibalsson, Arnór. (1983). Um sögu og sögukennslu [On history and history teaching]. *Morgunblaðið*, December 7, 1983, p. 25.

Hanson, J. S. and K. Howe (2011). "The Potential for Deliberative Democratic Civic Education". *Democracy and Education*, 19(2), 1–9.

Haraldsdóttir, Elsa. (2011). Efling gagnrýninnar hugsunar of siðfræði í íslenskum skólum [Strengthening of critical thinking and ethics in Icelandic schools]. Reykjavík: Institute of Philosophy at UI. Retrieved from: <https://gagnryninhugsun.hi.is/wp-content/uploads/Gagnrynin-hugsun-og-sidfraedi_Lokaskyrsla.pdf>

Haraldsdóttir, Elsa. (2015). Heimspekileg samræða í menntun: Rannsókn á tengslum heimspeki og menntunar í leik- og grunnskólum Garðabæjar 2013–2015 [Philosophical dialogue in education: A research on the relation between philosophy and education in preschools and elementary schools in Gardabaerr 2013–2015]. Reykjavík: Institute of Philosophy at UI. Retrieved from: <https://gagnryninhugsun.hi.is/wp-content/uploads/Rannso%CC%81knarverkefnium-tengsl-heimspeki-og-kennslu_15.pdf>.

Harber, C. (2004). *Schooling as Violence. How schools harm pupils and societies*, Routledge Falmer, Kohl, H. (1967) *36 Children*, New York, London: Penguin.

Hargreaves, Andy (2000). Nueva profesionalidad para una profesión paradójica. *Cuadernos de Pedagogía*, 290, 58–60.

Hart, R. (1997) *Children's Participation: the theory and practice of involving young citizens in community development and environmental care* London, Earthscan.

Harvey, D. (2007). Neoliberalism as Creative Destruction. *The ANNALS of the American Academy of Political and Social Science, 610*, 21–44.

Hatcher, R. (2012). Democracy and Governance in the Local School System. *Journal of Educational Administration and History*, 44(1), 21–42.

Hatcher, R. & Hirtt, N. (1999). The Business Agenda Behind Labour's Education Policy. In Allen, M., Benn, C., Chitty, C., Cole, M., Hatcher, R., Hirtt, N., and Rikowski, G. *New labour's education policy*. London: Tufnell.

Hernández, F. (coord.) (2006). *Cap a una escola secundària inclusiva: sabers i experiències de joves en situació d'exclusió.* Available in <http://hdl.handle.net/2445/15963>.

Hernández, F. & Sancho, J. M. (2004) *El clima escolar en los centros de secundaria: más allá de los tópicos*. CIDE, Madrid.

Hesse-Biber, S. (2010). Qualitative Approaches to Mixed Methods Practice. *Qualitative Inquiry, 16(6)*, pp. 455–468.

Hill, D. & Kumar, R. (eds.). (2009). *Global Neoliberalism and Education and its Consequences*. New York: Routledge.

Honneth, A. (1997) [1992]. *La lucha por el reconocimiento. Por una gramática moral de los conflictos sociales*. Barcelona: Crítica.

Hope, M. (2012) The Importance of Belonging: Learning from the Student Experience of Democratic Education, *Journal of School Leadership* 22 (4), pp. 733–750.

Hornby, G. & Lafaele, R. (2011). "Barriers to parental involvement in education: an explanatory model". *Educational review*, 63(1), pp. 37–52.

Hoy, W.; Tarter, J. C. & Kottkamp, R. B. (1991). *Open School/Healthy Schools: Measuring Organizational Climate,* Londres, Sage.

IDESCAT (2013). *Taxa de fecunditat 2009–2013*. Barcelona: Generalitat de Catalunya. Retrieved on March 25th from: <http://www.idescat.cat/pub/?id=aec&n=288>.

Indriðason, I. H., Önnudóttir, E. H., Þórisdóttir, H. and Harðarson, Ó. Þ. (2017), Re-electing the Culprits of the Crisis? Elections in the Aftermath of a Recession. *Scandinavian Political Studies, 40*(1), pp. 28–60. doi:10.1111/1467-9477.12081.

Jakobsdóttir, Katrín. (2011). Ávarp [Address]. In Ólafur Páll Jónsson and Þóra Björg Sigurðardóttir, *Lýðræði og mannréttindi* [Democracy and human rights]. Reykjavík: Ministry of Education, Culture and Science.

Jessop, B. (2002). Liberalism, Neoliberalism, and Urban Governance: A State-Theoretical Perspective. *Antipode, 34*(3), pp. 452–472.

Jessop, B. (2004). "Multi-level Governance and Multi-level Meta-governance". In Bache, I. and Flinders, M. *Multi-level Governance* (pp. 49–74). Oxford: Oxford University Press.

Jóhannesson, Guðni Th. (2015). Exploiting Icelandic History 2000–2008. In P. Durrenberger and G. Pálsson (editors) *Gambling debt: Iceland's rise and fall in the global economy*. Boulder CO: University Press of Colorado.

Jóhannesson, Ingólfur Á. (2006). "Strong, independent, able to learn more...": Inclusion and the construction of school students in Iceland as diagnosable subjects. *Discourse: Studies in the Cultural Politics of Education, 27*, pp. 103–119.Jones, K., Cunchillos, Ch., Hatcher, R., Hirtt, N. Innes, R., Johsua, S., and Klausenitzer, J. (2007). *Schooling in Western Europe. The New Order and its Adversaries*. London: Palgrave Macmillan.

Jónsson, Ólafur P. (2009). Lýðræði, réttlæti og haustið 2008 [Democracy, justice and the fall of 2008]. *Skírnir, 183*(2), pp. 281–307.

Jónsson, Ólafur P. (2011). *Lýðræði, réttlæti og menntun: Hugleiðingar um skilyrði mennskunnar*. [Democracy, justice and education: Consideration about the human condition]. Reykjavík: University of Iceland Press.

Jónsson, Ólafur P. (2012). Desert, liberalism and justice in democratic education. *Education, Citizenship and Social Justice, 7*(2), pp. 103–115. DOI: 10.1177/1746197911432596.

Jónsson, Ólafur P. (2014). Lýðræðisleg menntastefna: Sögulegt ágrip og heimspekileg greining [Democratic educational policy: Brief history and philosophical analysis]. *Icelandic Review of Politics & Administration, 10*(1), pp. 99–118.

Jónsson, Ólafur P. (2017). Lýðræði og borgaravitund: Hugsjón, stefna og tómarúm [Democracy and citizenship: Vision, policy and vacuum]. In Árnason, V. & Henryson, H. A. (editors) *Hvað einkennir íslenskt lýðræði? Starfsvenjur, gildi og skilningur* [How Does Democracy Work in Iceland? Practices, norms and understanding]. Reykjavík: University of Iceland Press.

Kaplan, I. (2008) Being 'seen' being 'heard': Engaging with students on the margins of education through participatory photography. In

Thomson, P. (Ed.) *Doing Visual Research with Children and Young People*. London: Routledge.

Kaplan, I. and Howes, A. (2004) 'Seeing through different eyes': Exploring the value of participative research using images in schools. *Cambridge Journal of Education*, 34 (2), pp. 143–155.

Kerr, D., Sturman, L., Schulz, W. i Burge, B. (2009). *ICCS 2009 European Report: Civic knowledge, attitudes, and engagement among lower-secondary students in 24 European countries*. Amsterdam: International Association for the Evaluation of Educational Achievement (IEA).

Kinna, R., Prichard, A. & Swann, T. (2016). Iceland's crowd-sourced constitution: Hope for disillusioned voters everywhere. *The Conversation*. October 28th 2016. <http://theconversation.com/icelands-crowd-sourced-constitution-hope-for-disillusioned-voters-everywhere-67803>.

Kohlberg, L. (1980) 'High school democracy and educating for a just society', in R. Mosher (ed) *Moral education: a first generation of research and development* New York, Praeger, pp. 20–57.

Krugman, Paul. (2010). The Icelandic post-crisis miracle. *The New York Times*, 30.06.2010.

Kymlicka, W. (1995a). *Multicultural Citizenship*. Oxford: Clarendon Press.

Kymlicka, W. (1995b). *The Rights of Minority Cultures*. London: Oxford University Press.

Labaree, D. (2011). How Dewey lost: The victory of David Snedden and social efficiency in the reform of American education. In D. Tröhler, T. Popkewitz & D. Labaree (Eds.), *Schooling and the making of citizens in the long nineteenth century* (pp. 163–188). New York: Palgrave Macmillan.

Lahire, B. (1995). *Tableaux des familles*. Paris, Seuil.

Landemore, Hélene. (2016) What is good constitution? Assessing the constitutional proposal in the Icelandic experiment. In T. Ginsburg and A. Huq (editors), *Assessing constitutional performance*. Cambridge: Cambridge University Press.

Landemore, Hélene. (2014). "We, All of the People. Five lessons from Iceland's failed experiment in creating a crowdsourced constitution". *The Slate*, 31.07.2014. <http://www.slate.com/articles/

technology/future_tense/2014/07/five_lessons_from_iceland_s_
failed_crowdsourced_constitution_experiment.html>.

Lareau, A. (2003). *Unequal childhoods: class, race and family life.*
Berkeley: University of California Press.

Lárusdóttir, Steinunn H. (2014). Educational leadership and market values: A study of school principals in Iceland. *Educational Management Administration & Leadership, 42*(4), pp. 83–103.

Latour, A. (2016). Stephen Colbert's New Word "Trumpiness" Is The
2016 Evolution Of "Truthiness", BUSTLE, July 19; <https://
www.bustle.com/articles/173568-stephen-colberts-new-word-
trumpiness-is-the-2016-evolution-of-truthiness>        Downloaded
20/01/2018.

Lawson, H. (2010) Beyond tokenism? Participation and 'voice' for pupils
with significant learning difficulties. In Rose, R. (Ed.) *Confronting
Obstacles to Inclusion: International Responses to Developing Inclusive Education.* London: David Fulton.

Lawy, Robert; Biesta, Gert; McDonnell, Jane; Lawy, Helen; Reeves,
Hannah (2010). "The art of democracy: young people's democratic
learning in gallery contexts". *British Educational Research Journal,*
36 (3), pp. 351–365.

Lawy, R. and G. Biesta (2006). Citizenship-as-practice: The Educational
Implications of an Inclusive and Relational Understanding of Citizenship. *British Journal of Educational Studies,* 54(1), pp. 34–50.

Lee, J.S. & Bowen, N. (2006). "Parent Involvement, Cultural Capital,
and the Achievement Gap Among Elementary School Children".
*American educational research journal,* 43(2), pp. 193–218.

Leitch, Ruth; Mitchell, Stephanie (2007). Caged birds and cloning
machines: how student imagery 'speaks' to us about cultures of
schooling and student participation. *Improving schools,* 10 (1),
pp. 53–71.

Levinson, M. (2012). The Civic Empowerment Gap. In *No Citizen Left
Behind,* ed. M. Levinson, Cambridge, MA: Harvard University
Press.

Ley Orgánica 1/1990, de 3 de octubre, de Ordenación General del Sistema Educativo. (LOGSE). *Boletín Oficial del Estado* núm. 238,
4 de octubre de 1990. Avalaible in <http://www.boe.es/buscar/doc.
php?id=BOE-A-1990-24172>.

Ley Orgánica 8/2013, de 9 de diciembre, de Mejora de la Calidad del Sistema Educativo (LOMCE,). *Boletín Oficial del Estado*, núm. 295, 10 de diciembre de 2013. Avalaible in <https://www.boe.es/buscar/act.php?id=BOE-A-2013-12886>.

Lippmann, W. (1939). "The indispensable Opposition", *Atlantic Monthly*, August, pp. 186–89; <http://croker.harpethhall.org/Must%20Know/Government/DemocracyLippmann.pdf>.

Lippmann, W. (1937). *The Good Society*. Boston: Little, Brown & Co.

Lippmann, W. (1927). *The Phantom Public*, New York: Macmillan; 13 Transaction Publishers, New Brunswick, New Jersey.

Lippmann, W. (1922). *Public Opinion*, Harcourt Brace and Company.

Lissovoy, Noah De (2018). Against Reconciliation: Constituent Power, Ethics, and the Meaning of Democratic Education, in Special edition eds Matthew Clark, Linda Hammersley-Smith, and John Schostak, *Power & Education.*

Loftsdóttir, Kristín. (2015). Vikings Invade Present-Day Iceland. In P. Durrenberger and G. Pálsson (editors) *Gambling debt: Iceland's rise and fall in the global economy*. Boulder CO: University Press of Colorado.

Luengo, F. (2006). El Proyecto Atlántida: experiencias para fortalecer el eje escuela, familia y municipio. *Revista de Educación*, 339, pp. 177–194.

Macedo, S. (1990). *Liberal Virtues: Citizenship, Virtue, and Community in Liberal Constitutionalism*. Nueva York: Oxford University Press.

Macpherson, C. B. (1973). Post-liberal-democracy? In *Democratic Theory: Essays in Retrieval*. Oxford: Clarendon Press.

Marinósson Grétar L. & Bjarnason Dóra S. (2014) Special education today in Iceland. In: A. F. Rotatory, J.P. Bakken, F.E. Obiakor, et al. (editors) *Special Education International Perspective: Practices Across the Globe Advances*. New York: Emerald Group Publsihing.

Marsh, J. (2011). *Class dismissed: Why we cannot teach or learn our way out of inequality,* New York: Monthly Review Press.

Marx, K. (1975) [1843]. "On the Jewish Question". In *Early Writing,* ed. K. Marx. Harmondsworth: Penguin Books.

Mayhew, K. C., and Edwards, A. C. (1936). *The Dewey School. The Laboratory School of the University of Chicago 1896–1903*. Introduction by John Dewey. New York and London: Appleton-Century Company Incorporated.

McNamara, S. and Moreton, G. (1995) *Changing Behaviour: Teaching Children with Emotional and Behavioural Difficulties in Primary and Secondary Classrooms*. London: David Fulton.

Messiou, K. (2017). "Research in the Field of Inclusive Education: Time for a Rethink?" International Journal of Inclusive Education 21 (2), pp. 146–159.

Messiou, K. & Hope, M. (2015) 'The danger of subverting students' views in schools, *International Journal of Inclusive Education*, 19, 10, pp. 1009–1021.

Messiou, K. (2012). Confronting Marginalisation in Education: A Framework for Promoting Inclusion. London: Routledge.

Messiou, K. (2008) Encouraging children to think in more inclusive ways. *British Journal of Special Needs Education*, 35 (1), pp. 26–32.

Messiou, K. (2006) Understanding marginalisation in education: The voice of children. *European Journal of Psychology of Education*, 21 (3) (special issue), pp. 305–318.

Messiou, K. (2003) Conversations with children: A pathway towards understanding marginalisation and inclusive education. PhD thesis. University of Manchester.

Milanovic, B. (2016). *Global inequality*. Hardvard University Press, Cambridge, MA.

Milne, R. (2016). Olafur Hauksson, the man who jailed Iceland's bankers. *Financial Times,* December 9th, 2016. <https://www.ft.com/content/dcdb43d4-bd52-11e6-8b45-b8b81dd5d080>.

Ministry of Education, Science and Culture. (2012a). *The Icelandic national curriculum guide for preschools*. Reykjavík: Author.

Ministry of Education, Science and Culture. (2012b). *The Icelandic national curriculum guide for compulsory schools: General section.* Reykjavík: Author.

Ministry of Education, Science and Culture. (2012c). *The Icelandic national curriculum guide for upper secondary schools: General section*. Reykjavík: Author.

Ministerio de Educación (2011). Educación, valores y democracia. *Revista de Educación,* n. extraordinario. Madrid: Secretaría General Técnica. Ministerio de Educación.

Ministerio de Educación (2003). Ciudadanía y Educación. *Revista de Educación*, n. extraordinario. Madrid: Secretaría General Técnica. Ministerio de Educación, Cultura y Deporte.

Mitra, D.L. & Serriere, S.C. (2012) Student voice in elementary school reform: Examining youth development in fifth graders, *American Educational Research Journal*, 49 (4), pp. 743–744.

Mitra, D. L. (2004). The significance of students: Can increasing 'student voice' in schools lead to gains in youth development? *Teachers College Record* 106 (4), pp. 651–688.

Mitra, D. L. (2003). Student voice in school reform: Reframing student–teacher relationships. *McGill Journal of Education*, 38 (2), pp. 289–304.

Mittler, P. (2000=. "From Exclusion to Inclusion." In Working Towards Inclusive Education: Social Contexts, edited by P. Mittler, 1–12. London: David Fulton.

Monceau, G. (2011). "La complexitat de les implicacions dels pares a l'escola o per què la participació dels pares no millora necessàriament els resultats acadèmics dels nens". A Collet, J.; Tort, A. (eds.) *Escola, famílies i èxit escolar*. Barcelona: Fundació Jaume Bofill.

Morrow, V. & Richards, M. (1996) The ethics of social research with children: An overview. *Children and Society*, 10 (2), pp. 90–105.

Nancy, J. L. (2011). Finite and Infinite Democracy. In *Democracy in what state?*, pp. 58–75. New York: Columbia University Press.

Neill, A. S. (1973). *Neill, Neill "Orange Peel": a personal view of ninety years*, (revised edition) London, Weidenfeld and Nicholson.

Nussbaum, M. (2011). *Creating Capabilities.The Human Development Approach*. The Belknap Press of Harvard University Press.

Nussbaum, M. (2010). *Not for profit: Why democracy needs the humanities*. Princeton: Princeton University Press.

Nussbaum, M. (2007) 'Cultivating Humanity and World Citizenship' *Forum Futures*, pp. 37–40.

OCDE (2013). *Equity and Quality in Education: Supporting Disadvantaged Students and Schools,* Avalaible in <http://dx.doi.org/10.1787/9789264130852-en>.

Ólafsson, J. (2016). Epistemic democracy – following the crowd's knowledge. *Iceland review of politics & administration, 12*(2), pp. 511–536.

Ólafsson, J. (editor). (2014). *Lýðræðistilraunir* [Democratic experiments]. Reykjavík: University of Iceland Press. English version of Ólafsson's introduction to the volume is available at: <https://www.academia.edu/35629734/J%C3%93_Democracy_Disaster_intro.pdf>.

Olivo, M.A., Alaniz, C. & Reyes, L. (2011). "Critica a los Conceptos de Gobernabilidad y Gobernanza. Una discusión con referencia a los consejos escolares de participación social en México". *Revista Mexicana de Investigación Educativa, 16*(50), pp. 775–799.

Olmedo, A. (2017). "Something old, not much new, and a lot borrowed: philanthropy, business and the changing roles of government in global education policy networks" *Oxford Review of Education* 43 (1), pp. 69–87.

Olmedo, A. & Wilkins, A. (2017). "Governing through parents: a genealogical enquiry of education policy and the construction of neoliberal subjectivities in England". *Discourse: Studies in Cultural Politics of Education* 38 (4), pp. 573–589.

Olmedo, A. & Wilkins, A. (2014). Gobernar la Educación a través de los Padres: Política Educativa y Construcción de Subjetividades Neoliberales en Inglaterra. *Profesorado: Revista de curriculum y formación del profesorado, 18*(2), pp. 99–116.

Olmedo, A. (2013). Policy-makers, Market Advocates and Edu-businesses: New and Renewed Players in the Spanish Education Policy Arena. *Journal of Education Policy, 28*(1), pp. 55–76.

Olmedo, A. (2008). From Democratic Participation to School Choice: Quasimarket Principles in the Spanish Educational Legislation. *Education Policy Analysis Archives, 16*(21), pp. 1–35.

Ong, A. (2007). Neoliberalism as a Mobile Technology. *Transactions of the Institute of British Geographers, 32*(1), pp. 3–8.

Ong, A. & Collier, O. (2005). *Global Assemblages. Technology, Politics and Ethics as Anthropological Problems*. Oxford: Blackwell.

Ovejero, F.; J. L. Martí and R. Gargarella (2004). La alternativa republicana. In *Nuevas ideas republicanas. Autogobierno y libertad*, ed. F. Ovejero *et al.* Barcelona: Paidós.

Ovejero, F. (2003). Dos democracias, distintos valores. Educar para la ciudadanía: perspectivas ético-políticas. *Contrastes. Revista Internacional de Filosofía*, 8, pp. 45–80.

Palaudàrias, J. M. (2002). Escola i immigració estrangera a Catalunya: la integració escolar. *Papers*, 66, pp. 199–213.

Palaudàrias, J. M. and J. Feu (1997). La acogida del alumnado extranjero en las escuelas públicas. Una reflexión necesaria para favorecer la integración plural. In *¿Educación o exclusión de la diversidad?*, ed. F. J. García Castaño and A. Granados. Granada: Universidad de Granada.

Parker, A., & Meo, A. (2012). "Reformas educativas y transformaciones del trabajo y la identidad profesional docente. El caso del sistema educativo estatal inglés: entre el cambio y la continuidad". *CPU-e, Revista de Investigación Educativa* 15, pp. 102–118.

Parra, J., García, M.P., Gomariz, M.A., & Hernández, M.A. (2014). Implicación de las Familias en los Consejos Escolares de los Centros. pp. 149–165. In Consejo Escolar del Estado. *La participación de las familias en la educación escolar*. Madrid: Ministerio de Educación, Cultura y Deporte.

Pengelly, M. (2017). Kellyanne Conway: 'alternative facts' was my Oscars blunder, *The Guardian,* March 4; <https://www.theguardian.com/us-news/2017/mar/03/kellyanne-conway-alternative-facts-mistake-oscars>. Downloaded 20/01/2018.

Peña, J. (2000). *La ciudadanía hoy. Problemas y propuestas.* Valladolid: Universidad de Valladolid.

Pettit, P. (1997a). *Republicanism: a Theory of Freedom and Government.* Nueva York: Oxford University Press.

Pettit, P. (1997b). Libéralisme et républicanisme. In *Dictionnaire d'éthique et de philosophie morale.* París: Presses Universitaires de France.

Prieto-Flores, Ò., Feu, J., Serra, C., & Lázaro, L. (2018). Bringing democratic governance into practice: policy enactments responding to neoliberal governance in Spanish public schools. *Cambdridge Journal of Education*, 48(2), 227–244.

Punch, S. (2002a) Interviewing strategies with young people: The 'secret box' stimulus material and task-based activities. *Children and Society*, 16 (1), pp. 45–56.

Punch, S. (2002b) Research with children: the same or different from research with adults? *Childhood*, 9 (3), pp. 321–341.

Rancière, J. (2011). Democracies against Democracy. In *Democracy in what state?*, pp. 76–80. New York: Columbia University Press.

Rancière, J. (2004). *The politics of aesthetics*, with an after word by Slavoj Zizek, translated with anintroduction by Gabriel Rockhill, London, New York, continuum.

Rancière, J. (1999). *Disagreement*, Minneapolis, University of Minnesota Press.

Rancière, J. (1987). *Le Maître ignorant. Cinq leçons sur l'émancipation intellectuelle*, Paris, Fayard; translated, with an introduction, by Kristin Ross, 1991 The ignorant schoolmaster. Five Lessons in Intellectual Emancipation. Stanford, California: Stanford University Press.

Ranson, S. (2008). The Changing Governance of Education. *Educational management, administration and leadership, 36*(2), 201–219.

Ranson, S., Arnott, M., McKeown, P., Martin, J., and Smith, P. (2005). The Participation of volunteer citizens in school governance. *Educational Review, 57*(3), pp. 357–371.

Ranson, S. (2003). Public Accountability in the Age of Neo-liberal Governance. *Journal of Education Policy, 18*(5), pp. 459–480.

Rawls, J. (1993). *Political Liberalism*. Nueva York: Cambridge University Press.

Reay, D. (2011). Schooling for Democracy: A Common School and a Common University? A Response to 'Schooling for Democracy'. *Democracy & Education*, 19(1), pp. 1–4.

Reay, D. (2005). "Mothers' involvement in their children's schooling: social reproduction in action?" In: G. Crozier and D. Reay (Eds.) *Activating Participation: Parents and Teachers working in Partnership*. Stoke on Trent: Trentham Books.

Resnick, L.B.; Spillane, J.P.; Goldman, P. & Rangel, E.S. (2010). 'Implementing innovations: from visionary models to everyday practice'. In Dumont, H. Instance, D. Benavides, F. *The nature of Learning. Using Research to Inspire Practice*. CERI/OCDE, Paris.

Rhodes, R. (2007). Understanding Governance: Ten Years On. *Organization Studies, 28*(8), pp. 1243–1264.

Rhodes, R. (1997). *Understanding governance: policy networks, governance and reflexivity*. Londres: Open University Press.

Richmond, J. (1982). *Becoming our own experts*, Talk Workshop Group, ILEA English Centre, London; <https://www.becomingourownexperts.org>.

Roberts, H. (2000). Listening to children: And hearing them. In P. Christensen & A. James (Eds.), *Research with children: Perspectives and practices* (pp. 225–240). London: RoutledgeFalmer.

Robertson, S., Bonal, X. and Dale, R. (2001). GATS and the Education Service Industry: The Politics of Scale and Global Re-territorialization. *Comparative Education Review*, 46(2), pp. 472–96.

Robinson, C. (2014) *Children, their voices and their experiences of school: what does the evidence tell us?* York: Cambridge Primary Review Trust.

Rollock, N.; Gilborn, D.; Vincent, C., Ball, S. (2015). *The colour of class*. London, Routledge.

Rosanvallon, P. (2013). *The Society of Equals*. Trans. Arthur Goldhammer. Cambridge Massachusetts and London, UK: Harvard University Press.

Rosanvallon, P. (2012). *Counter-Democracy. Politics in an Age of Distrust*, translated by Arthur Goldhammer, foreword by Gareth Stedman Jones, Cambridge: Cambridge University Press.

Rowbotham, S. (1979). 'The women's movement and organizing for socialism,' in S. Rowbotham, L. Segal; and H. Wainwright (eds) *Beyond the Fragments: Feminism and the Making of Socialism* London, Merlin Press.

Rubio, J. (2005). *Ciudadanos sin democracia. Nuevos ensayos sobre ciudadanía, ética y democracia*. Granada: Comares.

San Román, T. (1996). *Los muros de la separación. Ensayo sobre alterofobia y filantropía*. Madrid: Tecnos.

Sandel, M. (2009) 'A new politics of the common good', Lecture 4, BBC Reith Lectures, 30 June.

Sandel, M. (2004). "La república procedimental y el yo desvinculado". In *Nuevas ideas republicanas. Autogobierno y libertad*, ed. M. Canto-Sperber. Barcelona: Paidós.

Sandel, M. (1998). *Liberalism and the Limits of Justice*. Cambridge: Cambridge University Press.

Sandel, M. (1996). *Democracy's Discontent. America in Search of a Public Philosophy*. Cambridge: Harvard University Press.

Savater, F. (1999). *Diccionario filosófico*. Barcelona: Planeta.

School of Barbiana (1969). *Letter to a Teacher*, Harmondsworth, Penguin.

Schostak, J. F. (2018). "Towards a Society of Equals: Dewey, Lippmann, the Co-operative Movement and radical democracy undermining neoliberal forms of schooling" in Special edition eds Matthew Clark, Linda Hammersley-Smith, and John Schostak, *Power & Education.*

Schostak, J. F. (2014). Supersurveillance, democracy and cooperation – the challenge for teachers. *Asia-Pacific Journal of Teacher Education*, (4). 324–336.

Schostak, J, & Goodson, I. (2012). What's wrong with democracy at the moment and why it matters for research and education. *Power and Education, 4*(3), 257–276.

Schostak, J. F., and Schostak, J. R. (2012). *Writing Research Critically and Radically – the power to make a difference*, London, New York: Routledge.

Schostak, J. F. (1983/2012). *Maladjusted Schooling: Deviance, Social Control and Individuality in Secondary Schooling*, London, Philadelphia. Falmer. Re-issued 2012, 2014, Routledge.

Schostak, J. F. (1990). Practical Policy Making in a Primary School, *Journal of the Educational Research Network of Northern Ireland*, 3, 2–24.

Schostak, J. F. (1989). Developing More Democratic Modes of Teacher-Pupil Relationships: 'The Early Years Listening and Talking Project' *Journal of the Educational Research Network of Northern Ireland* 2, pp. 2–24.

Schulz, W., Ainley, J., Fraillon, J., Kerr, D. & Losito, B. (2010a). *ICCS 2009 international report: Civic knowledge, attitudes and engagement among lower secondary school students in thirty-eight countries*. Amsterdam: International Association for the Evaluation of Educational Achievement (IEA).

Schulz, W., Ainley, J., Fraillon, J., Kerr, D. & Losito, B. (2010b). *Initial findings from the IEA International Civic and Citizenship Study*. Amsterdam: International Association for the Evaluation of Educational Achievement (IEA).

Schulz, W., Fraillon, J., Ainley, J., Losito, B. & Kerr, D. (2008). *International Civic and Citizenship Education Study: Assessment framework*. Amsterdam: International Association for the Evaluation of Educational Achievement (IEA).

Sen, A. K. (2009). *The Idea of Justice*. Cambridge: The Belknap Press of Harvard University Press.

Sen, A. K. (1999). *Development as Freedom*. Oxford: Oxford University Press.

Serra, C. Palaudarias, J.M. Llevot, C. and Garreta, J. (2013). "Famílies immigrades i escoles. Dinàmiques de relació a Catalunya". In Secretaria per a la Immigració. *Recerca i Immigració V. Col·lecció Ciutadania i Immigració, 9*, pp. 123–139.

Serra, C. (2002). *Antropologia de l'educació: l'etnografia i l'estudi de les relacions interètniques en l'àmbit de l'educació*. Girona: Servei de Publicacions de la UdG.

Serramona, J. and T. Rodríguez (2010). Participación y calidad de la educación. *Aula Abierta*, 38(1), pp. 3–14.

Shier, H. (2001) 'Pathways to participation: openings, opportunities and obligations', *Children & Society*, 15, pp. 107–117.

Siddique, Haroon. (2011). Mob rule: Iceland crowedsources its next constitution. *The Guardian,* June 9th 2011. <https://www.theguardian.com/world/2011/jun/09/iceland-crowdsourcing-constitution-facebook>.

Sigurðardóttir, A. Kristín, Guðjónsdóttir, H., & Karlsdóttir, J. (2014). The development of a school for all in Iceland: Equality, threats and political conditions. In U. Blossing, G. Imsen, & L. Moss (eds.), *The Nordic education model: 'A school for all' encounters neo-liberal policy*. Dordrecth: Springer.

Sigurjónsson, Th. Ó. & Mixa, M. W. (2011). Learning from the "worst behaved": Iceland's financial crisis and the Nordic comparison. *Thunderbird International Business Review, 53*(2), pp. 209–223.

Simó, N.; Parareda, A. & Domingo, L. (2016). Towards a democratic school: The experience of secondary school pupils. *Improving Schools*, 19 (3), pp. 181–196.

Simovska, V. (2007). The changing meanings of participation in school-based health education and health promotion: the participants' voices. *Health Education Research*, 22 (6), pp. 864–878.

Simovska, V. (2004). Student participation: A democratic education perspective – Experience from the health-promoting schools in Macedonia. *Health Education Research*, 19 (2), pp. 198–207.

Skinner, Q. (2004). Las paradojas de la libertad política. In *Nuevas ideas republicanas. Autogobierno y libertad*, ed. F. Ovejero *et al*. Barcelona: Paidós.

Skúlason, Páll. (2008). Menning og markaðshyggja [Culture and market ideology]. *Skírnir, 182*(1), pp. 5–40.

Slee, R. 2011. The Irregular School. London: Routledge.

Special Investigation Commission. (2010). Skýrsla rannsóknarnefndar Alþingis um aðdraganda og orsakir falls íslensku bankanna 2008 [Report of the Special Investigation Commission on the processes leading to the fall of the Icelandic banks in 2008]. Reykjavík: Alþingi.

Spinoza, B. de (2004). *A Theologico-Political Treatise and A political Treatise*, Dover Philosophical Classics.

Stake, R. (2006). *Multiple Case Study Analysis*. New York: The Guildford Press.

Straume, I.S. (2016). Democracy, Education and the Need for Politics. *Studies in Philosophy and Education*, 35, pp. 29–45.

Subirats, J. (2010). Si la respuesta es gobernanza, ¿cuál es la pregunta? Factores de cambio en la política y en las políticas. *Ekonomiaz*, 74, pp. 16–35.

Sunstein, C. R. (2004). Más allá del resurgimiento republicano. In *Nuevas ideas republicanas. Autogobierno y libertad*, ed. F. Ovejero *et al*. Barcelona: Paidós.

Sutherland, G. (2006). Voice of change: embedding student voice work, *Curriculum Briefing*, 4(3), pp. 8–11.

Swedish Institute. (2013). *Education in Sweden*. Retrieved from <https://sweden.se/society/education-in-sweden/>.

Sylvester, D.W. (1974). Robert Lowe and the 1870 Education Act, History of Education, *Journal of the History of Education Society*, 3:2, pp. 16–26.

Taguieff, P. A. (1990). *La force du préjugé. Essai sur le racisme et ses doubles*. París: Gallimard.

Talisse, R. (2005). *Democracy after Liberalism*. New York: Routledge.

Tawney, R. H. (1964). *The radical tradition.* Harmondworth, UK: Penguin Books.

Taylor, C. (1994). The Politics of Recognition. In *Multiculturalism: Examining the Politics of Recognition*, ed A. Gutman. Princeton: Princeton University Press.

The Washington Times (2016). Stephen Colbert's 'truthiness' word describes campaign rhetoric, *The Washington Times*, August 18; <https://www.washingtontimes.com/news/2016/aug/18/stephen-colberts-truthiness-word-describes-campaig/>. Downloaded 20/01/2018.

Thomas, G. (2013). "A review of thinking and research about inclusive education policy, with suggestions for a new kind of inclusive thinking." *British Educational Research Journal* 39 (3), pp. 473–490.

Thomas, G. (2011). A typology for the case study in social science following a review of definition, discourse and structure. *Qualitative Inquiry, 17*(6), pp. 511–521.

Thomson, P. (2011) Coming to Terms with Voice. IN: Czerniawski, G. and Kidd, W. (eds.) *The Student Voice Handbook: Bridging the Academic/Practitioner Divide*. Bingley: Emerald Group Publishing Limited.

Thomson, P. (Ed.) (2008a) *Doing Visual Research with Children and Young People.* London: Routledge.

Thomson, P. (2008b) Children and young people: voices in visual research. In Thomson, P. (Ed.) *Doing Visual Research with Children and Young People.* London: Routledge.

Thornberg, R. and H. Elvstran (2012). Children's experiences of democracy, participation, and trust in school. *International Journal of Educational Research*, 53, pp. 44–54.

Tyack, David; Tobin, William (1994). The Grammar of Schooling: Why Has it Been So Hard to Change? *American Educational Research Journal*, 31(3), pp. 453–479.

Unger, R. (2004) *False Necessity: Anti-necessitarian Social Theory in the Service of Radical democracy* (2nd Ed) London, Verso.

University of Helsinki. (2006). *Department of Teacher Education. Subject teacher education.* Retrieved from <http://www.helsinki.fi/teachereducation/education/subjectteacher/index.html>.

University of Helsinki. (2006). *Department of Teacher Education.
Class teacher education.* Retrieved from <http://www.helsinki.fi/
teachereducation/education/classteacher/index.html>.

University of Helsinki. (2006). *Department of Teacher Education. Kin-
dergarten teacher and early childhood education.* Retrieved from
<http://www.helsinki.fi/tgeachereducation/education/kindergar-
tenteacher/studies.html>.

Vasak, K. (1984). Pour une troisième génération des droits de l'homme.
In *Études et essais sur le Droit International Humanitaire et sur les
principes du CICR en l'honneur à Jean Pictet.* ed, C. Swinarski, La
Haya: Martinus Nijhoff.

Vasak, K. (1977). A 30-year Struggle. The Sustained Efforts to Give
Force of Law to the Universal Declaration of Human Rights. *The
UNESCO Courier,* XXX, 11, pp. 29–32.

Verger, A. (2012). Framing and Selling Global Education Policy: the
Promotion of Public-Private Partnerships for Education in Low-income Contexts. *Journal of Education Policy, 27*(1), pp. 109–130.

Vincent, C. & Ball, S. (2007). "'Making Up' the Middle-Class Child:
Families, Activities and Class Dispositions" *Sociology* 41(6),
pp. 1061–1077.

Vincent, C. (2012). *Parenting: Responsibilities, Risks and Respect.*
London: Institute of Education, University of London.

Vincent, C. (2000). *Including Parents: Education, Citizenship and Parental Agency.* Buckingham: Open University Press.

Vincent, C. (1996). *Parents and Teachers: Power and Participation.*
London: Falmer.

Viñao, A. (2012). El Desmantelamiento del Derecho a la Educación:
Discursos y Estrategias Neoconservadoras. *AREAS, Revista Internacional de Ciencias Sociales, 31,* pp. 97–107.

Waller, W. (1932). *The Sociology of Teaching,* New York: John Wiley/
London: Chapman and Hall.

Weaver, A. (1989) 'Democratic Practice in Education: an historical
perspective,' *In* C. Harber and R. Meighan (eds) *The Democratic
School: Educational management and the practice of democracy*
Ticknall, Education Now, pp. 83–91.

Wilkins, A. (2016). *Modernising school governance: Corporate planning and expert handling in state education.* Routledge: London.

Wilkins, A. (2015). Professionalizing School Governance: the Disciplinary Effects of School Autonomy and Inspection on the Changing Role of School Governors. *Journal of Education Policy, 30*(2), pp. 182–200.

Willan, J. (2011). Susan Isaacs (1885–1948): her life, work and legacy, *Gender and Education*, 23, 2, pp. 201–210.

Williams, F. (1941). 'Introduction' *In* J. Macmurray *A Challenge to the Churches – Religion and Democracy* London, Kegan Paul, Trench, Trubner, V–VI.

Wolin, S. (2008). *Democracy Incorporated: Managed Democracy and the Specter of Inverted Totalitarianism*. Princeton University Press.

Wright, E.O. (2010). *Envisioning Real Utopias*. London/New York: Verso Books.

Young, I. M. (2000). *Inclusion and Democracy*. Oxford: Oxford University Press.

Zuzovsky, R. (2009). Teachers' qualifications and their impact on student achievement: Findings from TIMSS 2003 data for Israel. *IERI Monograph Series, 2*. Retrieved from: <http://www.ierinstitute. org/fileadmin/Documents/IERI_Monograph/IERI_Monograph_ Volume_02.pdf>.

# Social Strategies

## Monographien zur Soziologie und Gesellschaftspolitik
## Monographs on Sociology and Social Policy

Die Zielsetzung der Reihe *Social Strategies* ist es, Theorie und Praxis in soziologischen und gesellschaftspolitischen Problemstellungen zu verbinden. Dabei interessieren fundierte Analysen sowie konkrete Lösungsansätze und Handlungsvorschläge. Inhaltliche Schwerpunkte bilden die Bereiche soziale Ungleichheit sowie Konflikt und Kooperation im Kontext globaler Prozesse. Eine enge Zusammenarbeit besteht mit der Hochschule für Soziale Arbeit (Fachhochschule Nordwestschweiz), dem Basler Institut für Soziologie (Universität Basel) und dem dort angesiedelten Zentrum für Konfliktforschung. Daneben nimmt die Reihe aber auch Manuskripte von anderen Forscherinnen und Forschern auf. Die sozialwissenschaftlich orientierten Arbeiten sollen neben dem wissenschaftlichen auch ein breiteres, an soziologischen und gesellschaftspolitischen Fragen interessiertes Publikum ansprechen.

Publiziert werden Kongressberichte, Festschriften, Dissertationen und weitere Arbeiten, die sich interdisziplinär mit sozialen Fragen und Strategien auseinander setzen. Die Publikationssprachen sind deutsch, englisch und französisch.

**Social Strategies** is a series of monographs and proceedings. It deals with fundamental sociological questions and socio-political problems closely related to social reality. It analyses current day problems and shows, from a sociological viewpoint, how they can be overcome. The series covers the sphere of social change between the present day and the 'Utopian future' – something lacking in more recent sociological writings. Ideas directed towards the future may serve as guidelines.

Contributions to the series can be published in German, English and French.

La collection **Social Strategies** regroupe des monographies et travaux scientifiques traitant des questions sociologiques de base ainsi que des aspects socio-politiques de la réalité sociale. Elle analyse les problèmes contemporains et montre comment les sciences humaines peuvent les surmonter. *Social strategies* aborde le domaine des changements sociaux ente aujourd'hui et les «surlendemains utopiques». En se servant de conceptions tournées vers l'avenir comme point de repère, elle comble les lacunes sur ce sujet de la littérature sociologique récente. Des textes en allemand, anglais et français peuvent être publiés dans cette collection.

Vol. 24: **Marco Nese** Soziologie und Positivismus im präfaschistischen Italien (1870–1922). Basel 1993, IX + 184 Seiten.

Vol. 25: **Urs Fazis und Jachen C. Nett,** eds., Gesellschaftstheorie und Normentheorie. Symposium zum Gedenken an Theodor Geiger, 9.11.1891–16.6.1952. Basel 1993. VIII + 319 Seiten.

Vol. 26: **Urs Fazis** «Theorie» und «Ideologie» der Postmoderne. Studien zur Radikalisierung der Aufklärung aus ideologiekritischer Perspektive, Basel 1994. IV + 322 Seiten.

Vol. 27: **Karlheinz Hottes, Werner Gocht, Paul Trappe,** eds., Krisenkontinent Afrika – Ansätze zum Krisenmanagement, IAfEF-Klausurtagung 1994, Basel 1995, VII + 320 Seiten.

Vol. 28: **Christoph Bosshardt,** ed., Beiträge zu Transformationsprozessen und Strukturanpassungsprogrammen, i. A. des Interdisziplinären Arbeitskreises für Entwicklungsländerforschung (IAfEF), Basel 1997; VIII + 362 Seiten.

Vol. 29: **Christoph Bosshardt,** ed., Problembereiche interdisziplinärer Forschung; 30 Jahre IAfEF; Klausurtagungen in Freiburg i. Br. 1997 und Wien 1998, Bern 1999; VI + 380 Seiten.

Vol. 30: **Ueli Mäder,** Subsidiarität und Solidarität, Bern 2000; 304 Seiten.

Vol. 31: **Hans Neuhofer, Victoria Jäggi-Torra,** eds., Aktuelle Probleme der Stadt- und Landplanung; Bodenordnung in städtischen Verdichtungsgebieten und alpinen Regionen; im Auftrag der Europäischen Fakultät für Bodenordnung, Bern 2000; 260 Seiten.

Vol. 32: **Willy Kraus, Paul Trappe,** eds., Nachhaltige räumliche Entwicklung auf dem europäischen Kontinent – Interdisziplinäre Ansätze; im Auftrag der Europäischen Fakultät für Bodenordnung (FESF) und des Interdisziplinären Arbeitskreises für Entwicklungsländerforschung (IAfEF), Bern 2000; X + 458 Seiten.

Vol. 33: **Christoph Bosshardt,** Homo Confidens; Eine Untersuchung des Vertrauensphänomens aus soziologischer und ökonomischer Perspektive, Bern 2001; 285 Seiten.

Vol. 34: **Piotr Salustowicz,** ed., Civil Society and Social Development; Proceedings of the 6th Biennial European IUCISD Conference in Krakow 1999, Bern 2001; 422 pages.

Vol. 35: **Victoria Jäggi, Ueli Mäder und Katja Windisch,** eds., Entwicklung, Recht, Sozialer Wandel; Festschrift für Paul Trappe zum 70. Geburtstag, Bern 2002; 701 Seiten.

Vol. 36: **Erich Weiss und Tanja Zangger,** éds, 31ᵉ Symposium International FESF Strasbourg; Les régions en face de l'aménagement du territoire, du droit foncier et de la protection de l'environnement / Functions of the regions in the realms of spatial planning, landed property and environmental protection / Aufgaben der Regionen im Hinblick auf Raumplanung, Bodenrecht und Umweltschutz, Bern 2002; 473 Seiten.

Vol. 37: **Michael S. P. Freudweiler,** Soziale Normen in der multikulturellen Gesellschaft, Bern 2003; 286 Seiten.

Vol. 38: **Henrÿ Hagen und Rus͵en Keles,** éds, 32ᵉ Symposium International FESF Strasbourg; Des anciens et des nouveaux droits fonciers dans leur contexte culturel / Old and new land tenure rights in their cultural context / Zur Systematik alter und neuer Bodenrechte im kulturellen Kontext, Bern 2004; 257 Seiten.

Vol. 39: **Katja Windisch,** Gestalten sozialen Wandels; Die Entwicklungssoziologie Richard F. Behrendts, Bern 2005; 259 Seiten. ISBN 3-03910-366-0

Vol. 40: **Edmundas Kazimieras Zavadskas,** ed., 33ᵉ Symposium International FESF Strasbourg; Des développements récents dans la protection de l'environnement / Recent Developments in Environmental Protection / Neuere Entwicklungen im Umweltschutz, Bern 2005; 395 Seiten.

Vol. 41: **Daniela Berger-Künzli,** „Lieber Gott, bitte hilf mir. Ich sterbe dir sonst weg." Analyse spätmoderner Religiosität am Beispiel von frei formulierten Gebetsanliegen und Fürbitten, Bern 2006; 367 Seiten.